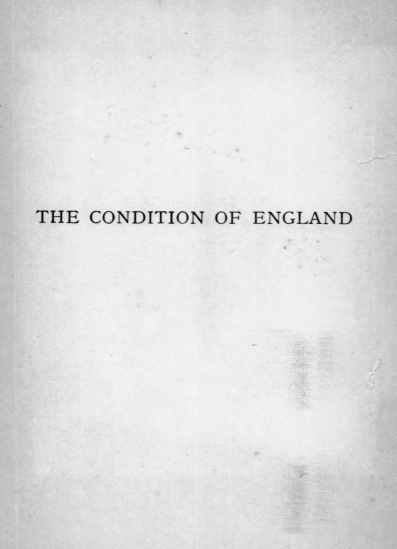

THE CONDITION OF ENGLAND

THE CONDITION
OF ENGLAND

BY

C. F. G. MASTERMAN

"WHETHER IN GENERAL WE ARE GETTING ON, AND IF SO
WHERE WE ARE GOING TO."

RUSKIN

METHUEN & CO.
36 ESSEX STREET W.C.
LONDON

First Published in 1909

TO

MY WIFE

PREFACE

" I 'VE got to a time of life," says the hero of a modern novel, " when the only theories that interest me are generalisations about realities." There are many contemporary observers who do not require advancing years and a wider experience of life to concentrate them upon so serious a study. It is not that they deliberately turn towards consideration of the meaning and progress of the actual life around them. It is that they cannot—with the best desire in the world—escape from such an encompassing problem. To those the only question before them is the present: the past but furnishing material through which that present can rightly be interpreted, the future appearing as a present which is hurrying towards them—impatient to be born. They ask for fact; not make-believe. With Thoreau, " Be it life or death," they will cry, " We crave only reality. If we are really dying, let us hear the rattle in our throats and feel cold in the extremities; if we are alive, let us go about our business."

The following pages offer an attempt to estimate some of these " realities " in the life of contemporary England. The effort might appear presumptuous, demanding not one volume but ten, the observation, not of a decade, but of a lifetime. I would plead, however, that any contribution may help in some degree the work of others in a more far-reaching and detailed survey. The right judgment of such an attempt should be directed not at its completeness, but its sincerity. In my former work as a critic and reviewer it was this test alone that I sought to apply to similar estimates of to-day and to-morrow. It is to this test alone that I now venture to appeal.

"Things are what they are. Their consequences will be what they will be. Why then should we seek to be deceived?" The custom of mankind to live in a world of illusion endows Butler's magnificent platitude with something of the novelty of a paradox. For many generations—perhaps since man first was—we have succeeded in believing what we wished to believe. The process has gone so far as to have excited a kind of reverse wave. We are supposed to wish to believe what we believe. We identify diagnosis with desire, and think that the prophet of evil is secretly rejoicing over the impending calamity. We are convinced that no man would assert that certain events are going to happen if he did not wish them to happen. If an observer anticipates a victory for Tariff Reform he is supposed to be weakening on Free Trade. If he proclaims a decline in religion he is deemed to be little better than an atheist.

I have no doubt wrongly estimated and anticipated events of the present and future, and gladly acknowledge the personal and tentative character of each particular assertion. I should like, however, to think myself free from the charge of disguising polemic as observation. I should like, in a word, to think that no one would be able to ascertain, merely from the following pages, whether their author was advocate of Free Trade or Protection, Socialist or Individualist, Pagan or Christian.

Portions of some of these chapters have already appeared—in substance — in the pages of *The Nation*, and I am indebted to the proprietors of that journal for permission to reproduce them. The book has been completed under circumstances of haste and pressure, for which I must ask indulgence. I would have delayed its publication until further leisure was possible, did I see any opportunity of that leisure being attained. But any one who has chosen to embark upon the storm and tumult of public affairs, must henceforth reconcile himself to the limitation of other interests to odd corners of time and short holidays avariciously husbanded. If I had delayed a study of modern England to a less hurried and more tranquil future, I might have found that it would be a very different England which I should then be compelled to examine.

C. F. G. MASTERMAN

Easter, 1909

CONTENTS

THE CONDITION OF ENGLAND

CHAPTER I

THE SPIRIT OF THE PEOPLE

WHAT will the future make of the present? That is a question which opens a wide field for speculation, but secures no certain reply. There is difficulty from two causes. The one is the imperfection of contemporary record, with its distortions or exaggerations of the life of to-day. The other is the inability of the life of to-day to picture its own appearance, even if accurately delineated, when set in historic background. So much of the future becomes then read into the present that (for example) altogether divergent elements in national life will be emphasised if that life be on the highway toward success, or hovering on the brink of calamity, or a cross section only of progress towards a national decay. The reconstruction of the past has been largely effected from the testimony of contemporary documents, each author setting out to write of his own personal experience. Yet with

I

all the material at our disposal, the vision of it is still fluctuating and changing; varying in the estimate of individuals, and from decade to decade. To some the days of declining Rome represent a period of tranquillity and human enjoyment; to others they appear as a tremendous warning of the triumph of the deadly sins. The Middle Age stands for one set of historians as a period of gold and innocence; with stately purposes, solemn processions, and widely diffused, if frugal, comfort; the whole illuminated by great dreams of adventure and aspiration. To another it presents itself as a prolonged delirium in which men wrestled in the darkness with fear and torment. To-day, perhaps too complacently, we assume that history will sharply distinguish our particular period of security from such troublous upheavals of Birth or of Death. We see ourselves painted as a civilisation in the vigour of early manhood, possessing contentment still charged with ambition; a race in England and Europe full of energy and of purpose, in which life, for the general, has become more tolerable than ever before. We would confess that we had not been able to "still the old sob of the sea," or compel Time to stand still in his courses, or abolish altogether those "two black birds of night," sighing and sorrow. But we would exhibit a people labouring and enjoying, more secure from plague, pestilence, and famine than in former ages, so accustomed to carry out unimpeded the labours of the day as almost to have forgotten the experience of a time when life itself was precarious and hazardous, and every morning an adventure into the unknown.

We would defend our Literature, our Art, our Architecture, as, if not indubitably inspired, yet respectable if judged by any but the highest standard; with an intelligence ever more widely diffused, much reading, some thought, even an original, or, at least, a courageous outlook towards the bigger problems of human existence and human destiny. Condemn our poverty, we confront it with our charity. Reveal the ravages of disease, cancer, appendicitis, complaints of the brain, nerves, and stomach, we retort with the revelation of our warfare against disease, maintained with a devotion and a determination unparalleled in all the past. If we have Atheisms, here are all our Churches; if Social Maladies, our Social Reformers. That any future estimate should associate us even in thought with the dying days of Rome or the delirium of the medieval twilight seems to us a proposition obviously incredible.

We have to remember, however, in such an estimate, that each generation stands in the roll-book of the centuries, not as it appears to itself, but as it appears to observers gazing, as from a distance, over a gulf of time. What records will survive, what evidence of existence, when all the pleasantness and amenity of little, comfortable, satisfied people have vanished over the limits of the world? Imagine, for example, the twentieth century interpreted to the twenty-fifth by its popular newspapers: to-day, more certainly than its popular drama, the abstract and chronicle of the time. England seen through the medium of its Sunday Press—the Press which to seven out of ten of its present inhabitants represents

the sole picture they possess of the world outside
their local lives—takes upon itself an appearance of
violence and madness. Men and women knife each
other in the dark. Children are foully butchered by
unknown assailants. Suicides sprinkle every page :—
now that a girl may die with another woman's husband ;
now that a family may escape the hell of unemployment ; now simply for weariness, because the whole
effort of life has lost significance and crumbled into
dust and ashes. The most insistent noise which
reverberates through their pages is the clicking of the
huge machine of English justice, as couples once
married in affection are torn apart, or a long procession of murderers, thieves, absconding solicitors,
fraudulent company promoters, are swept away into
the cold silence of the penal prison. The supply
seems never to run short. The various Courts are in
continuous sitting, and yet never overtake the work
so bountifully provided. Itinerant justices are even
compelled to journey round the countryside, arresting
their courses at the principal towns, in order more
speedily to deal with the continuous parade of
brutality, outrage, and unnatural crime. Is it possible, one can imagine the future historian demanding, that any one could have been in those days
altogether sane? as he pictures the decent wayfarer
stealing furtively through labyrinthine ways lest
ruffians should spring upon him in the dark, clutching
his difficult savings for fear that they should be
snatched from him ; with the terror of poverty yawning
before him, against which no prudence can guard, in
cities visibly given up to the dominion of lust and

greed. All this is in England: with a Sunday Press, if liberally providing the salt and flavour which so many colourless lives demand, yet on the whole committed to some standard of accuracy, some reflection of the fact in the record. In America, where such limitations are voted tiresome, the vision becomes gigantic, monstrous, like the Gargantuan architecture of its distorted cities. The observer who, in any future civilisation which may arise there, should attempt reconstruction of the barbaric past from a file of the New York Sunday editions, would find himself plunged into a region grotesque and hideous, like evil dreams.

But the survival of this peculiar literature is too impossible—perhaps too dreadful—an assumption. Let us believe that the great works will endure—the poetry, the fiction, the social studies and declamations of the representative people of the age. Are we in any better plight? Select ten, say, of the greatest writers of the Victorian era, and attempt from the picture which they present to effect a reconstruction of the Victorian age. The product is a human society so remote from all benignant ways as to demand nothing less than the advent of a kindly comet which will sweep the whole affair into nothingness. Our fathers led their decent, austere lives in that Victorian age which now seems so remote from us, making their money, carrying out their business and boisterous pleasure, inspired by their vigorous, if limited, creeds. They wrangled about politics and theology; they feasted at Christmas, and in the summer visited the seaside; they gave alms to the poor, and rejoiced that they lived in nineteenth-century England. But to the prophets of their age they were unclean from crown of head to sole of foot, a people who had visibly exhausted the patience of God. You may choose your verdict where you please —in Carlyle's "torpid, gluttonous, sooty, swollen, and squalid England," given up to the "deaf stupidities and to the fatalities that follow, likewise deaf"; or, in Ruskin's interpretation of the "storm cloud" as "a symbol of the moral darkness of a nation that has blasphemed the name of God deliberately and openly, and has done iniquity by proclamation, every man doing as much injustice to his brother as it was in his power to do." You may accept the condemnation kindly, as in Meredith's "folly perpetually sliding into new shapes in a society possessed of wealth and leisure, with many whims, many strange ailments, and strange fancies"; the condemnation plaintive, as in Arnold's "brazen prison," in which most men, with "heads bent o'er their toil," languidly "their lives to some unmeaning task-work give"; the condemnation defiant and rejoicing, as in Morris: "Civilisation which I *know* now is destined to perish; what a joy to think of." You may find it rising to a rather shrill shriek in the later Tennyson, with his protest against the city children—who "soak and blacken soul and sense in city slime"—with his calling upon vastness and silence to swallow up the noises of his clamorous, intolerable day. You may hear it sinking to a deep note of strong repudiation, in that vision of a city, "perchance of Death but certainly of Night," from the heart of which, in the pulpit of a great cathedral, a strange preacher proclaims the triumph of night and its despairs. One observer looking to the future will see "the whole life of the immense majority of its inhabitants, from infancy to the grave, a dreary routine of soulless, mechanical labor." Another will call for a cosmic cataclysm to quickly make an end. Another in a more chilling indifference will turn away from the unlovely sight as from a spectacle irrelevant, impossible. Literature has no tolerance for the existence of comfort and security which to so many people seems the last word of human welfare. And no reconstruction, from the works of genius, the great novelists, artists, critics, of the vanishing present, can provide any judgment much more satisfying to our pride than the judgment of summarised theft and fraud and violence which is the weekly enjoyment of many million readers.

We know—at once—that this is a one-sided verdict. Of ten thousand citizens, all but three or four will pass their lives unchronicled ; and these three or four —a murderer, an adulterer, an adventurer, a saint— will come to stand alone as lives whose existence is recorded. The remainder pursue their brave and patient labours, not too exacting in ideal, not too clamorous in pleasure, not at the end having very much to complain of, or being very eager to complain. So—in every civilisation, in every century, have passed the lives of the multitude of mankind. Yet it is change—obscure change in economic conditions, in aspirations, in faiths, in energies or lassitudes— which is responsible for the rise and fall of nations, for the variegated panorama of an ever-changing world. We have enjoyed in England security and settled society since the period of the great Civil War. For two hundred and fifty years ten generations have flourished and faded in a universe where regular government and an ordered apparatus of justice have guaranteed that life shall be reasonably safe, and that foresight shall attain reward. We are coming to believe that no circumstance will ever arise in which an insurance policy will not be honoured on presentation, and contracts entered into by the parents be fulfilled by the children. Yet during the whole of this period there have been cataclysms of change in the intimate life and convictions of the people which are more instinctive than opinions. So that the nineteenth-century civilisation is far removed from the eighteenth, and the twentieth from the nineteenth, in the estimate of the kingdom of the Soul. A study of those changes—a revelation and diagnosis of the hidden life of England — would be a study exceedingly worth attempting to-day. It would be a study which, passing from the external organisation, the condition of trade, the variation in fortune, would endeavour to tear out the inner secret of the life of this people : to exhibit the temper, mettle, response, character of an island race at a particular period of its supremacy. Changes in such temper and character are usually only revealed in times of national crisis : just as an individual only comes to "know himself" when confronted with the challenge of some overwhelming choice or anxiety. And as at that moment he reaps the fruit of the long obscure processes of sowing and ripening, so a nation in social upheavals, foreign perils, or some similar intrusion of reality, discovers in a moment also that it no longer possesses adequate forces of resistance, or that its religion, its boast of power, its patriotism, have been meaningless phrases.

"Contemporary England"—its origin, its varying elements of good and evil, its purposes, its future drift—is a study demanding a lifetime's investigation by a man of genius. But every tiny effort, if sincerely undertaken, may stimulate discussion of a problem which cannot be discussed too widely. It will study the most sincere of the popular writers of fiction, especially those who from a direct experience of some particular class of society—the industrial peoples, the tramp, the village life, the shop assistant, the country house—can provide under the form of fiction something in the nature of a personal testimony. It is assisted by those who to-day see instinctively the first tentative effort towards the construction of a sociology—investigation into the lives and wages, social character, beliefs and prejudices of various selected classes and localities. Biography is not without its contribution, especially the biography of typical men—a labour-leader who reveals himself as a conspicuous member of a labouring class at the base, or a politician who voices the scepticisms, manners, fascinations, and prejudices of a cultured, leisured society at the summit of the social order. The satirist and the moralist, if the grimace in the case of the one be not too obviously forced and bitter, and the revolt in the case of the other not too exacting and scornful, may also exhibit the tendencies of an

age. And there is always much to be learned from
those alien observers, each of whom, entering into
our midst a stranger, has set down his impression of
the life of our own people with something of the
freshness and curiosity of a child on a first visit to
Wonderland.

And here indeed it is largely upon foreign criticism
that we have to depend. We are familiar with
the "composite photograph" in which thousands of
superimposed likenesses result in the elimination of
personal variants, the production of a norm or type.
We seek a kind of mental or moral "composite
photograph" showing the average sentiment, the
average emotion, the average religion. And this is a
method of investigation far more familiar to Europe,
where introspection is regarded as a duty, than to
England, where introspection is regarded as a disease.
Most modern attempts at the analysis of the English
character have come from the European resident or
visitor. In books translated from the French, like
that of M. Boutmy, or from the German, like that of
Dr. Karl Peters, the Englishman learns with amazement that he presents this aspect to one observer,
that to another. His sentiments are like that of the
savage who is suddenly confronted with the looking-
glass; or, rather (since he is convinced that all these
impressions are distorted or prejudiced), like the
crowd which constantly gathers before the shop
windows which present convex or concave mirrors—
for the pleasure of seeing their natural faces weirdly
elongated or foreshortened. Yet we are compelled
to read such books. We are compelled to read all

such books. Even as a result of such unfair description we acknowledge the stimulus and challenge
which such description affords. We cannot help
being interested in ourselves. Sometimes, indeed,
these impartial minds are able to sting us into
anxiety by their agitation over things which we
generally accept as normal. Again and again the
foreigner and the colonial, entering this rich land
with too exuberant ideals of its wealth and
comfort, have broken into cries of pain and wonder
at the revelation of the life of poverty festering
round the pillars which support the material greatness
of England. A picture to which we have become
accustomed, which we endure as best we may, seems
to them a picture of horror and desolation. Again
and again we have found our material splendours and
extravagances which have developed by almost inconspicuous gradations year by year and generation
by generation, set out for surprise or condemnation,
by those who had maintained a tradition of simplicity,
even of austerity, in England's social life. Again and
again a revisit, after prolonged absence, has exhibited
some transformation of things of which those who
have been living in the current are hardly themselves conscious—a transformation effected by no
man's definite desires.

All such observations, however, are faced with
some fundamental difficulties. One of these is the
difficulty of ascertaining where the essential nation
resides: what spirit and temper, in what particular
class or locality, will stand to the future for twentieth-
century England. A few generations ago that difficulty

did not exist. England was the population of the
English countryside: the "rich man in his castle,"
the "poor man at his gate"; the feudal society of
country house, country village, and little country
town, in a land whose immense wealth still slept
undisturbed. But no one to-day would seek in the
ruined villages and dwindling population of the
countryside the spirit of an "England" four-fifths of
whose people have now crowded into the cities. The
little red-roofed towns and hamlets, the labourer in
the fields at noontide or evening, the old English
service in the old English village church, now stand
but as the historical survival of a once great and
splendid past. Is "England" then to be discovered in
the feverish industrial energy of the manufacturing
cities? In the vast welter and chaos of the capital
of Empire? Amongst the new Plutocracy? The
middle classes? The artisan populations? The
broken poor? All contribute their quota to the
stream of the national life. All have replies to give the
interrogator of their customs and beliefs and varying
ideals. All together make up a picture of a "roaring
reach of death and life" in a world where the one
single system of a traditional hierarchy has fissured
into a thousand diversified channels, with eddies
and breakwaters, whirlpools and sullen marshes, and
every variety of vigour, somnolence, and decay.

Again, no living observer has ever seen England in
adversity: beaten to the knees, to the ground. No
one can foresee what spirit—either of resistance or
acquiescence — latent in this kindly, lazy, good-
natured people might be evoked by so elemental a

challenge. England is often sharply contrasted with Ireland, and the Irish with the English people. What spirit would be manifest amongst the English people to-day if they had been subjugated by an alien conqueror, with their lands dispossessed, their religion penalised, their national ideals everywhere faced with opposition and disdain? Such an experience might have been stamped upon history if the Armada had reached these shores; it might have "staggered humanity" with unforgettable memories. Would an invaded England offer the resistance of an invaded Germany, or of an invaded Spain, in the Napoleonic Wars? How would we actually treat our "Communists" if they seized London after a time of national disaster and established a "Social" Republic? No one can tell what a man will do in such a shock as the Messina earthquake, or when the shells of the invader, without warning, crash through the ruins of his home. And no one can foresee what a nation will do in adversity which has never seen itself compelled to face the end of its customary world.

Again, we know little or nothing to-day of the great multitude of the people who inhabit these islands. They produce no authors. They edit no newspapers. They find no vocal expression for their sentiments and desires. Their leaders are either chosen from another class, or, from the very fact of leadership, sharply distinguished from the members of their own. They are never articulate except in times of exceptional excitement; in depression, when trade is bad; in exuberance, when, as on the "Mafeking" nights, they suddenly appear from nowhere to take possession of the city. England, for the nation or foreign observer, is the tone and temper which the ideals and determinations of the middle class have stamped upon the vision of an astonished Europe. It is the middle class which stands for England in most modern analyses. It is the middle class which is losing its religion; which is slowly or suddenly discovering that it no longer believes in the existence of the God of its fathers, or a life beyond the grave. It is the middle class whose inexhaustible patience fills the observer with admiration and amazement as he beholds it waiting in the fog at a London terminus for three hours beyond the advertised time, and then raising a cheer, half joyful, half ironical, when the melancholy train at last emerges from the darkness. And it is the middle class which has preserved under all its security and prosperity that elemental unrest which this same observer has identified as an inheritance from an ancestry of criminals and adventurers: which drives it out from many a quiet vicarage and rose garden into a journey far beyond the skyline, to become the " frontiersmen of all the world." [1]

But below this large kingdom, which for more than half a century has stood for " England," stretches a huge and unexplored region which seems destined in the next half-century to progress towards articulate voice, and to demand an increasing power. It is the class of which Matthew Arnold, with the agreeable insolence of his habitual attitude, declared himself to be the discoverer, and to which he gave the name of the

---

[1] F. M. Hueffer in " The Spirit of the People," a clever and suggestive analysis of Middle-Class England.

"Populace." "That vast portion of the working-class," he defined it, nearly forty years ago, "which, raw and half-developed, has long been half hidden amid its poverty and squalor, and is now issuing from its hiding-place to assert an Englishman's heaven-born privilege of doing as he likes, and is beginning to perplex us by marching where it likes, meeting where it likes, bending what it likes, breaking what it likes." "To this vast residuum," he adds, "we may with great propriety give the name of Populace." To most observers from the classes above, this is the Deluge; and its attainment of power—if such attainment ever were realised—the coming of the twilight of the gods. They see our civilisation as a little patch of redeemed land in the wilderness; preserved as by a miracle from one decade to another. They behold the influx, as the rush of a bank-holiday crowd upon some tranquil garden: tearing up the flowers by the roots, reeling in drunken merriment on the grass plots, strewing the pleasant landscape with torn paper and broken bottles. This class—in the cities—cannot be accused of losing its religion. It is not losing its religion, because it had never gained a religion. In the industrial centres of England, since the city first was, the old inherited faiths have never been anything but the carefully preserved treasure of a tiny minority. It is a class full of sentiment which the foreigner is apt to condemn as sentimentality. Amusing examples are familiar of its uncalculating kindliness. An immense traffic is held up for considerable time because a sheep—on its way to immediate slaughter—is entangled between two tramcars. The whole populace cheerfully submit to this inconvenience, sooner than consummate the decease of the unfortunate animal. In a certain pottery manufactory, the apparatus has been arranged for the baking process, and the fires are about to be lighted, when the mewing of a cat is heard from inside the kiln. The men refuse to proceed with the work. A whole day is spent in an endeavour to entice the cat out again ; and, on this proving fruitless, in the unloading of the kiln, in order to rescue the creature. When it is liberated, it is immediately hurled — with objurgations—into the river. The men were exasperated with the trouble which had been caused and the time wasted ; but they could not allow the cat to be roasted alive.

Next to this "sentimentality," so astonishing to Europe—because so irrational—comes the invincible patience of the English workman. He will endure almost anything—in silence—until it becomes unendurable. When he is vocal, it is pretty certain that things *have* become unendurable. I once had occasion to visit a family whose two sons were working on the railway when the dispute between directors and the union leaders threatened a universal disturbance. I inquired about the strike. There was an awkward pause in the conversation. " Jim won't have to come out," said the mother, " because he isn't on the regular staff." " Of course Jim will come out," said the father firmly, " if the others come out." " The fact is," they explained, after further silence, " we don't talk about the strike here ; we try to forget that there ever may be one." It was the experience of a thousand homes. There was no recognised or felt grievance. There was no clear understanding of the purpose and meaning of it all. But there were firmly planted in the mind two bedrock facts: the one, the tragedy that the strike would mean in this particular household; the other, the complete impossibility of any other choice but of the boys standing with their comrades in the day of decision. And this is England; an England which has learnt more than all other peoples the secret of acquiescence, of toleration, of settling down and making the best of things in a world on the whole desirable; but an England also of a determination unshaken by the vicissitudes of purpose and time, with a certain ruthlessness about the means when it has accepted the end, and with a patience which is perhaps more terrible in its silence than the violence of a conspicuous despair.

These and other qualities form an absorbing subject of study. A figure emerges from it all. It is the figure of an average from which all its great men are definitely variants. No body of men have ever been so "un-English" as the great Englishmen, Nelson, Shelley, Gladstone: supreme in war, in literature, in practical affairs; yet with no single evidence in the characteristics of their energy that they possess any of the qualities of the English blood. But in submitting to the leadership of such perplexing variations from the common stock, the Englishman is merely exhibiting his general capacity for accepting the universe, rather than for rebelling against it. His idea of its origin or of its goal has become vague and cloudy; definite statements of the average belief, set out in black and white by the average congregation, would astonish the average preacher. But he drives ahead along the day's work: in pursuing his own business, conquering great empires: gaining them by his power of energy and honesty, jeopardising them by his stiffness and lack of sympathy and inability to learn. So he will continue to the end; occupying, not in Mr. Pinero's bitter gibe the "suburb of the Universe"; but rather that locality whose jolly, stupid, brave denizens may be utilised for every kind of hazardous and unimaginable enterprise; fulfilling the work of another, content to know nothing of the reason of it all; journeying always, like Columbus, "to new Americas, or whither God wills."

It may be helpful to break up this composite figure of an "Englishman" into the various economic divisions of the present time, to examine what changes are fermenting amongst the rich, the middle stratum of comfort, the multitudinous ranks of the toilers, the dim hordes of the disinherited. A summary of science, art, literature, and religion in their influence upon the common life will indicate the changes most manifest, less in material conveniences than in the spirit of man. At the end arises the question of the future of a society, evidently moving in a direction which no one can foresee, towards experience of far-reaching change.

CHAPTER II

THE CONQUERORS

I

"ENGLAND is a sieve" is the cry of the astonished audience in Mr. Belloc's brochure on the fiscal question. "Poor old England is a sieve." They were filled with horror at the Tariff Reformer's revelation of the surplusage of imports over exports, and his vision of the golden sovereigns being drained from this country to pay for these undesirable incursionists. They already contemplated the time when the last piece of gold would have been transported to meet the demands of the insatiable "foreigner," and the whole country would suddenly realise that its pockets were empty—that it had spent all that it had. Undoubtedly similar if less pleasant arguments of a vigorous fiscal campaign have succeeded in shaking belief in England's prosperity. It is still possible in train or street, or places where men assemble, to find observers, with an air of sagacity, declaiming upon England's headlong rush towards poverty and the abyss. I remember listening for many hours, on the journey over the St. Gothard to Milan, to a fluent English traveller explaining to some astonished Italians that

England was steadily growing poorer year by year; less money accumulated, less money spent. Such are the follies of untrained minds, who are unable to read experience or to interpret figures. They cannot apprehend the astonishing facts of "super-wealth" as accumulated in this country; as accumulated in the past thirty years. That rate of accumulation has never been before paralleled: just as the expenditure which accompanies accumulation—for we are not a thrifty race — offers something new in a standard of whole classes. A serious study of the superfluous wastage of the nation might bring reassurance to all who are afraid of an enforced austerity of manners; even if it provides little gratification to those who would see expenditure devoted to desirable ends. Statistics present to the reader incredible arrays of increase: so much leaping forward of income-tax returns, unchecked by wars, borrowings, or trade depressions; nearly two hundred millions of the National Income divided amongst people whose individual incomes exceed five thousand a year. Where does it go to? How is it consumed? What asset of permanent value will be left behind as evidence of the super-wealth of the twentieth century? The answers to these questions are not entirely satisfactory. "Waste" is written large over a very substantial proportion of the national expenditure, and that far more in the private than in the public consumption. A Conservative leader once informed a meeting in Scotland that if all the rich men were abolished there would be no one left to give work to the poor people. That, however, was rather a popular method of combating Socialism, than a serious contribution to political economy. "To a retailer of news," says Mr. George Russell, "who informed him that Lord Omnium, recently deceased, had left a large sum of money to charities, Mr. Gladstone replied with characteristic emphasis, 'Thank him for nothing. He was obliged to leave it. He couldn't carry it with him.'" And what the rich man is to do with his money except to find employment, and how he is to escape the burden of death duties or graduated income tax in a world where every civilised nation has an eye upon his "super-wealth," are queries whose answer is conjectural.

The most obvious increase of this waste comes from the "speeding up" of living which has taken place in all classes in so marked a fashion within a generation. The whole standard of life has been sensibly raised, not so much in comfort as in ostentation. And the result is something similar to that in the insane competition of armaments which takes place amongst the terrified nations of the world. One year ten huge ironclads confront twenty. A decade after, fifteen huge ironclads of another type have replaced the first: to be confronted again with thirty of the new floating castles. So many millions have been thrown to the scrap heap. The proportion of power has remained unaffected. It is the same in the more determined private competition for supremacy in a social standard. Where one house sufficed, now two are demanded; where a dinner of a certain quality, now a dinner of a superior quality; where clothes or dresses or flowers, now more clothes, more

dresses, more flowers. It is waste, not because fine
clothes and rare flowers and pleasant food are in
themselves undesirable, but because by a kind of
parallel of the law of diminishing returns in agriculture, additional expenditure in such directions fails
to result in correspondent additions of happiness. In
many respects, indeed, the effect is not only negatively
worthless, but even positively harmful. Modern
civilisation in its most highly organised forms has
elaborated a system to which the delicate fibre of
body and mind is unable to respond. And the result
is the appearance (whimsical enough to Carlyle's
spectators "beyond the region of the fixed stars ") of
a society expending half its income in heaping up the
material of disease, to which the other half of its
income is being laboriously applied for remedy.

But the general effect (to the above-mentioned
dispassionate spectators) is of an extravagance of
wealth and waste which is only not insolent because
it is for the most part unconscious, the sport of blind
forces rather than the deliberate defiance of the limits
of human endeavour. It is not insolence or—as it
might have appeared in the olden days—a determination to rival the fabled immortals, which has charged
all our high roads with wandering machines racing
with incredible velocity and no apparent aim. Many
(such as W. E. Henley) demand " Speed in the face
of the Lord." Others are inflamed with the desire
for " driving abroad in furious guise," as an escape
from the *ennui* of a life which has lost its savour; as in
the tortured and bored procession in old Rome, for
the " easier and quicker" passing of the " impractic-

able hours." But a large proportion of those who have employed motor cars in habitual violation of the speed limit, and in destruction of the amenities of the rural life of England, have done so either because their neighbours have employed motor cars, or because their neighbours have not employed motor cars; in an effort towards equality with the one, or superiority over the other. When every man of a certain income has purchased a motor car, when life has become "speeded up" to the motor-car level, that definite increase of expenditure will be accepted as normal. But life will be no happier and no richer for such an acceptance; it will merely have become more impossible for those who (for whatever reason) are unequal to the demands of such a standard. And the same is true of the multiplication of meals; of the rise in the price of rent in certain districts of London, for example, because every one wants to live there; of numberless exactions and extortions which have grown up in a society whose members are "like wealthy men who care not how they give."

And mournfully enough this rather dull and drab extravagance of private living is accompanied by a severe scrutiny of any kind of public expenditure, and a resentful criticism of all efforts to stamp the memory of this age upon enduring brick and stone. The London County Council, housed in a few scattered hovels and warrens, proposed a year or two back to devote a few hundred thousand pounds to an "Hôtel de Ville," situate on the banks of the river opposite Westminster. And the opponents of the particular party in power had no difficulty in stirring up the wealthier classes into the fiercest protest against this attempt to leave the future with a permanent memorial of twentieth-century London. The one dignified and conspicuous building of the Victorian age—the Palace at Westminster—remains to-day scamped, truncated, and unfinished, because the nation, in a cold fit of retrenchment, was alarmed at the amount which it had already lavished upon it. Dr. Dill has shown in the Roman Peace, during the age of the Antonines and after, the people of the Empire turning with enthusiasm to great communal building; and every city setting itself to such achievements as remain to-day the wonder of the world. There is something of brutality, indeed, as well as something of large achievement, in the inadequacy of ends to means : as in the gigantic Pont du Gard, marching in its grandeur over a deep valley in order to conduct a tiny rivulet of water to a second-rate provincial city; or the enormous stone arenas which in every ruined Roman town mark the place of the communal games. But the brutality is charged with strength ; there is purpose in it, carried through with relentless tenacity; the purpose of the bending of Nature's stubborn resistance to the designs of man. What kind of building will represent for the astonishment of future eyes the harvest of the super-wealth of the British Peace? The signs are not propitious. A Byzantine Cathedral at Westminster, a Gothic Cathedral at Liverpool, a few town halls and libraries of sober solidity, the white buildings which to-day line Whitehall, and fill the passing stranger with bewilderment at a race "that thus could build," will be the chief legacies of this present generation. The thirteenth century gave us the Cathedrals; the sixteenth gave us the colleges at Oxford and Cambridge and the noblest of English country houses. These tiny Englands, with populations, in the aggregate, less than that of London to-day, and wealth incomparably smaller, have left us possessions which we can admire but cannot equal. "The work which we collective children of God do," complained Matthew Arnold, " our grand centre of life, our city for us to dwell in, is London! London, with its unutterable external hideousness, and with its internal canker of *publice egestas, privatim opulentia*, unequalled in the world." It was this contrast which gave point to a question which otherwise the plain man would put by as absurd: "If England were swallowed up by the sea to-morrow, which of the two, a hundred years hence, would most excite the love, interest, and admiration of mankind, the England of the last twenty years or the England of Elizabeth?"

Public penury, private ostentation—that, perhaps, is the heart of the complaint. A nation with the wealth of England can afford to spend, and spend royally. Only the end should be itself desirable, and the choice deliberate. The spectacle of a huge urban poverty confronts all this waste energy. That spectacle should not, indeed, forbid all luxuries and splendours: but it should condemn the less rewarding of them as things tawdry and mean. "Money! money!" cries the hero—a second-grade Government clerk—of a recent novel—"the good that can be done with it in the world! Only a little more: a little more!" It is the passionate cry of unnumbered thousands. Expenditure multiplies its return in human happiness as it is scattered amongst widening areas of population. And the only justification for the present unnatural heaping up of great possessions in the control of the very few would be some return in leisure, and the cultivation of the arts, and the more reputable magnificence of the luxurious life. We have called into existence a whole new industry in motor cars and quick travelling, and established populous cities to minister to our increasing demands for speed. We have converted half the Highlands into deer forests for our sport; and the amount annually spent on shooting, racing, golf — on apparatus, and train journeys and service — exceeds the total revenue of many a European principality. We fling away in ugly white hotels, in uninspired dramatic entertainments, and in elaborate banquets of which every one is weary, the price of many poor men's yearly income. Yet we cannot build a new Cathedral. We cannot even preserve the Cathedrals bequeathed to us, and the finest of them are tumbling to pieces for lack of response to the demands for aid. We grumble freely at halfpenny increases in the rates for baths or libraries or pleasure-grounds. We assert —there are many of us who honestly believe it— that we cannot afford to set aside the necessary millions from our amazing revenues for the decent maintenance of our worn-out " veterans of industry."

To the poor, any increase of income may mean a day's excursion, a summer holiday for the children ;

often the bare necessities of food and clothes and shelter. To the classes just above the industrial populations, who with an expanding standard of comfort are most obviously fretting against the limitations of their income, it may mean the gift of some of life's lesser goods which is now denied; music, the theatre, books, flowers. Its absence may mean also a deprivation of life's greater goods: scamped sick-nursing, absence of leisure, abandonment of the hope of wife or child. All these deprivations may be endured by a nation—have been endured by nations—for the sake of definite ends: in wars at which existence is at stake, under the stress of national calamity, or as in the condition universal to Europe a few hundred years ago, when wealth and security were the heritage of the very few. But to-day that wealth is piling up into ever-increasing aggregation: is being scrutinized, as never before, by those who inquire with increasing insistence, where is the justice of these monstrous inequalities of fortune? Is the super-wealth of England expended in any adequate degree upon national service? Is the return to-day or to posterity a justification for this deflection of men and women's labour into ministering to the demands of a pleasure-loving society? Is it erecting works of permanent value, as the wealth of Florence in the fifteenth century? Is it, as in the England of Elizabeth, breeding men?

No honest inquirer could give a dogmatic reply. The present extravagance of England is associated with a strange mediocrity, a strange sterility of characters of supreme power in Church and State. It is accompanied, as all ages of security and luxury are accompanied, by a waning of the power of inspiration, a multiplying of the power of criticism. The more comfortable and opulent society becomes, the more cynicism proclaims the futility of it all, and the mind turns in despair from a vision of vanities. It gives little leadership to the classes below it: no visible and intelligent feudal concentration which, taught in the traditions of Government and inheriting strength and responsibility, can reveal an aristocratic order adequate to the immense political and economic necessities of the people. Never, especially during the reaction of the past twenty years, were fairer opportunities offered to the children of wealthy families for the elaboration of a new aristocratic Government of a new England ; and never were those opportunities more completely flung away. Its chosen leaders can offer nothing but a dialectic, a perpetual criticism of other men's schemes, clever, futile, barren as the east wind. The political creed which it embraces—the Protectionist system which is going to consolidate the Empire and make every wife's husband richer—is almost entirely dependent for its propagation upon aliens from outside; politicians, economists, journalists, bred in an austerer life amongst the professional classes, and now employed by a society which seems without capacity to breed leaders of its own. It can compete for the pictures of great masters, but it leaves the men of genius of its own day to starve. It continues, now as always, garnishing the sepulchres of the prophets which its predecessors have stoned. It maintains large country houses which offer a lavish hospitality ; but it sees rural England crumbling into ruin just outside their boundaries, and has either no power or no inclination to arrest so tragic a decay. It fills vast hotels scattered round the coasts of England and ever multiplying in the capital, which exhibit a combination of maximum expenditure and display with a minimum return in enjoyment. It has annexed whole regions abroad, Biarritz and the Riviera coast, Austrian and German watering-places, whither it journeys for the recovery of its lost health, and for distractions which will forbid the pain of thinking. It plunges into gambles for fresh wealth, finding the demands of its standards continually pressing against its resources ; seeking now in South Africa, now in West Australia, now in other Imperial expansions, the reward which accompanies the conversion of the one pound into the ten. At best it is an existence with some boredom in it ; even when accompanied by actual intellectual labour : the management of an estate and its agents, directorships, or the overlooking of public and private philanthropies. At worst, more perhaps in America than in England, where the standard has not so much been overthrown as never securely established, it becomes a nightmare and a delirium.

Delirium would seem to be the fate of all societies which become content in secured wealth and gradually forget the conditions of labour and service upon which alone that security can be maintained.

" They describe," says Bagehot of the French memoirs,
" a life unsuitable to such a being as man in such a
world as the present one : in which there are no high
aims, no severe duties, where some precept of morals
seems not so much to be sometimes broken as to be
generally suspended and forgotten—such a life, in
short, as God has never suffered men to lead on the
earth long, which He has always crushed out by
calamity or revolution." Those who are familiar with
the methods of dissipation of much of the new wealth
of America—methods creeping across the Atlantic
—are familiar also with a life " unsuitable to such a
being as man." This society is only distinguished
from that which was consumed in the French Revolution, by absence of the wit and grace and polished
human intercourse which in part redeemed so selfish
and profitless a company. The pictures given from
time to time possess a note of exaggeration. They
flare a fierce white light upon a certain group
of rich people, with no toleration of shadows or half
tones. The thing stands ugly, in its pitiless glare,
a vision not good to look upon. Yet the essential
facts remain. The picture is only not a caricature,
because the life it describes is itself a caricature.
The forces which have moulded it have driven it
inevitably along certain paths : resistance is useless.
For in America enormous wealth—not only beyond
" the dreams of avarice," but in such aggregations
of millions as make it inconceivable even to its
possessors—has descended upon a tiny group of
persons who have exploited the resources of a continent. The first generation accumulated these great

possessions, in a fierce hand-to-hand conflict in which strength and cunning triumphed, and polish and pleasantness of manner and kindliness counted for nothing at all. To the second generation is given the spending of it. There are few traditions of social service. There are no feudal or communal responsibilities of social obligation. Charity is resented by the recipient and tiresome to the giver. The founding of Universities becomes too commonplace to attract. Settlements are voted drab and unsatisfying. Religion has become a plaything. All other avenues being thus closed, there remain but a self-indulgence which in itself breeds satiety, and a competition of luxurious display, which, in its more advanced stages, passes into an actual insanity. The second generation here is often weaker than its fathers. The fierce will-power which ensured financial success in the most terrific financial struggle that the world has ever seen, has exhausted the capacities of the family lineage. It has been raised on the principle of "doing as one likes." It pursues its existence through an unreal, fantastic world, in a luxurious expenditure as fantastic as a veritable "Dance of Death."

Mr. Upton Sinclair, Mr. Frank Norris, Mrs. Wharton, and other American novelists have presented pictures of the luxurious waste and extravagance of a plutocracy which have been scornfully repudiated by its members. Yet almost every individual incident or place in "the Metropolis"—"Castle Havens," Newport, the queer palaces of New York, the crude scattering of fortunes easily won in scratching the earth or wrecking a railway—could be paralleled in the actual society of America. Many could even be paralleled in England, where millionaire company promoters, on their hectic path between poverty through prosperity to prison or suicide, will purchase so many miles of good English land, build round it a great wall ten feet high, construct billiard rooms under a lake, remove a hill which offends the view. " He was kind to the poor," they wrote on the grave of one of them, who had devastated the middle classes with the promise of high interest for investment, guaranteed on his prospectuses by the names of Proconsuls and Ambassadors of world-wide fame. The disease may not have attained its full consummation in this country ; that is in part because of a standard which, though crumbling, still struggles to survive ; in part because the wealth accumulation is less sudden and overwhelming : in part also because we are satisfied with less bizarre manifestations of the always unsatisfied demand for pleasure. Yet we have parallels, even in this country to " Castle Havens." " It had cost three or four millions of dollars, and within the twelve-foot wall which surrounded its grounds lived two world-weary people who dreaded nothing so much as to be left alone." The house had many gables, in the Queen Anne style : from the midst of them shot a Norman tower decorated with Christmas tree wreaths in white stucco : overlapping this was the dome of a Turkish mosque rising out of this something like a dove-cot : out of that, the slender white steeple of a Methodist country church : on top a statue of Diana. " Has there ever been any insanity

come. In Mr. Hueffer's entertaining novel of New York, a rich man's son, scandalised at the method by which his father obtained his super-wealth, attempts restitution to the victims. They one and all indignantly repudiate his "charity." One and all they ask to "come in" on the ground floor in any future flotations and manipulations which he may be designing. They reject the return of the proceeds of piracy. All they desire is a partnership in future piratical raids against a person or persons unknown.

It is a society organised from top to bottom on a "money" basis, a business basis, with everything else as a side show. The men listen to President Roosevelt's fierce words about the Trusts and Corporations. They have no resentment. It is "only Teddy's way." It cheers up the people with the hope that something will be done, while they themselves are secure in the knowledge that everything which can be done is in the control of the money power. When they find a reformer whom they can silence by force, they crush him. If they cannot crush him, they purchase him. If he can neither be crushed nor purchased, they ignore him. Religion is easily woven into the scheme of things, and pleasantly harmonised with the accepted way of living. The Bishop of London preaches in Wall Street, eloquently urging the business men to regard their wealth as a stewardship from God. Far from resentment, the business men abandon the Stock Exchange gamble for a quarter of an hour, press round the bishop to shake his hand. "Bishop," they say, "that discourse of yours made us feel real good." Then they return to the Stock Exchange gamble. A prominent preacher is lured over at an immense salary from England to preach to a church of the wealthy. He braces himself for a great effort, and denounces their riches, their works, and their ways. He expects an outbreak of indignation. He discovers instead a universal congratulation. The wealthy and their wives flock to his church, hoping to hear some more. The receipts of the pew rents double. They talk of raising his salary. The more he denounces, the more they applaud. The experience indeed is common to all similar societies: since the day when the prophet complained that his listeners crowded to hear him as he denounced their vices, "and so," he reproaches himself, "thou art unto them as a very lovely song, of one that hath a pleasant voice and can play well on an instrument."

Only some realities cannot be altogether excluded. Change and Death knock with gaunt hands, and refuse all proffered monetary bribes. Here a frantic millionaire, going blind, offers two million dollars to any one that can cure him. The high gods remain indifferent to the challenge. Teeth drop out, hair drops off; old age creeps on apace: the wealthiest are trembling at the approach of the end. The visitor to "The Metropolis" from the south beholds "a golf course, a little miniature Alps, upon which the richest man in the world pursued his lost health, with armed guards and detectives patrolling the place all day, and a tower with a search-light whereby at night he could flood the grounds with light by pressing a button." A motor accident, an occasional sensational divorce case, the death of a child, tear down suddenly all the blinds and cushions, revealing the richest as unprotected as the poorest in a universe altogether indifferent to such slight things as man's profit and gain. Outside, an occasional crisis, the panic fear of people to whom wealth means attainment, that their wealth is vanishing, brings the accumulation of vast fortune toppling to the ground. There follows a crop of suicides: then the machine recovers and swings forward again on its blind, staggering progress nowhither. The secret places of the world are ravaged, the wise men subpœnaed, all cunning invention subsidised, that some alchemy may be found which will resist the ravages of time, preserve a beauty that is departing, stay the inexorable chariots of the hours. There are even attempts to turn the flank of the enemy: by "Christian Science" liberally supported, to abolish, if not disease, at least its sufferings; by "Psychical Research," to communicate with a company pursuing a similar ineffectual existence beyond the grave. "What is it all worth?" is the question which lurks in the background, refusing to be stifled; which drives occasional revolters, wearied of the repetition of these pleasures, into efforts after philanthropies, or to shoot wild beasts in remote places, or even into political and religious adventure. So they come and after a little while they go, none knowing whence or whither: a company of tired children, flushed and uncomfortable from the too violent pursuit of pleasure: who thought, in the snatching of what things seemed desirable in a life given over to enjoyment, to effect an attainment which has ever been jealously denied to the family of mankind.

But here, after all, in England or America, is only the life of the few.   If their existence is conspicuous it is because in distortion and dangerous cases there can be most clearly realised the ravages of disease. In England for the most part wealth is encased and preserved in a wall of social tradition; and the majority of men, however opulent, have some interests and occupations which redeem them from the mere blind pursuit of pleasure.   Yet in England it is becoming increasingly questioned how far this wealth is providing permanent benefit to the community. It is expended in the maintenance of a life—a life and a standard—bringing leisure, ease and grace, some effort towards charities and public service, an interest, real or assumed, in literature, music, art, social amenity, and a local or national welfare.   But it offers little substantial advantage, in endowment, building, or even direct economic or scientific experiment. The percentages of legacy bequeathed to charity or to education are lamentably low; and of these percentages most are deflected into charity or religion in its least remunerative forms.   Philanthropy is large and liberal, but the aggregate of poverty remains unaffected by it, or even, to the minds of the intimate observer, deepened.   Much of it appears less as the effort of intelligence and compassion than as the random and often harmful attempt to satisfy a conscience disturbed by penury adjacent to plenty.

Social experiments involving thought as well as money—a Bournville, a Toynbee Hall, a Limpsfield colony for epileptics, a hospital for the new cure of consumption—are still sufficiently rare as to attract attention. A few thousands bequeathed to miscellaneous institutions out of a fortune of many hundred thousands is still so unusual as to evoke considerable newspaper adulation. The fact is, that the necessary expenditure upon an accepted standard of living is so exacting and so continually increasing with the increase of new demands, that little superfluity remains for adventure in social or charitable effort. Some of the wealthiest landlords have been reducing their pensions on their estates, now that the State provides five shillings a week; in part, perhaps, in order that the recipients should not be demoralised by this enormous access of fortune; but in part because they can see other channels into which this expenditure may at once be deflected. Families with incomes of many thousands a year— caught in the cog-wheels of this vast machine, this swollen definition of essential things—find a real difficulty in making " both ends meet." Most—in a calm hour—will deplore it. The old look back with regret to an austerer day, to the time when central London had no Sunday restaurant, and it was only necessary for the few to know the few. The young— or the more thoughtful of them—look forward with foreboding, wondering how long the artisan, the shop assistant, the labourer, the unemployed, will content to acquiesce in a system which expends upon a few weeks of random entertainment an amount that would support in modest comfort a decent family for a lifetime.

"The most unpremeditated, successful, aimless Plutocracy"—so it appears to one shrewd observer— "that ever encumbered the destinies of mankind." He sees it continually being recruited from below. Companies rise like bubbles, expand, burst, carrying with them into the upper air their promoters and the parasites which follow in their train. Now it is the gold mines of South Africa which offer a particular crop of amiable, ignorant, generously spending persons to swell the general extravagance. Now from America comes the importation of millions which are scattered in the home country in various forms of elaborate expenditure. Now old-established businesses are renovated, purchased, floated on the market inordinately "boomed"; with subsequent collapse to the shareholders, with substantial margin of profit to the "undertakers." Those who retain the wealth thus cleverly won, settle down in the English countryside to make the money circulate, and generally to have a good time. Now, again, the more feverish industry and energy of the new cities pile up a monopoly value of millions upon the land which is "owned" by private persons: who find themselves, as they rise and sleep, suddenly inundated with a steady flow of money which is exacted as tribute from the working peoples. So, in various ways, the enrichment of a new wealthy class which is compensating for its newness by liberal hospitalities, and the effort of some old-established rich families not to be pushed under in display by these alien intruders,

has " set a pace " which is driving the whole of modern
life into a huge apparatus of waste. Numbers go
down in the competition: then the country estates
are sold and pass into the hands of South African
millionaires or the children of the big traders, or the
vendors of patent medicines. Others find themselves
continually in debt, adventuring into the City as
directors of companies, or attempting to obtain unearned increase by following in the train of the great
adventurers. Sometimes, as in the South African pro-
motions of 1895, the whole of a society flings itself into
a furious gambling mania, from which the few astute
suck no small advantage, and ultimately attain the
honour which is the reward of great possessions.
There are many who endeavour to keep their heads
in this confused tumultuous world, who still cherish an
ideal of simplicity, and upon exiguous income will
maintain a standard of manners and intelligence.
More and more, it would appear, these are destined to
capitulate: to be compelled to "give in" and accept
the new expenditure, or to be pushed aside as outside
the main current of successful life. The vision of this
new " Plutocracy " appears to be drifting steadily away
from the vision which, at any historic time, has been
held to justify the endowment of leisure and comfort,
and the control of great fortunes, as a trust for the
service of mankind.

For this " Plutocracy," though accepting distinction
in art, in literature, in the governance of Empire, as
a matter of evidence to-day itself contributes but
little to these desirable ends. Mr. Mallock can
laboriously demonstrate—in counter reply to the

demands of Socialism—that the wealth of the world is in the main increased by the inventor, the individual, the ingenious multiplier of energy and discoverer of scientific appliances. Many of the richer classes accept such a demonstration as an infallible proof of the justice of present wealth distribution. Other writers can justify an opulent and leisured class above, for the provision of clever and energetic persons who will cultivate the tradition of statesmanship, or encourage disinterested experiment in advancement of knowledge or the service of humanity. But the actual rulers of Empire, the men of science, the great soldiers, the great artists and writers, as a matter of fact very rarely appear as the children of, or are rewarded by the qualifications for entrance into, the governing classes. The wills and legacies presented day by day in the newspapers are themselves a judgment and refutation of any attempt to demonstrate parallel between achievement and material acquisition. At the summit are usually names of obscure unknown persons, who bequeath, with sundry small diversions into charity or hospitals, the bulk of their hundreds of thousands to their relatives. Here a successful brewer, there a speculator in land, again a "financier" in the city, or a landlord who has not even had the enterprise to speculate, but merely placidly drawn his rents from the developing town or half a countryside; or again, the owners of large trade organisations now run by skilled and alert managers as limited liability companies : these form the staple material of the huge accumulations which make up the bulk of those hundreds of millions which regularly pass every year from some few hundred persons to some few other hundreds. Quite low down in this list of obscure wealthy, conspicuous if they attain six figures, and often falling below five, are the men who have created and have served; authors of European distinction, generals with ten campaigns to their name, politicians who have devoted their lives to public affairs, men of science who have effected discoveries for which all humanity is richer. Under no kind of analysis does examination of these names and figures provide any co-ordination of wealth and capacity, or wealth and national or imperial or humanitarian service. The observer has not only to lament the paucity of talent amongst the children of families with high past record of spacious and splendid renown. He is not compelled to turn his attention in perhaps unfair emphasis to that section of society which regards its possessions as a trinket or plaything, and, amid an atmosphere of frivolity, is engaged in squandering its brief existence through every variety of passionless pleasure. It is enough for him, in analysing the ordinary undistinguished accumulation of great wealth, to note the balance of social service on the one hand, of remuneration on the other; and to wonder how long the obscure multitudes who labour with so scanty a return, in order that these may enjoy, will continue to be satisfied with what (to them) appears so improvident a bargain. And if this detached observer, inspired neither by hate nor envy, were asked to summarise the social advantage of all this heaped-up wealth

expended by the few who have attained, he would
be compelled to find it in a social convenience and
amenity; in the provision of opportunity, embedded
in pleasant surroundings and with bodily discomforts
as far as possible removed, for entertaining conversation.

So, concentrating themselves especially in London,
for an annual campaign of association, there gather
every year the companies of the successful. They
have expended some half their days in tranquillity
and quiet places—in rural England, in high Swiss
mountain valleys—anywhere in which the too exasperated material of the human mind can be nursed
back into some semblance of sanity. They gather,
from the four winds, into the tumult of the capital, to
occupy the remaining half of the year in deliberate
tearing the fabric of that mind to pieces in an orgy
of human intercourse. It is effort directed at the
highest pressure, with no interspaces of silence in
which to learn, to suffer, or to enjoy. It is the effort
of those few who have attained success in a race where
the majority are content with existence and endurance, to exhibit the magnitude of that success in a
transitory experience of too violently accelerated life.
For these months nobody is ever alone; nobody ever
pauses to think; no one ever attempts to understand.
All quick and novel sensations are pressed into the
service of an ever more insistent demand for new
things. Parliament pays its tribute, in a labyrinth of
dining-rooms and a famous terrace, which is an annexe
—as the Empire is an annexe—to the activities of
this restless energy. What passes for British Art in

a Royal Academy and other exhibitions; the Opera,
dragging European singers to stimulate an audience numbed by the whirl of circumstance; any
unexpected appeal, a decadent French play, actors
from an earlier, simpler, passionate South, an
audacious novel or two, a passing scandal, serve
to infuse the concoction with some lambent vitality.
But, for the most part, it is talk—talk—talk; talk
at luncheon and tea and dinner; talk at huge, undignified crowded receptions, where each talker is
disturbed by the consciousness that his neighbour
is desirous of talking to others; talk at dances and
at gatherings, far into the night; with the morning
devoted to preparation for further talking in the day
to come. It is talk usually commonplace, sometimes
clever, occasionally sincere; of a society desirous of
being interested, more often finding itself bored, filled
with a resolute conviction that it must "play the
game"; that this is the game to be played, that it
must be played resolutely to the end. Elemental
things occasionally intrude, marriages, and those
unexpected deaths which refuse to postpone themselves to a more convenient out-of-season. What
does it all mean? No one knows. What does it all
come to? Again, no one knows. To many it stands
for the inevitable, as the factory life is inevitable to
some, the field drudgery to others. A few it stimu-
lates with a consciousness of power in human intercourse and the subtle sensation of rejoicing in a
crowd. To a tiny remnant alone it presents the
appearance of a complicated machine, which has
escaped the control of all human volition, and is

progressing towards no intelligible goal; of some
black windmill, with gigantic wings, rotating un-
tended under the huge spaces of night.

It is not illuminated by high ardours. It is not
disfigured by great crimes. The criticism of its
" smartness," its vulgarity, its selfishness, advanced
largely by women novelists and unfamiliar critics, is
based upon a biassed reading of values. There are
those who are pushing to get in, as there are those
who are pushing to get out. There are egoisms here
as in all human energies; revolts which drive their
victims outside the accepted standards; reactions
which find expression in a petulance or a despair.
Neither to-day nor to-morrow will this strange turmoil
stand for anything conformable to the record of various pleasure-loving societies, which from time to time
have lived and flourished and died. But if its vicious-
ness be but the palest reflection of similar past efforts,
its activities and devotions are also set in grey. It
has none of the fury of passionate pleasure which
accompanied the decline and fall of Rome; but it has
little of the large utterance, and magnificence of
artistic display, and consciousness of occupying a great
arena in the world's affairs, which speaks from every
day's record of that long autumn of decay. It has
few of those feverish and almost unintelligible lusts
and cruelties which make the story of the Early
Renaissance in Italy like the memory of evil dreams.
But, on the other hand, it will neither stamp upon the
stone and marble of its dwelling-places, nor store
up upon the walls of its cities and opulent houses,
nor write in the life-history of its men and women,

that harvest of an artistic beginning and a rich individual experience which makes the Renaissance appear as one of the wonder-ages of the world. To-day, here, in England, it plays and trifles with large forces which, if it once understood, it might flee from in terror and dismay. Its social and philanthropic enterprises are fairly ample; it bestows considerable sums on public and private charities, shepherding its friends into drawing-room meetings to listen to some attractive speaker—an actor, a Labour Member, a professional humorist—pleading for pity to the poor. It discusses the possibility of social upheavals in that dim, silent, encompassing life in which all its activities are embedded—the incalculable populations, which set the society that matters in the midst of a rude and multitudinous society that does not count. It plays in good humour with light schemes of Social Reform; wondering, like the pleasant salons of Paris in the new age of gold before the Revolution, whither events are tending; convinced, as these salons also were convinced, that nothing can alter the effectual standards of its world. It plays with religion; listening to the agreeable discourses of one popular preacher, urging kindliness and charity and toleration to all men; amused at the violence of another, denouncing all its works and ways; a little disturbed by a third, feeling the sudden intrusion of the cold hand of a universe in which all its standards are unknown. "Sydney Smith talking," wrote Carlyle in his diary, "other persons prating, jargoning. To me, through these thin cobwebs, Death and Eternity sat glaring." Only

in an occasional solitary hour, in that magic twilight
of a London summer evening, or in the flare of a
dim dawn over the sleeping city, do such disturbing
visitants tear the silence as with a sudden cry.

It is an aggregation of clever, agreeable, often
lovable people, whose material wants are satisfied
by the labour of unknown workers in all the world,
trying with a desperate seriousness to make something of a life spared the effort of wage-earning.
It is built up and maintained in an artificial, and
probably a transitory, security—security which has
never been extended in the world's history to more
than a few generations. It will continue with each
until each drops out, if uncomplaining, a little
fatigued, and the fresh recruits take the place of
the deserters and the dead.

No study is more disheartening, none more disturbing, than the study of those companies of
human beings, which in various periods of social
security have attempted in similar fashion to play
with the purposes of life. " Some set their hearts on
building and gardening," wrote Tavannes of the
Court of the Valois, "on painting or reading or the
chase. They run after an animal all day and get
their faces torn in the woods ; or they trot from
morning till evening after a ball of wool ; or they
spend the day and the night in games of hazard, from
which they rise without any great reluctance ; or they
buy arms and horses, and never use them." " Sadness
and melancholy without a legitimate cause," he declares, "are their own just punishment ; a failure
to recognise the grace of God which has made us

immortal." More than an age of Adventure, more even than an age of reckless Wickedness, does time judge and condemn an age of ineffectual Pleasure.

> Where are the braveries, fresh or frayed?
>   The plumes, the armours—friend and foe?
> The cloth of gold, the rare brocade?
>   The mantles glittering to and fro?
> The pomp, the pride, the royal show?
>   The cries of war and festival?
> The youth, the grace, the charm, the glow?
>   Into the night go one and all.

Mane floreat, et transeat: vespere decidat. Et custodia in nocte—" As a watch in the night."

II

"Conquerors" they appear to the critic abroad: "the Island Pharisees" to the critic at home. Many attempts have been made in recent times to describe in fiction this new leisured life of England: the particular contemporary aspect of that Fair "wherein it was contrived should be sold all sorts of Vanity, and that it should last all the year long." There is something of it in the *Egoist*, something also in the extraordinary analysis by Mr. Henry James of the meaning of situation in various companies of rich, idle persons whose utility or significance in any rational universe it is difficult to apprehend. Some of the younger novelists, with less detachment and with less acceptance, have attempted interpretation, not of the moods of the moment, but of the meaning of a whole society. Mr. Galsworthy, for example, in a rather fierce indictment

—gazing at the struggle for continuance amongst the successful, like a spectator gazing at a struggle of ants or bees—has drawn up an impeachment of the country house and conventional life of successful England. His hero enters this society from abroad, examining it, as if for the first time, with curious eyes, without any background of the fortifying curriculum of the accepted English education. He is excited to questioning and resentment by the ironical smiles and comments of a foreigner, a chance acquaintance in a third-class carriage, who, having rejected everything, swallowed "all the formulas," has no attitude but that of irony towards the folly of human things. He attempts to allay that resentment by personal examination of the various phases of the life of the "Conquerors." He wanders desolately from the oppression of the club to the oppression of an artistic and literary gathering ; and thence to the futility of the philanthropic attempt to elevate the lower classes by chess and coffee and bagatelle. He notes the well-fed, bullet-headed, jovial crowds in the streets, the wives and husbands who have settled down to a routine of affection, the wives and husbands who have settled down to a routine of dull hatred and acceptance. The complacency of it all, its satisfaction, its docility, its absence of high purpose and adventure, haunt him like a nightmare. He essays the countryside with no better result. He stays a night with a lonely vicar. He beholds a warder guarding the huge convict prison—symbol of the unsuitability of Christianity to practical affairs. He walks the English roads with an energetic Indian civilian, who is very content to run the machine, without caring to inquire whether the machine is worth running at all. Finally, in the atmosphere of the English country house, serene and dominant, and triumphantly content, he realises that he is not of this company. Some disturbing madness has come upon him, which compels him to inquire, where other men are content to enjoy. And that way lies madness — or the struggle up a hill path, difficult and extended, towards some new form of sanity. So he brands them with some contempt and some anger as " Pharisees "—the island Pharisees, who have mistaken the accident of their own favoured circumstances for the reward of merit, and now present an invincible complacency to all the arrows of outrageous fortune. In such a condemnation he is something less than just to a race which has been considerably misjudged and misunderstood. The men and women which fall under the lash of Mr. Galsworthy's satire have none of the historic characteristics of the Pharisee. Their ancestors may have thanked God that they were not as other men are. These are but astonished that the distinction was noticeable or important. The "other men " have vanished from the picture. They would be acknowledged to be of common blood, common faith, common nationality. But they so readily pass unnoticed that it would seem a work of supererogation to drag them on to the stage at all. The standard of life which is only maintained by the labour of obscure persons becomes accepted as normal ; to be received without questioning. It is

less easy, indeed, to excite questions than to pro-
pound answers. In the study of the psychology of
"Space" and "Time" the student is familiar with
the difficulty, not of explanation but of inquiry : "here
is space, here is time—What is all the pother about?"
is the attitude of the plain man. And "here is human
life, as we know it," is the attitude of the "plain
man" in the class where is accepted as fixed and
unalterable, that the services of many shall minister
to the comfort of the few. The "Conquerors" have got
far beyond the stage of the Pharisee. They are the
children's children of those rather crude exponents of
complacency and pride. They reveal no ostentatious
complacency and pride. Their attitude is rather one
of acceptance. It is not that they thank God that
they are not as other men are. It is that they can
imagine no conceivable readjustment of the universe
which could make other men as themselves ; or
themselves different. They are enterprising, but
they shun adventure. They are kind, with no real
possibility of sympathy. Enormous shut doors
separate them from the real world : and they bend
the world to their desires. "Doubts don't help you,"
says one of Mr. Galsworthy's characters. "How
can you get any good from doubts? The thing
is to win victories." "Victories?" is the reply.
"I'd rather understand than conquer." But the
"Island Race" has preferred to conquer rather than
to understand. And wisdom is justified of all her
children.

Once or twice, indeed, the critic is willing to suggest that perhaps the choice is not so mad a one

after all. The ironical foreigner who prefers to resist, beg, cringe, and criticise, presents a figure not wholly heroic. He has fallen back on facts. He has sucked the salt and rind of life. He has deliberately contracted himself out of the universe of make-believe which he sees encompassing the people amongst whom his lot is cast. He enjoys his weakness and his laughter: the machine moves on; doing the work of the world. And these people, as he sees them—with their blindness to real issues, their carefully tended gardens, and the gates so severely padlocked which guard the pathways to waste spaces outside—may perhaps after all have learned the lesson of compromise in a world of frantic possibilities. The garden must be cultivated: cultivated, even if the sun which so pleasantly encourages its flowers to pass into kindly fruit is in reality a furnace of incredible fury; and the earth, of which this garden is a tiny segment, running along an illimitable inane towards no intelligible goal. "Spirit ruins you," declares the little foreign barber, condemned always to shave paupers in the cellars of a Rowton lodging-house. "In this world what you want is to have no spirit." The *drôle* Irish actor dies drunk in squalor, all because he has something in him "which will not accept things as they are, believing always that they should be better." "When he was no longer capable of active revolution he made it by getting drunk. At the last this was his only way of protesting against society." And occasionally, from the heart of the mechanical routine, there comes evidence that

understanding is there—that understanding is possible : that not grossness or obtuseness or selfishness,
as in the first hasty verdict, but the deliberate determination *not* to face the realities is the real motive
power which keeps the system from falling into
decay. For if the realities be faced, the bottom
falls out of the world ; and man, naked, shivering,
and alone, is suddenly left defenceless, confronting
the fire and the darkness. The hero of one of Mr.
Galsworthy's novels finds his uncle, a shrewd, insen-
sitive man of business, criticising the modern uncen-
sored drama. "'What's right for the French and
Russians, Dick,' he said, 'is wrong for us. When
we begin to be *real* we only really begin to be
false.' 'Isn't life bad enough already?' he asks.
It suddenly struck Shelton that, for all his smile,
his uncle's face had a look of crucifixion. He stood
there very straight, his eyes haunting his nephew's
face ; there seemed to Shelton a touching muddle in
his optimism—a muddle of tenderness and of in-
tolerance, of truth and second-handedness. Like
the lion above him, he seemed to be defying Life
to make him look at her." [1]

"Defying Life to make him look at her" has been
the effort of all societies which have been removed
for a time from the immediate necessities of labour,
hunger, and cold. That defiance of life is not so
mad a thing as it at first appears. It attempts,
and to a certain extent with success, to create a
possible existence for an average which can never be
far removed from the conventional. It works : that

[1] *The Island Pharisees.* J. Galsworthy.

is its justification; this gospel of the Second Best, which substitutes a placid friendliness for love's high ardour, and prettiness for beauty, and a compromise of cruelty and kindliness for social justice, and a standard of convention for the demands of a compelling religion. It is assailed in scornfulness and bitterness and passion, by the advocates of these various flaming emotions; by the religious prophets who demand sincerity; by the social prophets who cry for equality and compassion; by the artists who wish to challenge the unveiled Truth; by the great lovers who are outraged by this ignoble treatment of the "Lord of Life of terrible aspect." But the thing swings forward, indifferent or but politely tolerant of the clamour; because its inhabitants know that the secure second best is a wiser choice (for them) than the hazards of an effort towards a doubtful larger attainment. Most of those who have demanded less limited horizons, and pressed forward to sail on uncharted seas, and adventured "beyond the sunset," have vanished and been heard of no more. There is surely justification for any who in the face of such disasters confine their voyages to the familiar creeks and havens, and never willingly forsake the shelter of the shore.

And still to other nations—less successful in the economic struggle, less immovably confident in attainment—these people appear as "the Conquerors": dominating the world with a certain serene confidence in the justice of their supremacy which is at once enviable and exasperating to the critic from outside. The Englishman abroad is inclined to gush a little

at the fascination of the foreign freedom, especially at
the charm and beauty of the South. He finds here
manners, and an immemorial tradition of courtesy,
and a less slavish devotion to material ends. But the
South itself is under no such illusion. To these it is
the English who are the people that have attained.
Italy, Spain, Hungary, Bulgaria, are all desirous of
unravelling the secret and accepting the standard of
the dominant race. Even the writers of literature,
although they may mingle a delicate irony with
their praise, yet are content to emphasise the defici-
ences of their own people; in the contrast presented
to them by the immigrant English who settle in their
coasts, and maintain their own life and manners unconscious of the life and manners of their neighbours.

It is as a conquering race, secure, imperturbable,
profoundly careless of opinion outside, that the
astonished foreigner encounters the Englishman
abroad. "I see them at work," writes M. Marcel
Prevost, from Biarritz, "and never perhaps have I better
known and understood their Anglo-Saxon energy than
here, on the French soil, in a French hotel, kept not
by Germans or Swiss, but by the French of the Midi."
He applauds even while he criticises. He mingles his
irony with admiration. He sees the Conquerors, not
triumphant over the conquered, not consciously brutal
to the conquered, but simply brushing them aside as
irrelevant; never, indeed, seeing them at all. He
sees, in fact, this English colony contemplating certain
cities of France, not as a land with centuries of history
beaten into its soil, but as a place where the amenities
of climate enable them to transplant into a Southern

air a portion of England. The French—even in the towns of the stranger, where the French colony is numerous, in London or in Barcelona, for example— never give the impression of a civic garrison engaged by the Mother Country. Whilst a few hundreds of English people in a French town, " obstinately speaking nothing but English, inhabiting only English lodgings, dressing only in the English fashion, practising their religion, their sports, and their games, with an easy ostentation, end by persuading us," he ironically complains, " that we are the strangers—or at least the conquered nation." It is this mingling of security and indifference that fills him with despair. In Biarritz, Pau, Dinard—he might have said in the whole *côte d'azur* of the Riviera—" the English have conquered us," he declares. *Excellent milieu pour étudier leurs procédés de conquête.*

In the attempt to analyse the secret of this supremacy, he fixes attention especially upon three points. First, the English are at home abroad. When we go to foreign lands, says M. Prevost, it is the stranger who interests us, his manners and habits, his peculiarities, the ways in which he differs from us. When the Englishman goes abroad, the customs of the country, the opinion of the people amongst whom he lives, count for nothing. He comes to Biarritz to live his life, the traditional English life, made up of bounteous feeding, of violent physical exercise, of clubs, and of bridge. He describes the types which he found at the Hotel Victoria, all entirely complacent, all self-sufficient, all just blandly tolerant of the occasional presence of the native inhabitant in this frontier post of Empire. "Yes; all those people are entirely at home there. It is I who am the stranger, the profane, since I look upon them with curiosity, since I wish to learn something from them." This accusation is an old one: accepted since the famous definition of the Continent in the verdict of the British tourist, as "ruins, inhabited by imbeciles": since the refusal of the English lady to speak French in Paris, because, as she protested, "it only encourages them." Here at least, amid much that has changed, the type is unchangeable. The conquering race cannot understand the conquered. No conquering race ever has understood the conquered: except when, understanding, its Imperial rule has begun its decline. If the English in India, it has been said, commenced to understand India, the episode of English rule in India would be nearing its close. The second "instrument of invasion," this acute observer finds in a "Discipline of Life, unanimously accepted." Their plan of conquest is traced in advance. They stamp their life upon the life of the invaded cities: demanding, and in consequence readily obtaining, those things which they judge indispensable to the discipline of their existence. These include especially *l'installation hygiénique* and *l'installation sportive*. At Biarritz to-day, the villas which are not entirely sanitary do not let. This is a more effective pressure than any bye-law of a local authority. They create—through their demands—hot air and vapour baths, certain conditions of ventilation, electric light, *le seul qui ne "mange pas d'oxygène" disent-ils*. They insist also upon their sports: golf, tennis, polo, hunting, shooting. They

even patronise automobilism, whilst declaring, says
M. Prevost slyly, "that it is not a true sport; they
accuse it of not being an English sport." To this
they join their religion, or at least the outward
manifestation of their religion. (One thinks of English "chaplains abroad.") Given also to this an
imperious complacency of costume, and all the
materials are offered to provide the Anglican colony
abroad with the impression of *un corps d'occupation
ayant son uniforme, ses titres, ses chefs. Ces sont bien
des conquérants.*

But beyond these superficial truculencies the
observer may find a deeper interpretation of the
cause of these triumphs. He sees the English, in
these new Englands that they have made abroad, less
intelligent, less generally cultivated than the French;
less cultivated, less scientific, artistic, and laborious
than the Germans. Yet it is these "barbarians," not
the French or the Germans, who have attained, almost
without effort, the overlordship of the world. He
ascribes this attainment to the fact that to-day the
English are the only people who have truly national
manners and characteristics. In a different order of
things, but in equal measure, they exercise upon the
manners of the world the Authority which the French
exercised in the eighteenth century; when even those
who hated them were compelled to copy them.
"Manners and Customs in France," he asks dejectedly, "what is it that can be developed to-day under
this title? We have no longer 'Manners and Customs.' But the English retain their manners and
customs with a stubborn placidity." "You can love

—more or less—certain qualities of this conquering people," he concludes, " but how is it possible not to admire its strong national discipline?" "That is what ought to be learnt from it," he exhorts his fellow-countrymen, " rather than ways of smoking or rules of play."

There is much sound common sense under this quiet irony and badinage. The qualities which have produced an English domination of Biarritz or Cannes are the qualities which have given to the race an Empire dominant over four hundred millions of variegated peoples. The qualities which have made them respected rather than loved at the continental watering-places are the qualities which would cause their subject peoples for the most part to contemplate the abandonment of their rule without regret. Strength, energy, and a certain crudity make up the blend of all Imperial races. It was so with the Romans: a conspicuous efficiency, a justice equally impartial and indifferent; aloofness with a certain disdain in it; an exercise of power almost startling in the disproportion of end to means. It is the vigour of a clumsy giant; sometimes exercising his strength in beneficent enterprise, in effecting desirable acts which no weaker agent can perform; sometimes— and generally unwittingly—crushing with heavy hoof things of whose value he has no conception. No Conquering Race can possess much power of introspection, of self-examination. "They do not fret and whine about their condition," says Whitman of the animals. He could equally have said it about the English. No Conquering Race can possess patience:

else it passes into the acquiescence of the South, whose favourite word is " to-morrow," or the acquiescence of the East, which is content to let the thundering legions pass, and to plunge in thought again. No Conquering Race can possess irony: else it will uncomfortably suspect that its conquered peoples are secretly laughing at it, and this suspicion will excite it to resentment and reprisal. No Conquering Race can possess humour: for then one day it will find itself laughing at itself; and that day its power of conquest is gone. Those who would help mankind must not expect much from them, is the half sad, half cynical verdict of worldly wisdom. Those who would rule mankind must not expect much from themselves beyond rulership, is the lesson of history upon all Imperialisms. Above all, those who would do the work of the world must not trouble themselves very greatly with the inquiry whether the work of the world is worth the doing. If there are signs of menace in the present outlook they arise from just this fact: that a race which has conquered is now passing, it would seem, into a race that is comfortable; that the frivolous pursuit of pleasure rather than of wickedness, and the maintenance of a too exacting standard of material welfare is threatening to replace an older salutary simplicity; and that the reproach of Juvenal to Rome is not without justification in twentieth-century London, when he accused its successful peoples of having eaten of the herb of Sardinia. *Moritur et ridet*;—it laughs and dies.

For its efforts at conquest, however annoying to those who resent its domination, are enterprises of no

mean or timid order. No nation need be ashamed
of Empire on a large scale, or apologise for the over-
lordship of a Continent. To-day's criticism deplores
the weakening or vanishing of the qualities by which
such conquest was attained: in an aristocratic caste
which is merging itself in a wealthy class, and undergoing weakening in the process. It is not from the
" Conquerors " but from a rather harassed and limited
Middle Class that the " Empire builders" are now
drawn: a Lord Macdonnell from the home of a peasant
farmer in Ireland, a Cecil Rhodes from an English
country parsonage. The men who are administering
with varying success British East Africa and Northern
Nigeria, and the huge machine of government in
India, are mainly the children of the professional
families, drawn abroad by love of adventure or
absence of opportunity at home. There is little
danger in England of any general popular uprising
against aristocratic privilege, or even against a system
which has concentrated in few hands so dispropor-
tionate a percentage of the national accumulation.
But there may be danger of a kind of internal collapse
and decay, in the deflection of vigour and intellectual
energy to irrelevant standards and pleasures; in the
inadequacy of that vigour and energy before nations
ever becoming better equipped in the world struggle,
and determined to make desperate efforts for the
supreme position. The invocation to "wake up"
is supposed to be addressed mainly to the working
peoples, whose extravagant thirst for alcoholic
refreshment, and whose Trade Unions, encouraging
an enforced idleness, are creating, in this theory,

a falling-off in commercial and industrial efficiency.
But far more than among the "rude mechanicals," a
facing of realities is needed among the classes who
have conquered and attained; who now, absorbed in
the difficult art of living under elaborate standards, find
little superfluous energy or wealth remaining for the
setting of the house in order. A variable and random
philanthropy is the substitute for Social Reform. A
buying-off of the more energetic from below by honours
and titles liberally bestowed, prevents the attack
upon a whole class by the resentment of energy and
intellect excluded from privilege. Free patronage
and a liberal entertainment of authors, critics, play-
wrights, musicians, and ambitious politicians, removes
the menace of an intellectual proletariat exciting
anger and envy amongst the dim millions of the
industrial populace. It has the sense also to know
the limits of its interferences; to know that its power,
inadequate to constructive effort, rests on inhibitions
rather than activities. The rather ignoble rôle played
by the House of Lords during the past decade reveals
its weaknesses. It will allow changes which it profoundly dislikes, when compelled by fear. It will
resist changes in action when that fear is controlled.
It will altogether abandon the effort to initiate
changes where change is essential. It can do little
but modify, check, or destroy other men's handiwork.
It has no single constructive suggestion of its own to
offer to a people confronting difficult problems, and
harassed by the obligations of necessary reorganisa-
tions. It can neither breed leaders nor ideas. And
because of this ultimate sterility—though it has all

the cards in its hands and every material force in its
favour—its power may gradually pass and be destroyed; to appear in history as one more aristocracy
declining, not through the batterings of external
enemies, but from the fretting and crumbling of an
internal decay.

Its fear to-day is Socialism: Socialism which it
does not understand, but which presents itself as
an uprising of the uneducated, suddenly breaking
into its houses; their clumsy feet on the mantel-
piece, their clumsy hands seizing and destroying all
beautiful and pleasant things. So it lies awake at
night, listening fearfully to the tramp of the rising
host: the revolt of the slave against his master.
From Socialism—as a code of economic organisation,
ordering life on a military, disciplinary, and rational
basis—it has perhaps less to fear than it sometimes
imagines. For this "Socialism" is farther away in
time than many ardent Socialists suppose. And
if "Socialism" were consummated, there might
be found under its rigorous régime more tenderness
to an aristocratic caste and tradition than is anticipated by those who are terrified at the promise of its
advent. These people, indeed, have less to fear from
a demand for equality, than from a demand for
efficiency: from the enforced necessity, either in a
hazardous national crisis abroad, or in some stress
of economic adversity at home, for the rule of energy
and intelligence. The demand of the Napoleonic
system—"the declared principle," to "seek talent
wherever it may be found"—might make havoc of
the supremacy of the children of the "Conquerors";

might drastically determine that some less ruinous proportion of the national wealth was expended on aimless conventions and enjoyments. It may be desirable that the land of England, for example, shall be held in the hands of private owners, instead of being owned by the whole community. It seems to be increasingly questioned whether the land of England shall continue to be held by its present private owners : whether the landed classes of this country, in any ultimate standard of profit and loss, can justify the trust and high calling which has placed the welfare of the rural population in their keeping, and now sees little return but a decaying, deserted countryside. There is much, again, to be said for a Second Chamber in Government. There is little to be said for the present Second Chamber, except that in practice it appears to have disproved all its theoretical advantages : abstaining where in theory it ought to have struck, and striking where in theory it ought to have abstained. Aristocracy in England has been kindly and generous. Even as in part transformed into a plutocracy, it provides little of that attitude of insolence to the less fortunate which is the surest provocation of revolution. The action of a section of the motoring classes, indeed, in their annexation of the highways and their indifference to the common traditions, stands almost alone as an example of wealth's intolerable arrogances, and has certainly excited more resentment amongst the common people than any extravagance of pleasure or political reaction. It is only in such manifestations as those of enjoyment deliberately associated with careless injury to the general convenience, that there is revealed the remotest possibility of a deliberate "class war" between the rich and the poor. Feudal England is dying, and the attempt to transform a caste basis of land and breeding into a caste basis of material possession seems doomed to failure. But it will fail less from external assault than from the inability of the inheritors of great fortune to maintain the energies and devotions through which that fortune has been made. "The Conquerors" will leave little bitterness behind them. There may even remain, in the memory of a more exacting age to come, a pleasant recollection of those who upheld, in time of tranquillity, a standard of manners and a tradition of kindliness, duty, and courage before life's lesser ills. From public schools, which profess to teach "character" rather than to stimulate intelligence, through universities encouraging large expenditure on comfort, limitless bodily exercise, and an exiguous standard of intellectual effort, they pass to the "truly national manners and characteristics" which M. Prevost so much admires. In country residence, in solid aggregation in the metropolis, in lesser imitative effort amongst the provincial cities, they have cherished a code of hospitality, courtesy, criticism, mild and generous interest in public and private affairs. If that code is in part vanishing before the influx of the new "Super-wealth," it yet exhibits, in the present generation, a still active power of assimilation. Not for conspicuous crimes, for selfishness, for class exclusiveness, or for insolence will this society be judged and condemned by the progress of time. It will pass—if it passes—because it is mistaking abnormal and insecure experience for the normal and secure; because an unwillingness to face reality is gradually developing a confusion between reality and illusion; because in its prosperity it may be stricken with blindness to the signs of the time.

CHAPTER III

THE SUBURBANS

THEY are easily forgotten: for they do not strive or cry; and for the most part only ask to be left alone. They have none of those channels of communication in their possession by which the rich and the poor are able to express their hostility to any political or social change. The Landed Classes or the brewing interests, on the one hand, find newspapers energetic in fighting their cause; on the other, see themselves securely entrenched in a "Second Chamber," which offers them a permanent majority. The Working Classes can organise into unions, subsidise members of Parliament and a Labour Party, make themselves both respected and feared. No one fears the Middle Classes, the suburbans; and perhaps for that reason, no one respects them. They only appear articulate in comedy, to be made the butt of a more nimble-witted company outside: like "Mr. Hopkinson," who is aspiring to transfer his residence from Upper Tooting to Belgravia, or the queer people who dispute — in another recent London play—concerning the respective social advantages of Clapham and Herne Hill. Strong in numbers, and in possession of a vigorous and even tyrannical convention of manners, they lack organisation, energy, and ideas. And in consequence they have been finding themselves crushed between the demands of the industrial peoples on the one hand, and the resistance of the "Conquerors" on the other. They act only when their grievances have become a burden impossible to be borne. They act without preparation, without leadership, without preliminary negotiation. They rise suddenly, impervious to argument, unreasoning and resolute. And the result is often a cataclysm which would be almost ludicrous if it were not both random and pitiful.

Such action, for example, was revealed in the complete overturn of London's system of government which took place in the spring of 1908, after a continuous rule of nearly twenty years of administration by one party. Lord Randolph Churchill ended his political career because he had "forgotten Goschen." The Progressive Party ended its political career in the Metropolis because it had forgotten the Middle Classes. It recognised, indeed, and estimated not unfairly, the strength of the rich, the artisans, the unskilled labourers. These three classes are prominent factors in the modern European polity. But it had forgotten the dimensions and latent power of those enormous suburban peoples which are practically the product of the past half-century, and have so greatly increased, even within the last decade. They are the creations not of the industrial, but of the commercial and business activities of London. They form a homogeneous civilisation,—detached, self - centred,

unostentatious,—covering the hills along the northern
and southern boundaries of the city, and spreading
their conquests over the quiet fields beyond. They
are the peculiar product of England and America ;
of the nations which have pre-eminently added commerce, business, and finance to the work of manufacture and agriculture. It is a life of Security ; a
life of Sedentary occupation ; a life of Respectability ;
and these three qualities give the key to its special
characteristics. Its male population is engaged in all
its working hours in small, crowded offices, under
artificial light, doing immense sums, adding up other
men's accounts, writing other men's letters. It is
sucked into the City at daybreak, and scattered again
as darkness falls. It finds itself towards evening in
its own territory in the miles and miles of little red
houses in little silent streets, in number defying
imagination. Each boasts its pleasant drawing-room,
its bow-window, its little front garden, its high-
sounding title—" Acacia Villa," or " Camperdown
Lodge "—attesting unconquered human aspiration.
There are many interests beyond the working
hours : here a greenhouse filled with chrysanthe-
mums, there a tiny grass patch with bordering
flowers ; a chicken-house, a bicycle shed, a tennis
lawn. The women, with their single domestic servants, now so difficult to get, and so exacting when
found, find time hang rather heavy on their hands.
But there are excursions to shopping centres in the
West End, and pious sociabilities, and occasional
theatre visits, and the interests of home. The children
are jolly, well-fed, intelligent English boys and girls ;

full of curiosity, at least in the earlier years. Some of them have real gifts of intellect and artistic skill, receiving in the suburban secondary schools the best education which England is giving to-day. You may see the whole suburbs in August transported to the more genteel of the southern watering-places; the father, perhaps, a little bored; the mother perplexed with the difficulty of cramped lodgings and extortionate prices. But the children are in a magic world, crowding the seashore, full of the elements of delight and happy laughter.

The rich despise the Working People; the Middle Classes fear them. Fear, stimulated by every artifice of clever political campaigners, is the motive-power behind each successive uprising. In feverish hordes, the suburbs swarm to the polling booth to vote against a truculent Proletariat. The Middle Class elector is becoming irritated and indignant against working-class legislation. He is growing tired of the plaint of the unemployed and the insistent crying of the poor. The spectacle of a Labour Party triumphant in the House of Commons, with a majority of members of Parliament apparently obedient to the demands of its leaders, and even a House of Lords afraid of it, fills him with profound disgust. The vision of a "Keir Hardie" in caricature—with red tie and defiant beard and cloth cap, and fierce, unquenchable thirst for Middle Class property—has become an image of Labour Triumphant which haunts his waking hours. He has difficulty with the plumber in jerry-built houses needing continuous patching and mending. His wife is harassed by the

indifference or insolence of the domestic servant.
From a blend of these two he has constructed in
imagination the image of Democracy—a loud-voiced,
independent, arrogant figure, with a thirst for drink,
and imperfect standards of decency, and a determination to be supported at some one else's expense.
Every day, swung high upon embankments or buried
deep in tubes underground, he hurries through the
region where the creature lives. He gazes darkly
from his pleasant hill villa upon the huge and smoky
area of tumbled tenements which stretches at his
feet. He is dimly distrustful of the forces fermenting
in this uncouth laboratory. Every hour he anticipates the boiling over of the cauldron. He would
never be surprised to find the crowd behind the red
flag, surging up his little pleasant pathways, tearing
down the railings, trampling the little garden; the
"letting in of the jungle" upon the patch of fertile
ground which has been redeemed from the wilderness. And whatever may be the future, the present
he finds sufficiently intolerable. The people of the
hill are heavily taxed (as he thinks) in order that the
people of the plain may enjoy good education, cheap
trams, parks, and playgrounds; even (as in the
frantic vision of some newspapers) that they may be
taught Socialism in Sunday schools, with parodies
of remembered hymns. And the taxes thus extorted
—this, perhaps, is the heart of the complaint—are all
going to make his own life harder, to make life more
difficult for his children. The man of forty has
already sounding in his ears the noise of the clamour of the coming generations. And these coming

generations, who are going to push him roughly out of his occupation, and bring his little castle in ruins to the ground, are being provided with an equipment for the struggle out of the funds which he himself is compelled to supply. He is paying for his own children's start in life, and he is having extorted from him the price of providing other people's children with as good a start in life, or a better. He has to lay by for his old age in painful accumulation of pence and shillings, every one of which he can ill spare. And he now finds the old age of the loafer and the spendthrift—so he interprets recent legislation on the subject—bountifully provided for. He wonders where it is all going to stop. He is becoming every day more impatient with the complaining of the poor. He refuses to mourn over the sufferings of the factory girl when he is offering a desirable position as general "help" and can find no applicant. He believes that the "unemployed" consist exclusively of those who are determined to go softly all their days at the public expense — the expense of himself and his class. He is labouring at his dismal sedentary occupation so many incredible hours a day, while these men are parading their woes in exuberant rhetoric at the street corner. And as he labours there enters into his soul a resentment which becomes at times almost an obsession; in which all the disability of his devitalised life is concentrated into revolt against the truculent demands of "the British working man."

He has had enough of it. He is turning in desperation to any kind of protection held out to him. His ideals are all towards the top of the scale. He is proud when he is identifying his interests with those of Kensington, and indignant when his interests are identified with those of Poplar. He possesses in full those progressive desires which are said to be the secret of advance. He wants a little more than he can afford, and is almost always living beyond his income. He has been harassed with debts and monetary complications; and the demands of rent and the rate-collector excite in him a kind of impotent fury. In that fury he turns round and suddenly strikes down the party in possession, glad to vote against the working man, whom he fears; and for a change, which he hopes may lighten his present burden; and against a Socialism which he cannot understand. So in an unexpected whirlwind of ferocity, a Progressive Party, hitherto unconquerable, finds itself almost annihilated. The general effect is that of being suddenly butted by a sheep.

It is no despicable life which has thus silently developed in suburban London. Family affection is there, cheerfulness, an almost unlimited patience. Its full meaning to-day and the courses of its future still remain obscure. Is this to be the type of all civilisations, when the whole Western world is to become comfortable and tranquil, and progress finds its grave in a universal suburb? Or is the old shaggy and untamed earth going to shake itself suddenly once again and bring the whole edifice tumbling to the ground? It has no clear recognition of its own worth, or its own universe, or the scheme of the life

of the world. It is losing its old religions. It still
builds churches and chapels of a twentieth-century
Gothic architecture: St. Aloysius, reputed to be dan-
gerously "High," because its curates wear coloured
scarves; the Baptist Chapel, where the minister maintains the old doctrines of hell and heaven, and
wrestles with the sinner for his immortal soul; the
Congregational Church, where the minister is abreast
with modern culture, and proclaims a less exacting
gospel, and faintly trusts the larger hope. But the
whole apparatus of worship seems archaic and unreal
to those who have never seen the shaking of the solid
ground beneath their feet, or the wonder and terror
of its elemental fires. There are possibilities of havoc
in this ordered and comfortable society which cannot
easily be put by. The old lights have fallen from
the sky, existence has become too complex and
crowded for the influences of wide spaces reaching to
a far horizon. Summer and winter pass over these
little lamplit streets, to-day the lilac and syringa,
to-morrow the scattered autumn leaves, in an experience of tranquillity and repose. But with the ear to
the ground there is audible the noise of stranger
echoes in the labyrinthine ways which stretch beyond
the boundaries of these pleasant places; full of restlessness and disappointment, and longing, with a
note of menace in it; not without foreboding to
any who would desire, in the security of the
suburbs, an unending end of the world.

Why does the picture of this suburban life, presented by however kindly a critic, leave the reader
at the end with a sense of dissatisfaction? The

query is aroused by examination of its actual condition.   It is excited not only by works written
in revolt, such as those of Mr. Wells or George
Gissing, but also by the writings of Mr. Keble
Howard and Mr. Shan Bullock and Mr. Pett Ridge
and others, who have attempted, with greater or less
success, to exhibit a kindly picture of suburban
society.   At first this society appeared in literature
as depicted by cleverness, delighting in satire at
the expense of bourgeois ideals.   Its historians were
always in protest against its limitations, its complacencies, its standards of social success and intellectual attainment.   But in later time this somewhat
crude attitude of scornful superiority has passed.
Many writers with an intimate knowledge of suburban
and   English   Middle   Class   provincial   life   have
attempted a sympathetic and truthful description :
the sincere representation of a civilisation.   But in all
their efforts the general effect is of something lacking ; not so much in individual happiness, or even in
bodily and mental development, as of a certain communal poverty of interest and ideal.   The infinite
boredom of the horrible women of "The Year of
Jubilee"—with its vision of Camberwell villadom
as idle and desolate as Flaubert's vision of French
provincial bourgeois life in "Madame Bovary"—has
been replaced by a scene of busy activity, with interest
in cricket and football results, "book talk," love-
making, croquet and tennis parties for young men
and women.   And yet at the end, and with the best
will in the world, one closes the narrative with a
feeling of desolation ; a revolt against a life which,

with all its energies and satisfactions, has somehow lost from it that zest and sparkle and inner glow of accepted adventure which alone would seem to give human life significance. Civilise the poor, one complains, expand their tiny rubbish yards into green gardens, introduce bow - windows before and verandahs behind; remove them from the actual experience of privation, convert all England into a suburban city—will the completed product be pronounced to be "very good"?

It is not the simplicity of suburban life which is at fault. Simplicity in writing, or in character, is as difficult of attainment as it is worth the attaining. And in so far as simplicity here exists—character cut on elemental lines, or occupied with elemental things—it provides an antidote to the complexities or cynicisms of other classes. No one, except the vulgar, despises a Middle Class existence because it has substituted a high tea for an elaborate dinner, because it uses speech to reveal rather than to conceal thought, or because it refuses to torture itself with analysis and emotion which are the products of mind divorced from the ancient sanities of existence. Nor, again, is the narrow separation from poverty and the abyss a cause for any legitimate contempt, which makes the business of life for so many of them in their tiny two-storeyed villas an enterprise hazardous and insecure. Rather is the observer conscious, where this struggle exists, that there has entered into the atmosphere the breath of salt wind, bracing if austere, which can provide a more heroic sustenance than the atmosphere in which such tests and challenges are denied. We may compare, for example, two of Mr. Bullock's stories of suburban life; the one, in which he traces the attempt of a "twopenny clerk" to provide for the needs of a family on an exiguous and precarious income; the other, in which a prosperous family who have attained security set themselves to the business of living under such favourable conditions. There is humour in the struggles of Robert Thorne, as of all similar millions of Robert Thornes, in his attempt to maintain his hardly-won standard of decencies and modest comfort. There is resistance to hard circumstance which the most critical onlooker will applaud —in the little boxes for the division of income, labelled "Necessities," "Outings," "Savings"—the first so rarely permitting any overflow into the second and third; in the revolt against the shabby clothes and difficulties created by unexpected illness; in the necessities of a clerk, who is also a man, wheeling the perambulator on Peckham Rye, or scrubbing the front doorsteps furtively after night-fall. But the humour is of the ancient, not of the modern, significance; a humour not without tears in it, with admiration also at the courage and determination which could yet be content, and under such conditions, with "the glory of going on and still to be." For here is the sense of battles; and battle, whether against deliberate foes, against the inimical force of Nature, or the indifference of the crowd to the individual survival, is always stimulating and bracing. And it is the battle depicted by Mr. Davidson in his "thirty bob a week"; the "naked child against a hungry wolf," "the playing bowls upon a splitting wreck," "daily done by many and many a one" in a tenacious struggle, against the enemies of human welfare, which illuminates and glorifies the monotonous streets of suburban England.

But where this "struggle to live" has passed into a "struggle to attain," the verdict is less enthusiastic. For that struggle to attain too often means absorption in ignoble standards, and an existence coming more and more to occupy a world of "make believe." When the family is in a position of assured comfort or of affluence, the houses ample stuccoed or pseudo - Georgian edifices, and the breadwinners in posts of established security in the commercial or financial houses of the city, the atmosphere often becomes stifling and difficult. It may be that such a condition is in itself unsuitable to mankind in the life of so uncertain and transitory a world: that existence which is occupied with sedentary labour in an artificially constructed aggregation of human beings herded in the same narrow grooves, is an existence of necessity carrying with it the seeds of futility and decay. Certainly the two chief accusations against the product of such an existence would be of an imperfect standard of value about the things which exist, and of a lack of demand for the existence of things at present unattained. It is a wrong estimate of the significance—of rank, of birth, of wealth, of various material accumulations—which produces the more desolating ingredients of suburban life. Listen to the conversation in the second-class carriages of a suburban railway train, or examine the literature and journalism specially constructed for the suburban mind; you will often find endless chatter about the King, the Court, and the doings of a designated "Society"; personal paragraphs, descriptions of clothes, smile, or manner; a vision of life in which the trivial and heroic things are alike exhibited, but in which there is no adequate test or judgment, which are the heroic, which the trivial.   Liberated from the devils of poverty, the soul is still empty, swept and garnished; waiting for other occupants.   This is the explanation of the so-called "snobbery" of the suburbs.   Here is curiosity, but curiosity about lesser occupations ; energies,—for the suburbs in their healthy human life, the swarms of happy, physically efficient children, are a storehouse of the nation's energy,—but energies which tend to scatter and degrade themselves in aimless activities; "random and meaningless sociabilities" which neither hearten, stimulate, nor inspire.   So into a feud with a neighbour over a disputed garden fence, or a bustling and breezy church or chapel's mundane entertainment, or a criticism of manners and fashion, dress and deportment, will be thrown force and determination which might have been directed to effort of permanent worth, in devotion to one of the great causes of the world.

Beyond these incorrect standards of value there is a noticeable absence of vision.   Suburban life has often little conception of social services, no tradition of disinterested public duty, but a limited outlook beyond a personal ambition.   Here the individualism of the

national character exercises its full influence: unchecked by the horizontal links of the industrial
peoples, organising themselves into unions, or by the
vertical links of the older aristocracy with a conception of family service which once passed from
parent to child. Religion—if that were vital and
compelling—would provide in part a vista of larger
horizons. When and where religion existed—even
in its rigid conception of heaven and hell and a
straight way of salvation—it offered some universes
for contemplation beyond the orderly suburban road
and the well-trimmed suburban garden. It is to be
feared, however, that in the prevailing cloudiness
about ultimate things which is developing in the
modern world, religion has been tending more and
more to resolve itself into social institutions, " Pleasant
Sunday Afternoons," or exercise of the less adventurous forces of suburban philanthropy. What remains?
A public spirit in local affairs which is deplorably
low, which sends a minute percentage of voters to
Council or Guardian Elections, and accompanies a
perpetual contempt for present municipal mismanage-
ment with a refusal of the personal effort required
to make that management clean and efficient. An
outlook upon Imperial affairs which is less a conception of politics than the acceptance of a social
tradition: which leaves suburban seats securely
Conservative not because the Conservative creed is
there definitely embraced, but because Conservatism
is supposed to be the party favoured by Court, society,
and the wealthy and fashionable classes. And too
often an essential ignorance supplemented by an

6

arrogance which refuses advice and despises opposition. The result is a not too reputable product of modern civilisation: that dense and complacent "Imperial citizen" who despises "the foreigner," and could set right or improve upon generals in the field or admirals on the ocean, and is satisfied with its universe and its limitations because it has resolutely closed all doors and windows through which there might appear the vision of larger other worlds. It is this particular suburban figure—with custom dominant, accepted and inherited students of judgment, contempt for the classes below it, envy of the classes above, and no desire for adventure or devotion to a cause or an ideal—which has become too representative a figure of a laborious and praiseworthy race of men. Against this type of "honest man" have warred the anarchists, the artists, the advocates of new moralities, the opponents of the accepted way. In revolt against the dominion of so questionable a citizen, we are perhaps inclined to forget the mitigating features: the good nature and ready generosity, the cleanliness of life, the still unbroken family tradition; all animated by that resolution, not so much deliberate as unconscious, to "make the best of it," in a world of incalculable purposes; in which, indeed, some cloudiness of vision or some unusual courage would seem to be necessary if the struggle is to be continued at all.

Yet in the crumbling and decay of English rural life, and the vanishing of that "yeoman" class which in Scotland provides a continuous breeding ground

of great men, it would seem that it is from the
suburban and professional people we must more
and more demand a supply of men and women of
capacity and energy adequate to the work of the
world. Sufficiently vulnerable to criticism as they
appear to-day, finding no one who will be proud of
them because they are not proud of themselves, they
yet offer a storehouse of accumulated physical health
and clean simplicities of living. Embedded in them
are whole new societies created by legislation and a
national demand, whose present development is full of
interest, whose future is full of promise. Here is, for
example, the new type of elementary teacher—a figure
practically unknown forty years ago—drawn in part
from the tradesmen and the more ambitious artisan
population, and now, lately, in a second generation,
from its own homes. It is exhibiting a continuous
rise of standard, keen ambitions, a respect for intellectual things which is often absent in the population amongst which it resides. Its members are not
only doing their own work efficiently, but are everywhere taking the lead in public and *quasi*-public
activities. They appear as the mainstay of the
political machine in suburban districts, serving upon
the municipal bodies, in work, clear-headed and
efficient; the leaders in the churches and chapels,
and their various social organisations. They are
taking up the position in the urban districts which
for many generations was occupied by the country
clergy in the rural districts; providing centres with
other standards than those of monetary success,
and raising families who exhibit sometimes vigour

of character, sometimes unusual intellectual talent. A quite remarkable proportion of the children of elementary schoolmasters is now knocking at the doors of the older Universities, clamouring for admittance; and those who effect entrance are often carrying off the highest honours. This process is only in its beginning; every year the standard improves; these "servants of the State" have assured to them a noteworthy and honourable future. Again, there is no doubt that the conception of social service is making progress against the resistance of whatever is solid in the suburban tradition of individualism and indifference. Even the Socialist no longer turns from the Middle Classes in disgust. He is coming to regard them as the most fruitful field for his propaganda. The women—or a remnant of them—are finding outlet for suppressed energy and proffered devotion in an agitation for the vote. Sixpenny reprints of proof or disproof of religion, the world's classics in neat shilling volumes, sevenpenny novels, and a variety of printed matter are irrigating the suburbs with a fresh flood of literature. It is not impossible to conceive of a time when a Middle Class will definitely build up a standard of its own: no longer turning to a wealthy and leisured company above it for effective imitation of a life to which it is unsuited. Becoming conscious, for the first time, that it possesses elements to contribute to the stream of national life which can be provided neither by the rich nor the poor, it may gain that collective respect and pride in itself which it has not yet achieved. Abandoning its panic fear of the industrial peoples, it may find itself treating with them as an equal, exacting terms in return for its alliance. At best it may even resist the stampedes of those who find the support of the " Middle Classes " always easily obtainable for an agitation against the Income Tax or in favour of municipal reaction, or for any system which will "broaden the basis of taxation" by shifting it from the shoulders of the rich to the shoulders of the poor.

This fissure in the alliance between the Middle Class and the wealthy—the most absurd and irrational of all alliances, in which the advantage is all sucked by the one, and the burden borne by the other—would long ago have been demanded by the suburbans themselves but for one remarkable element in their present condition. Revolution, or at least vigorous progress, may always be predicted when in the case of any particular class the standard of comfort is permanently beating against a limitation of income, and permanently in revolt against such limitation. Such a conflict seemed inevitable a few years ago in the case of the Middle Classes. The " intellectual proletariat " was evidently being created, which could never obtain full satisfaction for its desires. It would fret always at its limitations. Its fretting would become vocal in a clamorous demand for economic change. And the "intellectual proletariat" has been the historic leader of all political and social revolutions. The process of its creation, however, seems likely to be checked, and in a curious fashion. The pressure is being reduced, not by any lowering of the standard of comfort demanded by the

individual, for that is steadily rising in suburban England, but by the limitation of the family, pursued
as a deliberate method of adjusting expenditure to
income. The headlong collapse in the birth-rate of
this country during the past twenty years—a fall
greater than that in any other nation in Europe
—is a collapse to which all classes save the very
poorest are probably contributors. There are no
exact figures available, of allocation to one section
rather than to another. But there is much to indicate that this decline has gone far amongst those
suburban populations in which a few years ago the
discrepancy between the standard of comfort and the
means available for its satisfaction was most conspicuous. The endurance of a continual indebtedness
and frustration of desire, the indignation which will
convert that endurance into a hunger for reform, the
anger and envy against more prosperous people which
is excited by the contrast of human inequalities under
such conditions of torment, is being assuaged, not by
reform itself, nor by any accepted reduction of the
individual demands, nor by any falling back upon
supernatural consolations. It is being averted by the
repudiation of marriage, or its postponement, or its
acceptance without the accompaniment of children.
Here is a kind of ingenious method of turning the
position, of climbing through the window when the
door is closed. Judgment may vary between approval or regret, in accordance with the point of view
of the critic. The nation must inevitably suffer from
an artificial restriction of children amongst those very
classes and families who should be most encouraged

to produce them; who offer the best chances of raising, from a healthy stock and in simple homes, the
men and women who will be the most desirable
citizens of the future. And a nation is in a serious
condition if its better stocks are producing smaller
families or no families at all, and its least capable are
still raising an abundant progeny. An appreciable
amount of human discontent, on the other hand, is
doubtless arrested by this method of eluding Nature's
blind struggle for existence; and those who have
vested interests in contentment—who see changes
bringing them less opportunity of life's good things—
will, no doubt, hail with approval so satisfactory a
method of averting the operation of "natural" law.
By such limitation of family the standard of comfort
is reduced to the level of the income, and the clerk
and professional classes can be identified with the
prevailing order, instead of becoming centres of social
upheaval.

But this limitation involves deliberate and artificial
repudiation of paternity and motherhood, and as such
is condemned by most ethical systems and by the
Christian Church. Its widespread operation, now
guaranteed by figures which may be deplored, but
which cannot be denied, in itself reveals the considerable undermining process which suburban religion has undergone. Once again, therefore, it is
necessary to notice this element of weakening supernatural sanctions: to inquire how far this process has
gone, and whither it is tending. There will be
no immediate catastrophe; for custom and convention will carry on the apparatus of organised

belief long after the driving power of definite conviction has vanished, like a machine still running
down after the motive power has ceased.   There are
renewed rallies in each generation, especially at the
time of adolescence ; revivals under the inspiration of
American evangelists, or advocates of new theologies,
or vigorous teachers who blend theology with politics,
humour, or social entertainment.   It may still be confidently affirmed to-day that, of all the various sections
of English society, the suburban and Middle Class
retains most resolutely its ancient religious convictions.
These convictions are here more vigorously preserved
than in the class below them, to whom, as a whole,
religion has not yet come, or in the class above them,
whose attitude towards Christianity has always been
one of kindly patronage rather than of accepted
allegiance. Yet it would be idle to overlook the
ravages which have even here been made.   These
ravages must not be sought merely amongst the small
bodies in open opposition, ethical societies and the
like, or the much larger bodies in open indifference,
such as the multitude of Sunday cyclists or the patrons
of Sunday music.   They will be found also amongst
those who still own outward allegiance to the faith of
their fathers, and still think themselves to be orthodox
believers.   " Some thirty years ago," writes the Bishop
of Birmingham," there was a sort of Protestant religion,
with a doctrine of the Trinity, of Heaven and Hell,
of Atonement and Judgment, of Resurrection and
Eternal Life, which for good or evil could be more or
less assumed.   Such a standard has gone.   I seriously
doubt whether nearly half the grown men of the

country could seriously say that they believed that Christ is God, or that He really rose on the third day from the dead. It is not that they have become Unitarians. It is that their religious opinions are in complete chaos."

The drift of this "chaos" in modern thought is, indeed, as noticeable amongst those who still cling to religious exercises and sing the hymns of childhood as amongst the larger populations who regretfully or defiantly, or more often in sheer apathy, have abandoned these ancient traditions and ceremonies. And just as, in Denison's famous verdict, our large organised charities are less a sign of our compassion than of our indifference, so it may be that the noise of fierce fighting amongst rival religions, the queer competition which Mr. Charles Booth discovered even in the remotest slums of London for the bodies and souls of their denizens, may be less an evidence of religious fervour than a manifestation of an ebbing vitality.

Yet the edifice collapses slowly, and in silence. No one can tell, at any definite moment, how far the disintegrating process has gone. Few records would be more illuminating than candid confessions, such as the confession recently made by Mr. Wells in his *First and Last Things*, honestly set down by quite ordinary people, in a casual street of a suburban terrace, of what they believed. If the industrious householders of " Homelea," " Belle View," " Buona Vista," " Sunnyhurst," and " The Laurels," contiguous dwellings in Beaconsfield Road, Upper Norwood, were thus deliberately to face their convictions, the result might be surprising to the clergy of St. Aloysius and

St. Clotilde, and the ministers of the Wesleyan Methodist Church and the Baptist Chapel, beneath whose discourses, attired in long black coats, they sit in decorous silence Sunday after Sunday, seemingly as docile and acquiescent as their fathers before them.

The loss of religion would not, indeed, be so serious a matter if it were being replaced by any other altruistic and impersonal ideal. Such have been found in a conception of patriotism, in efforts towards a social redemption, even in a vision of duty, sometimes hard and rarefied, which occupies its mind with the difficulties of the day. It is to be feared that these are not universal amongst the suburban peoples. Their lives are laborious and often disappointing. The rise in the price of the material things which they regard as essential is steady and continuous. House rent, and the rates laid upon house rent, clothes, food, the demands for small enjoyments, with the debt which often accompanies a too radiant conception of the possibilities of fixed income, leave little margin for superfluous expenditure. And as with the body, so with the soul. Considerable hours spent in not too exacting but conspicuously cheerless occupations, the natural harassments of Middle Class poverty, and the misfortune of loss or sickness, which is always unexpected and generally unprovided for, leave little surplusage of mental energy to be devoted to larger issues. Those who are intimate with the modern phases of suburban life think that they can detect a slackening of energy and fibre in a generation which is much occupied with its pleasures. It is a common complaint with the fathers that none of their children seem prepared to work in the manner in which they worked in the older days. It is a common complaint with the whole of a passing generation—the big manufacturers who built up England's commercial supremacy, the veterans who remember the strenuous middle-class existence of Victorian England—that the whole newer time thinks that it has little to do but to settle down and enjoy the heritage which has been won. The young men of the suburban society, especially, are being accused of a mere childish absorption in vicarious sport and trivial amusements.

It is curious to find this accusation driven home by just that variety of newspapers which has most completely exploited the nascent hunger of the sedentary boyhood of these classes for the excitements of gambling and adventure. The cheap and sensational Press found here a field ripe for its energies. It attained an immense commercial success from the provision of the stuff which this population demanded. Now the cleverest of its promoters are beginning to be a little alarmed at the results of its handiwork, and to eye with foreboding or with disgust the youth that has been moulded by its ideals. Under the circumstances, resentment at such scolding would appear not unnatural. In a popular play, designed to encourage or to ridicule Volunteering, the creature of this "Yellow Press" was recently revealed in all his vacuous vulgarity ; and the "Yellow Press" itself turned in anger to assail its own darling and docile offspring. The retort, indeed, could be final and complete. "We have been nourished," these could say, "in this unreal world of impudence, nonsense, vicarious sport and gambling. We began with our boys' papers and guessing competitions. We were insensibly led on to efforts after a pound a week for life by estimating the money in the Bank of England on a certain day, or amassing gain in hundreds of pounds for guessing missing words or the last line of 'Limericks.' On the Sabbath, committed by our parents to some such literature as the Sunday Syndicated Press, we found there the same cheery game, smeared with a grease of piety; rewards and prizes here for guessing anagrams on Bible cities, or acrostics representing Kings and Queens of Israel. We were led on to talk and read and chatter about 'sport,' in biography of various football heroes, in descriptive reports of football matches, ever deepening in imbecility, until they rivalled the language of the lunatic asylum; stuff that uses its own phraseology, about 'netting the muddied orange' and 'the ubiquitous spheroid,' and 'impelling the pill between the uprights.' Our thoughts and growing interest were sedulously directed away from consideration of any rational or serious universe. We were exhorted to demonstrate patriotism by 'mafficking,' and informed that when we fell into the fountain at Trafalgar Square and subsequently embraced a policeman, we were performing a virtuous action. Then we are denounced because this universe of foolishness and frivolity has rendered us utterly unfit to face real things. Our slight world crumbles before such a challenge, as the daylight judges and condemns the scene of a night's orgie." "This short, slender, pale man," says M. Hanotaux of Taine in 1870, "munching his throat lozenges, with squinting grey eyes behind his thick glasses, had at last seen things which astonished him—dying men, flowing blood, burning cities." Dying men, flowing blood, and burning cities intruded suddenly into a world which is fashioned out of such emptiness and vanity exhibit but the same judgment as is revealed to the discerning mind through every passing hour.

And no one can seriously diagnose the condition of the "Suburbans" to-day without seriously considering also the influences of this chosen literature. There is nothing obscene about it, and little that is morally reprehensible. But it is mean and tawdry and debased, representing a tawdry and dusty world. You can see it in illustration. Photographs of the *Englishman's Home*, showing the products of spectacular sport and silly gambling, falling amid their falling houses, face the picture of a negro on a raised platform pummelling an American, with tier upon tier of white, vacant faces—the Australian spectators—gazing with fierce approval. The reader passes—in such publications—from one frivolity to another. Now it is a woman adventurer on the music-hall stage, now the principal characters in some "sensational" divorce case, now a serial story in which the "bounder" expands himself, and is triumphant in an unreal universe. In the midst of all comes an appeal which, if it were to excite even a limited response, would sweep all this nonsense away, and land in bankruptcy the vast apparatus of newspapers which exploit and encourage the hunger of the suburban crowd. The work of corruption—the word is not too violent—in the matter of frivolous gambling competitions, is a systematic whole, beginning with the papers designed for boys and children. From absorption in these, with occasional rewards of five or ten shillings, a box of paints, or a bicycle, the growing youth passes to the "Limerick," the picture puzzle, and the missing-word competition. At the end this newspaper world becomes—to its victims—an epitome and mirror of the whole world. Divorced from the ancient sanities of manual or skilful labour, of exercise in the open air, absorbed for the bulk of his day in crowded offices adding sums or writing letters, each a unit in a crowd which has drifted away from the realities of life in a complex, artificial city civilisation, he comes to see no other universe than this—the rejoicing over hired sportsmen who play before him, the ingenuities of sedentary guessing competitions, the huge frivolity and ignorance of the world of the music hall and the Yellow newspaper. Having attained so dolorous a consummation, perhaps the best that can be hoped for him is the advent of that friendly bullet which will terminate his inglorious life. Were this accomplished, the next day his own newspapers, the high priests of his religion, will rejoice over his death, and shamelessly gird at him for being what he is—the faithfullest of worshippers at their shrine.

This is the less desirable side of suburban life: a set-off against its many excellences. It probably represents but a passing phase in a progress towards intelligence and a sense of real values. That progress would be aided by any loosening of the city texture by which, and through improved means of transit, something of the large sanities of rural existence could be mingled with the quickness and agility of the town. At least the most hostile critics will acknowledge in these regions a clean and virile life: forming, when criticism has done its worst, in conjunction with the artisan class below, from which it is so sharply cut off in interest and ideas, the healthiest and most hopeful promise for the future of modern England.

CHAPTER IV

THE MULTITUDE

THE Multitude is the People of England: that eighty per cent. (say) of the present inhabitants of these islands who never express their own grievances, who rarely become articulate, who can only be observed from outside and very far away. It is a people which, all unnoticed and without clamour or protest, has passed through the largest secular change of a thousand years: from the life of the fields to the life of the city. Nine out of ten families have migrated within three generations: they are still only, as it were, commencing to settle down in their new quarters, with the paint scarcely dry on them, and the little garden still untilled. How has the migration affected them? How will they expand or degenerate in the new town existence, each in the perpetual presence of all? That is a question of as profound interest in answering as it is difficult to answer. The nineteenth century—in the life of the wage-earning multitudes—was a century of disturbance. The twentieth promises to be a century of consolidation. What completed product will emerge from its city aggregation, the children of the crowd? You must learn of them to-day, as I have said, from outside: from the few observers who have lived amongst them and recorded their experience; from the very few representative men, with articulate utterance, which they have flung up from amongst themselves. You must examine masses of documents and statistics embodied in Government publications, or tentative efforts towards a sociology: recording how they live, and eat and drink, and obtain shelter, and marry and are given in marriage; the particulars of their upbringing, how they seek or elude religions and charity, and escape from the laws which are passed for their protection, and enjoy and suffer, and live and die. The mass of this chaotic and undigested evidence waits for the observer who will create from it some general picture of the life of the English people. And when all these statistics and cold facts are assimilated, there yet remains the further inquiry of the temper and spirit of a race subjected to such forces; hampered and limited by the narrow walls between which they labour and endure.

The tangible things come first, in some such evidence as that provided by Government investigation, in the Blue Book bearing a forbidding title, the "Cost of Living of the Working Classes." It shows them, gathered into astonishing cities, working for variable wage. It reveals the dwellings which they seek to transform into homes. It follows their wages from production to distribution, in the cost of their daily economy, the manner in which they divide up their exiguous incomes, the amounts they think it worth while to allot to shelter, to food, and to pleasure.   It analyses over a thousand "family budgets," each giving details of how much is spent weekly on butter, tapioca, or treacle.   It shows the rate of birth and the rate of death : varying from city to city, both materially changing.   It gives, in fact, in outline only, that blurred image of a huge and industrial population whose complete apprehension would furnish the key to many of the pressing problems of to-day.

Here are the houses in which for a season they abide; in part the product of their own volition, in part the creation of external changes which they can but little control.   They have had no choice in these constructions.   Their demands and desires have scarcely counted in the provision made for them. Their impetuous need was shelter : shelter "on the spot," around the sites of the new factories which had sucked them up from the deserted countryside.   And they were thankful to take what was offered them by those men who foresaw the changes which were coming, and could accumulate fortunes in the rapid provision of immediate necessities.   Swept into aggregations by the demand of the newest industries, the clay and stone has been hastily fashioned into place for human habitation.   And now these stand to-day, made by, and yet making, the temper and characteristic of the people.   Here the normal standard is a four-roomed cottage; there, "back to back " houses ravage the health of their inhabitants ; here again huge piles of tenements encompass the bewildered occupants in a kind of human ant-heap; there the ancient dwelling of the wealthy or comfortable classes have been "swarmed out" by the busy people. Carlyle pictured mankind flowing, as it were, through the visible arena of material things. A wave of humanity beats through these solid constructions; it vanishes, another succeeds. "Orpheus built the walls of Thebes by the mere sound of his lyre. Who built these walls of Weissnichtwo, summoning out all the sandstone rocks to dance and shape themselves into Doric and Ionic pillars, squared ashlar houses, and noble streets?" All cities are thus built "to music." What discordant melody to-day is responsible for the creation of Jarrow, or Salford, or Canning Town?

England at once, under such an analysis, separates itself into divergent parts. There is rural England, still largely unaffected by modern science and invention, except by the loss of population, drained away; the agricultural labourers, the fishermen, and the artisans of the sleeping provincial towns. There is urban England in hastily created industrial centres, vocal with the clanging of furnaces and the noise of the factories; but still a population in manageable aggregation, set in open spaces, never far from green fields under a wide sky. And there is London: a population, a nation in itself; breeding, as it seems, a special race of men; which only is also produced, and that in less intensive cultivation, in the few other larger cities — Glasgow, Manchester, Liverpool— where the conditions of coagulation offer some parallel to this monster clot of humanity. Everywhere, indeed, this million-peopled, exaggerated London sets at defiance the generalisations drawn from the

normal town areas.   House rent is immensely higher.
The mean weekly price for two rooms in London is six
shillings, in the provinces a little more than one half;
for four rooms the variation is between nine shillings
in the one, five shillings in the other. A portion of
this surplus is the booty of more highly paid labour.
The greater part vanishes in the increased value of
the land, heaped up by the mere fact of aggregation,
and flowing away into the pockets of many affluent
and fortunate persons. London has been normally
Tory; defiant of " Socialism," defiant of change. The
cause of this cannot be found entirely in the existence
of a metropolis and capital of the Empire living
a parasitic existence on tribute levied upon the
boundaries of the world. For in most of the great
capitals of Europe the advocates of revolutionary
programmes find to-day their most fruitful fields of
propaganda. It may perhaps best be understood in
the apprehension of an actual picture of visible
things. The answer is hidden in these strings and
congestions of little comfortable two-storeyed red and
grey cottages, which multiplied with such amazing
rapidity in the preceding generation; pushing their
tentacles from factory or industrial centre out over
the neighbouring fields, and proclaiming with their
cleanliness and tiny gardens and modest air of comfort, a working population prosperous and content.
One type of dwelling, indeed, is found to be more or
less prevalent through all the urban aggregation.
That is the small four or five-roomed cottage, containing on the ground floor a front parlour, a kitchen,
and a scullery built as an addition to the main part

of the house; and on the upper floor the bedrooms, the third bedroom in the five-roomed house being built over the scullery. And in such dwelling-places, if anywhere, is concealed the secret of the future of the people of England. Abroad, the self-contained "flat," the gigantic tenement, in which the single family is embedded in a cliff of bricks and mortar, is more and more coming to be the staple dwelling of the working classes. Broad, tree-planted avenues, with fast electric locomotion, cut through carefully planned cities of storey piled on storey. The whole effect is grandiose and spacious, if it lacks the picturesqueness of that enormous acreage of chimney-pots and tiny tumbled cottages which is revealed in a kind of smoky grandeur from the railway embankments of South and East London—the desperate efforts made by a race reared in village communities to maintain in the urban aggregation some semblance of a home. Such is the shelter; what of the food? The price of bread varies. Family budgets of the weekly incomes are extraordinarily suggestive of the struggle which takes place in the industrial areas of the city. Classified according to amount of net receipts, they reveal an ever-growing proportion devoted to the essentials of bodily nutriment; until, at the bottom, where the income appears permanently below the "living wage," there is practically no margin left when the food demand is satisfied. "For the incomes below thirty shillings, two-thirds of the total income is spent on food, "declares a Board of Trade investigator," while in the case of the incomes of forty shillings and above, about fifty-seven per cent. is spent on food."

Amongst the poorest, actually one-fifth of the total
food expenditure is spent on bread and flour:
a conclusive statistic condemning those who lightly
justify a tax on imported corn on the ground
that so much stale bread is committed to the pig-
sty. Tea, in these lowest incomes, demands nine-
pence farthing a week, and sugar eightpence. It is
expenditure on the margin, counted in farthings, a
life exceedingly difficult to realise amongst those
to whom a few coppers more or less means no
appreciable difference.

Variations—from town to town—in a civilisation
which is in all essentials homogeneous, and a life of
easy flow from one labour centre to another, tend to
lessen or to vanish. Yet there still are apparent local
variations in wages which appear to be independent
of variations in wealth or in prices. Again there are
most remarkable differences in habits, customs, pro-
ductivity, and statistics of birth and death. Why
(for example) should Middlesborough have the highest
birth-rate of England? Why indeed, the cynical
might ask, should any children be born in Middlesborough at all, considering the more than dismal
picture which investigation discloses of existence in
that feverish industrial centre? There is appalling
wastage of life force in these percentages of
infant mortality, especially in the factory centres
—soiled, useless child lives, whose existence stands
for no intelligible significance in any rational scheme
of human affairs. There are statistics of mortality
which reveal so many years knocked off human life
in the transition from the life of the field to the life

of the factory. And there is the evidence also, amongst the industrial peoples as amongst the classes above them, of perhaps the most remarkable change which is operating to-day in modern England: in the tumbling down of the birth-rate with ominous rapidity, until nothing but a similar reduction of the death-rate, with the increase of sanitation and the limitation of disease, seems to stand between the two meeting in a henceforth stationary population. Is the vitality of the race being burnt up in mine and furnace, in the huddled mazes of the city? And is the future of a colonising people to be jeopardised, not by difficulties of over-lordship at the extremities of its dominion, but by obscure changes in the opinion, the religion, and the energies at the heart of the Empire? These and other subjects confront even a superficial examination of the material condition of England. Karl Marx was wrong in his defiant assertion that economic causes were the sole factors in the transformations of history. He would have been right had he asserted that many startling over-turnings of opinion, in political and social, and even religious change, can ultimately be traced back to the economic condition of obscure masses of the common people. The majority are in regular labour in summer and winter, tearing from coal and furnace and factory the vast industrial wealth of England. Their disabilities are imperfect houses set often in quite needlessly squalid surroundings: the possibility of finding, through no fault of their own, their labour no longer required; specific diseases and risks of specific accidents which are associated with various

specific occupations. Their advantages are a rate
of payment higher for shorter hours of work than is
at present prevailing (in the majority of trades) in any
other country of Europe. The artisan is far better
fed than the agricultural labourer, is more intelligent,
quicker and more active, with greater pleasures
available in popular entertainment, or a Saturday
half-holiday, or a week at the seaside. Yet his
span of life is shorter and his work more precarious.
He possesses little opportunity for the accumulation
of property. He has no "stake in the country,"
and has no permanent possession, lacking even a tiny
plot of land which he can bequeath from father to
child. His effects—on his decease—are generally
negligible. The Multitude, with a substantial although
inadequate share of the income of the country, possesses but an infinitesimal proportion of its capital.

In such surroundings and despite such drawbacks,
there labours a hardy race of men, whose efforts, in
skill, perseverance, and indefatigable industry, have
earned them supremacy in the markets of the world.
It is an industrial order in transition, evidently being
swept forward by forces beyond individual control,
to a condition in the future which would be almost
inconceivable to the present. It is a population of
weekly wage-earners which has struggled out of
servitude into independence, but which still remains
goaded into activity by fear—not of the lash of the
overseer, but of the grim and implacable forces of
hunger and cold. Slavery, Serfdom, Poverty: these,
says the author of the *Nemesis of Nations*, form
three stages in the changing condition of the social

basis of civilisation. "Poverty" is the foundation
of the present industrial order. It is a poverty
which is removed, for the most part, from actual
lack of physical necessities, though it is always never
far distant from such a privation. It is rather
"industrialism" — the "proletariat" — a state of
human affairs for which we have in English no
defining title. In working it provides others with
leisure, and the complex and refining influences
which leisure can bring. It works in the city
aggregations, always twisting threads, or clanging
machinery, or stoking effectual fires. Its products
post o'er land and ocean without rest — swinging
steel bridges over the rivers of East Africa, furnishing
Nicaragua with carpets, or encasing the women of
Upper Burmah in Lancashire cotton fabrics. What
is the meaning of it all? What is the end of it all?
We cannot tell the meaning outside; the future of
a world when the "iron age" has become triumphant,
and man, a midget, controlling by his intelligence
huge and ponderable forces, will be lost in the
labyrinths of his enormous machines. Certain forms
of American activity on the shores of Lake Michigan,
or in the devastated North-East of Pennsylvania,
provide sufficient forecast of such a future. Nor
can we tell the meaning (as it were) inside: in
the lives of those two differentiated classes which the
modern industrial life is daily creating; the life of
those who enjoy, on the one hand, in Pleasure
Cities, in all branches of eager and sometimes
morbid amusement; and the life of the new
race which will be evolved out of these strenuous

gnomes who labour in the heart of the city congestions.

Of very special interest, however, is the testimony
of those who have endeavoured to get behind the
form of cottage or quality of food, to apprehension
of the actual life of the people who dwell in the one
and are nourished by the other. Such efforts have
been made, and not unsuccessfully, by Lady Bell at
Middlesborough, by Mr. Charles Booth in London,
by Mr. Reynolds amongst his friends the Devon
fishermen, by Mr. Reginald Bray from his block
tenement in Camberwell. They all bear testimony
concerning a life novel to humanity, whose development and future is still doubtful.

Lady Bell, in her study of such life in a prosperous
northern centre, goes near to provide a bird's-eye
view of the city "proletariat" in its present uncertain
state. It is a town erected almost in two nights and
a day by the demands of the new iron manufacture.
Its hundred thousand population are practically all
workers. It exists solely for the purpose of trans-
lating human energy into material values. Its
inhabitants have been sucked in like the draught
in its own blast furnaces: from the neighbouring
countryside, from the neighbouring townships, from
Scotland and Ireland, and places far afield. Round
the furnaces there have rapidly heaped together
mazes of little two-storeyed cottages. The furnaces,
the grey streets, a few public buildings, all set in
a background of greyness, in a devastated landscape,
under a grey sky—that is the proletarian city. Lady
Bell set herself (in her own happy phrase) to reveal

what the Iron Trade, which people outside "know but by name, perhaps, as a huge measuring gauge of the national prosperity, is in reality, when translated into terms of human beings." She takes her readers through the great furnaces and down into the interiors of the little houses. She exhibits the habits, manners, pleasures, and pains of the people. She shows in one chapter the literature patronised by this population; in another the people at work; in another the people at play. Again, she will describe the lives of the children, the lives of the wife and mother, the influences of sickness, accident, or old age. The slave populations who built Babylon, or upon which the Athenian oligarchy which called itself a Democracy essayed philosophy and beauty, remain to-day more as a myth than as a memory. The poverty populations, upon which are built to-day England's unparalleled accumulation, will stand in the future, with at least a corner of their lives lifted. Such a corner will interpret to a less harassed age a life once peopling these waste places, which will then be but ruins and a memory.

Here is a population in many respects more fortunate than its fellows. Its wages are high; its hours of work are few. Its life, though exacting and laborious, demanding, perhaps, from human nature more than human nature can readily give, is more exhilarating than the long hours in the humid air of the cotton factory, or the perpetual scribbling in an underground office cellar. It is wrestling continually with the iron: tearing it out of the ironstone, directing rivers of molten metal into their proper

channels, bending the intractable stone and the huge
forces of heat and affinity to the will of man.   And
in life also it is wrestling with huge forces which it
but dimly understands, poised on a perilous pathway
from which one slip means utter destruction.   " The
path the iron worker daily treads at the edge of the
sandy platform, that narrow path that lies between
running streams of fire on the one hand and a sheer
drop on the other, is but an emblem of the Road of
Life along which he must walk.   If he should
stumble, either actually or metaphorically, as he
goes, he has but a small margin in which to recover
himself."   There is a less defensible side of the
people's life in the enormous disproportion of attend-
ance at public-houses and at places of religious
worship;   the universal prevalence of betting and
gambling;   the thoughtlessness and wastefulness
which often produces economic collapse;   the ignorance of child-rearing and the laws of health;   the
darker side of the artificial restriction of families.
But these become explained rather than condemned
by the revelation of the contrast in the condition of
child-bearing in one of these crowded, tiny homes
with the condition in the surroundings of those who
live in another universe.   Boys and girls of fourteen
or younger are turned loose to pick their way through
the most difficult period of life, just at the season
when the boys and girls of another class are most
completely surrounded with careful and humane
influences.   The married woman of the working
classes, " handicapped as she is by physical conditions
and drawbacks, with but just bodily strength enough to

encounter the life described," may be defended against
the fluent criticism of "her more prosperous sisters—
whose duties are divided among several people, and
even then not always accomplished with success."

So is being heaped up the wealth of the world.
Under darkened skies, and in an existence starved
of beauty, these communities of men and women and
children continue their unchanging toil. Is the price
being paid too great for the result attained? The
cities have sucked in the healthy, stored-up energies
of rural England; with an overwhelming percentage
to-day of country upbringing. Must they ever thus
be parasitic on another life outside, and this nation
divide into breeding-grounds for the creation of
human energies and consuming centres where these
energies are destroyed? The standard of longevity
has pitifully fallen in such places from that prevalent
amongst the agricultural labourers. Workers formerly
too old at sixty are now too old ten years earlier.
The men are scourged by specific diseases; the
mortality of the children is appalling. One is apt
to be surprised, says Lady Bell, of the iron workers
of Middlesborough, to find how many of the workmen are more or less ailing in different ways. "But
we cease to be surprised when we realise how apt
the conditions are to tell upon the health even of
the strongest, and how many of the men engaged in
it are spent by the time they are fifty. To say that
this happens to half of them is probably a favourable
estimate." Of the women, Lady Bell brushes aside
with a welcome contempt that newspaper and
drawing-room cant which explains that a beneficent

Providence has made the working classes insensible to pains and conditions which other classes would find intolerable. " It is not only bringing children into the world that affects the health of the working women. It is an entire delusion to believe that they are, as a rule, stronger, hardier, healthier, than the well-to-do. Their life is a continuous toil. They rarely go outside the doors of their houses, except for Saturday marketing and Sunday-evening exercise. Recreation, the stimulus of changed garments, rest during the day, or the other minor comforts which other classes find so necessary, are not for them. They are mostly convinced that it is wrong to sit down and read a book at any hour of the day. Their interests, not unnaturally, turn towards the stimulus of drinking, and of betting and gambling— two elements which at least can give colour in a life set in grey." [1]

Every observer, in this and its hundred similar fellows, can see family affection, endurance, kindliness, and patience beyond all praise ; a resistance (even in the last extremity) to the triumphant powers of darkness. What is more difficult to show is any interpretation of the whole business, an ideal which can illuminate the present disability, or a vision in which to-day's efforts will appear intelligible in the light of an end. Lacking such vision, the verdict of a nineteenth-century prophet still sounds mournful over much of industrial England that abides unchanged. " The two most frightful things I have ever yet seen in my life," wrote Ruskin, " are

[1] *At the Works. Lady Bell.*

the south-eastern suburbs of Bradford, and the scene from Wakefield Bridge, by the chapel; yet I cannot but more and more reverence the fierce courage and industry, the gloomy endurance, and the infinite mechanical ingenuity of the great centres, as one reverences the fervid labours of a wasp's nest, though the end of all is only a noxious lump of clay."

Yet all England has not yet been roofed over and become subservient to furnace and factory: and there are other observers who find amongst the labouring populations, especially amongst those who are compelled to face danger and to cultivate endurance, an excellence denied to classes sometimes deemed more fortunate. We may pass from the blackness and almost uncouth violence of Middlesborough to the jolly fishermen of the South Coast: to find not the iron trade, but the ocean harvest, "translated into terms of human beings." Mr. Reynolds, who has lived amongst such a fishermen's colony in a Devonshire watering-place, can give encouraging testimony to the happiness found there, the generosity, the standards of the poor; to a definite and remote civilisation, which gazes out upon the activities of the wealthier classes above it, sometimes with wonder, sometimes with a little envy, certainly with no hatred or predatory aim.

Sixty years ago, Disraeli described the rich and poor of England as two nations. To-day, even national distinctions seem less estranging than the fissure between the summit and basis of society. "Their civilisations are not two stages of the same civilisation, but two civilisations, two traditions which have grown up concurrently." And a similar testimony is expressed by many who have intimate and first-hand knowledge of the life of the hand worker. "The more one sees of the poor in their own homes," is the verdict of Miss Loane, a witness of varied and peculiar experience, "the more one becomes convinced that their ethical views, taken as a whole, can be more justly described as different from those of the upper classes than as better or worse." Most present-day failures in legislation and social experiment are due to neglect of this fact. It has been assumed that the artisan is but a stunted or distorted specimen of the small tradesman; with the same ideals, the same aspirations, the same limitations: demanding the same moulding towards the fashioning of a completed product. We are gradually learning that "the people of England" are as different from, and as unknown to, the classes that investigate, observe, and record, as the people of China or Peru. Living amongst us and around us, never becoming articulate, finding even in their directly elected representatives types remote from their own, these people grow and flourish and die, with their own codes of honour, their special beliefs and moralities, their judgment and often their condemnation of the classes to whom has been given leisure and material advantage. The line is cut clean by both parties, neither desiring to occupy the territory of the other. "There is not one high wall, but two high walls, between the classes and the masses," declares this witness; "and that erected in self-defence by the exploited is the higher and more difficult to climb."

The scene is laid in the huddled cottages of a fisher village of a South Coast watering‑place. The observer penetrates behind the appearance—to the normal visitor—of a rather squalid fishing suburb, with swarms of untidy children, and the fishermen, deferential, seeking patronage of the brisk or bored holiday-maker. He has lived amongst them and loved them. He has convinced them that he has no desire to do them good. He comes to their life having "swallowed all the formulas" with a perhaps exaggerated contempt for the "intellectuals" and the upholders of the middle-class moral code. He is enchanted by the life he finds there, despite all its discomforts. In the existence of the poor, in an experience fixed on the hard rind of life, tasting to the full its salt and bitter flavours, he finds a sincerity and an adventure denied to the more secure classes above. Always faced by elemental facts, and demanding a continuous courage for the maintenance of an unending struggle, these men and women exhibit clean-cut, simple qualities which vindicate their existence before any absolute standard of values.

The poor are inclined to suspect and dislike the classes just above them, the tradesmen. Nowhere is the moral standard more divergent than between the frugal, laborious, and rather timid assiduities of the lower middle class on the one hand, and on the other the reckless, generous, improvident life of the working peoples. To the "gentleman," the attitude of the sea-folk is different. He is despised for his ignorance. He is sometimes regarded as fair game for deceit or extortion, outside the moral standard of the home

8

community, just as the coloured peoples are regarded as outside the recognised codes of civilisation to-day. Yet there is little envy of his riches and enjoyments, and even a certain admiration, so long as he conforms to certain accepted laws of kindliness. "'An 'orrible lie!' between two poor people is fair play from a poor man to a wealthier, just as, for instance, the wealthy man considers himself at liberty to make speeches full of hypocritical untruth when he is seeking the suffrage of the free and independent electors, or is trying to teach the poor man how to make himself more profitable to his employer." The "gentlemen" are permitted idleness, luxuriousness, and the freest self-indulgence without criticism; but anything from them in the nature of meanness is resented. Haggling, for example, over the hire of a boat, is an unpardonable offence. The fishermen, on their occasional holidays, spend their savings lavishly and without question; why should not the "gentle-men" do the same? "When Tony goes away himself, he pays what is asked; regrets it afterwards, if at all; and comes home when his money is done. 'If a gen'leman,' he says, 'can't afford to pay the rate, what du 'ee come on the beach to hire a boat for— an' try to beat a fellow down? I reckon 'tis only a *sort o' gen'leman* as does that!'"

And this, indeed, is only congruous with that changed estimate of moral values which prevails amongst the poor. Mr. Reynolds, amongst his Devon fishermen, finds the same general summing-up of moral guilt or excellence as Miss Loane has found in the mean streets of the great cities.

"Generosity ranks far before justice, sympathy before truth, love before chastity, a pliant and obliging disposition before a rigidly honest one. In brief, the less admixture of intellect required for the practice of any virtue, the higher it stands in popular estimation." It is the emotional, indeed, against the intellectual: to one point of view, life in an incomplete condition of development; to another, life lived nearer to its central heart. Certainly, in the combination of Christian and ethical dicta which make up the popular moral code of modern civilisation, the standard of the poor is nearer to the Christian standard. One can see how many of the New Testament assertions have been fashioned from the common democratic mind, as Socrates and Plato from the aristocratic. Yet religion counts for little in the scheme of human affairs. There is, indeed, nothing of a definite denial; the fishing village would be scandalised by any truculent disproof of Christianity. The children go regularly to Sunday school; their parents believe in God and in a better time coming. But the general spirit reveals that widespread and prevailing uncertainty, and conviction of uncertainty, which to-day is the most dominant attitude in face of ultimate problems. "Tony" the fisherman pronounces religion to be "the business of the clergy, who are paid for it, and of those who take it up as a hobby, including the impertinent persons who thrust hell-fire tracts upon the fisher-folk. 'Us can't 'spect to know nort about it,' says Tony. ''Tain't no business o' ours. May be as they says; may be not. It don't matter, that I sees. 'Twill be all the same in a hundred years' time, when we're a-grinning up at the daisy-roots.' " [1]

It was thought, says Mr. Charles Booth, of a certain experiment in East London, that as the poor were not going to the churches, they would attend the Hall of Science. When the Hall of Science was opened, it was as deserted as the churches. The people wanted neither religion nor its antidote. All they wanted was to be left alone. All that the poor want, runs the popular Socialist declaration, is that the rich shall get off their backs. All that the poor want, would be a truer aphorism, is to be left alone. They don't want to be cleaned, enlightened, inspected, drained. They don't want regulations of the hours of their drinking. They assiduously avoid the hospitals and parish rooms. They don't want compulsory thrift, elevation to remote standards of virtue and comfort, irritation into intellectual or moral progress. In that diverting novel, the *Lord of Latimer Street*, the peer who owns the neighbourhood, disguised as a lodger in a block of scandalous tenements in Bermondsey, announces with pride that the philanthropic landlord is going to pull them down and convert the site into a recreation-ground for the people. The result is an awakening of universal fury amongst the residents in these deplorable abodes. Why can't he leave them alone? They pay their rents without complaining. They are not jealous of his enjoyments. They are not endeavouring to seize his money or despoil his goods. Why can't he go and spend the

[1] *A Poor Man's House. Stephen Reynolds.*

money at Monte Carlo or Newmarket "as the other lords do," as indeed they would like to do, if they were lords? Many who are conscious that the poor want to be left alone are not convinced that they ought to be left alone. Yet it is doubtful if much personal interference can be of any practical service. The effect of our meddling is similar to the effect of the preaching of Western morals in the East. The old faiths are destroyed. The new faiths are not assimilated. Mr. Reynolds, certainly, has no doubt on the matter. He is scornful concerning the boom of Elementary Education. He dislikes the preaching of thrift. Amongst the poor, "extreme thrift, like extreme cleanliness, has often a singular dehumanising effect. It hardens the nature of its votaries, just as gaining what they have not earned most frequently makes men flabby. Thrift, as highly recommended, leads the poor man into the spiritual squalor of the lower middle class." He is willing to make almost any sacrifice for his friends, if only they can retain their chief vindicating quality—that insouciance or contempt for life's ills and dangers which enables them ever to take the thunder and the sunshine with a frolic welcome. He finds this greatly characteristic of his fishermen: he probably would find less manifestation of it in the difficult darkness of the cities, where Fear, rather than Courage, is the driving force of common humanity. But, however much Churches may talk about sin and virtue, "we know well in our hearts," says this observer, "that pluck and courage are the great twin virtues, and that cowardice is the fundamental sin." He finds amongst the poor not only

the " will to live," but the " courage to live "; not only
endurance of existence, but exultation in it.   They are
not afraid of life.   They keep something of the adventure which takes all risks : the resolute action which
cannot even see the risks it is taking.   With Stevenson,
they will have nothing to do with the negative virtues.
With the original Christian axiom—as Renan saw it
—they reveal that " the heart of the common people
is the great reservoir of the self-devotion and re-
signation by which alone the world can be saved."

II

This " daring and courage," however, is the pre-
rogative of individuals ; specially equipped, or selected
(as it seems) by a life trained from the earliest years
to confront hostile forces in the open air and sunshine ; skilled and heartened by combats with the sea.
How far can such characters be identified in the
Crowd : the special product of modern industrial
civilisation ?   Those who would attempt a diagnosis
of the present must find themselves more and more
turning their attention from the individual to the
aggregation : upon the individuals which act in an
aggregation in a manner different from their action
as isolated units of humanity.   We have to deal, in
fact, not only with the Crowd casually collected in
sudden movement by persons accustomed to live
alone, but with whole peoples which in London and
the larger cities are reared in a Crowd, labour in a
Crowd, in a Crowd take their enjoyments, die in a
Crowd, and in a Crowd are buried at the end.

"Has there been a row?" asked a journalist of a gathering at Westminster summoned by "Suffragettes" and unemployed leaders. "No," was the cheerful reply, "but we still 'ave 'opes." It is a crowd which "still 'as 'opes" that forms the matrix or solid body of these agglomerations of humanity whose doings to-day excite some interest and some perplexity amongst observers of social change. In the midst are the criminal and the enthusiast, those who are openly at war with Society, those who are battered by its complications and troublous demands, those, again, in whom devotion to some ideal cause burns like a flame at the heart. But these are all encompassed and embedded in the multitude of the unimportant: gathered from nowhere, journeying nowhither, swaying and eddying, swept into random groups and whirlpools, choking for a moment all the city ways, and in a moment leaving them all silent and deserted; the city Crowd which has seen little that is encouraging at the present, but "has hopes" of something wonderful yet to be revealed.

You may see it in the dim morning of every London day, struggling from the outskirts of the city into tramcars and trains which are dragging it to its centres of labour: numberless shabby figures hurrying over the bridges or pouring out of the exits of the central railway stations. You may discern in places the very pavements torn apart, and tunnels burrowed in the bowels of the earth, so that the astonished visitor from afar beholds a perpetual stream of people emerging from the middle of the street, seemingly manufactured in some laboratory below. It flows always along the high road of the huge town in the daytime, like a liquid unprecipitated, or a river in even stream carrying down dust to the sea. But at any moment an unexpected incident, tragic or trivial, may change the liquid from clear to cloudy, or reveal, like the river suddenly banked in obstruction, the débris and turgid elements which it has hitherto borne along so buoyantly. A motor omnibus stands still, a cab horse collapses, men's voices are raised in altercation, an itinerant agitator demands work for all, or announces the day of judgment. Immediately a knot appears in the texture of the wood, a whirlpool in the water. The multitude of the unimportant gather together, "having hopes." With incredible rapidity appear amongst them the criminal, the loafer, the enthusiast; the stream of busy persons has become transferred into the city Crowd.

There is a note of menace in it, in the mixed clamour which rises from its humours and angers, like the voice of the sea in gathering storm. There is the evidence of possibilities of violence in its waywardness, its caprice, its always incalculable mettle and temper, forming in the aggregate a personality differing altogether from the personalities of its component atoms. Satisfied, curious, eager only for laughter and emotion, it will cheer the police which is scattering it like chaff and spray, mock openly at those who have come with set purposes, idle and sprawl on a summer afternoon at Hyde Park or an autumn evening in Parliament Square.

But one feels that the smile might turn suddenly into fierce snarl or savagery, and that panic and wild fury are concealed in its recesses, no less than happiness and foolish praise. But more than the menace, the overwhelming impression is one of ineptitude; a kind of life grotesque and meaningless. It is in the city Crowd, where the traits of individual distinction have become merged in the aggregate, and the impression (from a distance) is of little white blobs of faces borne upon little black twisted or misshapen bodies, that the scorn of the philosopher for the mob, the cynic for humanity, becomes for the first time intelligible. Separate the drops and particles of it, follow each man homeward through the various ways of the city labyrinth—at the end you will find Humanity in its unchangeable and abiding existence: a tiny suburban home with cottage and garden, a tenement in a cliff of workmen's dwellings, a "child's white face to kiss at night," a "woman's smile by candle light." In each individual is resistance, courage, aspiration; a persistence which carries through the daily task with some energy and some enjoyment, and not entire discredit at the end. But immediately the mass of separate persons has become welded into the aggregate, this note of distinction vanishes. Humanity has become the Mob, pitifully ineffective before the organised resistance of police and military, and almost indecently naked of discipline or volition in the comparison; gaping open-mouthed, jeering at devotions which it cannot understand, like some uncouth monster which can be cajoled and flattered into imprisonment or ignoble action; like the Crowd which in all ages has rejoiced, one day at the crowning, the next at the crucifixion, of its King.

Why is it that this writing down of values takes place when mankind is thus collected into aggregations: that the spirit of the mob is so much less reputable than the spirit of its separate components? In part, perhaps, because the trivial and vacant elements are uppermost amongst a city race whose aspirations and purposes are independent of organised collective energies and aims. They have gathered for recreation, to be amused; for curiosity, to be surprised; for companionship, in a region where night has its empire, not without its terrors, just beyond the boundaries of their limited experience. The tragedy of common life is apparent, a modern philosopher has declared, not where poverty is the heritage of all but the few, or because existence offers at best a struggle uncertain and austere; but whenever that life is closed within limited horizons, and moved by no ideal springs. The visionary who cherishes the hope of a renovated society in which all shall be satisfied, the woman who flings herself into prison in the expectation that through her sacrifice the freedom of women will be attained, is a figure to the outward eye, indistinguishable in its obscurity from the multitude around who jeer and wonder and applaud. But these visionaries and enthusiasts possess a secret denied to their fellows, which gives their little lives a significance absent from the encompassing multitude; in the sense of consecration to a purpose, a meaning, and a goal.

Meantime that spirit abides but in the few; and

the Crowd remains, to-day as yesterday, an instrument which the strong man has always used and always despised in the using. The new features of it come from the change that has gathered men from the countryside and the tiny town and hurried them into the streets of an immense city; henceforth always to move in a company, each tied as with a chain to his fellows, never to stand alone. In such a transformation there would seem some danger of the normal life of man becoming the life of the Crowd, with features intensified and distorted when collected in tumult or demonstration. We seem to see in the experience of a generation an increasing tendency thus to merge the individual in the mass, more frequent and unfailing response to the demand for agitation, which, in fact, is an excuse for absurdity or violence. Man, always seeking to escape from himself, found various channels of egress; in drink, in religious emotion, in political energy. He has now found that he can escape from himself by merely linking up with others like himself to become units in a Crowd. The secret is perhaps most clearly apprehended in America, where the Crowd consciousness is excited as deliberately as the religious emotion of a revivalist meeting; and after due preparation an aggregate of human beings suddenly breaks into carefully fermented lunacy. So that selected delegates of the political parties—men, being selected, it would seem, for special calculation, intelligence, and prudence—will shout at Denver or Chicago meaningless cacophinations for an hour and a half on end, march round and round the hall playing instruments and singing discordant songs, or suddenly take off their coats, or stand on their heads, or beat each other with bits of board. It is the experience of the flagellants and pilgrims of medieval times, with hysteria no longer left to chance, but organised as a fine art. In our own "mafficking," in the tearing to pieces of the City Volunteers, in unemployed demonstrations, even in a spectacle so diverting and yet so foreboding as the "sieges of St. Stephen's" by the "Suffragettes," there are traces of similar if less exaggerated emotion: as man, communicating the infection of the Crowd consciousness to his fellow-men, suddenly abandons his individual volitions and restraints, and loses himself in the volition of the Crowd. A note of hysteria may seem to be an inevitable accompaniment of a city life so divorced from the earth's ancient tranquillity as never to appear entirely sane. And the future of the city populations, ever "speeded up" by more insistent bustles and noises and nervous explosions, takes upon itself, in its normal activities, something hitherto abnormal to humanity. We shall probably encounter more appeals to the multiplied power of assembly, more determination to find a short cut in lawlessness towards attainment, more passive and active resistance in attempts at government by violence rather than government by reason. Others, besides the unemployed or the women, will make this visible protest before all men by exhibition of their willingness to face ridicule, discomfort, physical injury, and even martyrdom in their ardour for the triumph of their cause. In a vision across the centuries, with time foreshortened, even material things take upon themselves the quality of motion : and the cities may be seen rising and falling, in growth, in triumph, and decay, like the fire that flares and in a moment fades. In similar vision the streets of those cities are always filled with this tumultuous and curious Crowd : restless, leaderless, astonished at itself and at the world, finding little intelligible either in the universe without or the universe within. Before which assembly in perpetual session there pass the phantom figures of those who appeal for its favour and its judgment : at first to a Crowd contemptuous, then to a Crowd acquiescent and astonished, ultimately to a Crowd applauding : themselves members of it, yet standing always separate and apart ; because they alone are working towards an end.

The definite excitement, and the deflection of that excitement into certain prepared channels, seems likely to become one of the arts of the political game. It is only in the last few months that those who have been studying the latest methods of electioneering have elaborated a new system of appeal to a new race of men. The old discussion by argument, commonplace posters, and literature, even the cheery riotings of rival mobs, is already voted as a thing stale and outworn. Instead, we are to see an effort to capture, not individuals as individuals, but the Crowd as a Crowd. It is the first noteworthy recognition in politics that this creature has a personality— a personality altogether different from the personalities of its independent members. The first successful start was effected in the spring of 1908 in the

Crowd, at its very centre and crown, in a bye-election
in the heart of London. A particular segment of its
grey streets, in no way different from its half-century
of neighbours, had been chalked round with entirely
artificial boundaries, and labelled the Parliamentary
constituency of Peckham. And it was in this forbidding and desolate neighbourhood that the new electioneering set itself the high test of hypnotising, not
each single Imperial citizen who happened to live in
Peckham, but Peckham itself—the very heart of it—
the Peckham Crowd.

The report of this novel and entertaining crusade
soon spread from Peckham to its neighbours : what
would appeal to Peckham would also appeal to them ;
and every evening an appreciable percentage of the
four millions which lie around Peckham, and in whose
streets Peckham is embedded, poured into the centre
of disturbance. There they soon fell under the spell
so sedulously prepared for them. They surged up
and down the narrow ways, chaffing each other,
cheering the candidates, keen, alert, glad each to find
himself in the heart of a London Crowd. Any man
or woman upon whom fell the itch of speech secured
a box, mounted on it, held forth to those who would
listen, on teetotalism, or vaccination, or the wickedness of the Government, or the variable price of beer.
And the Crowd listened, as it may be seen listening
to any distorted nonsense in the public parks on
Sunday afternoons : with an aspect of intense seriousness, the respect which the inarticulate Englishman
instinctively feels for the voluble. Party feeling was
supposed to run high, the newspapers on each side

called shrilly for the defeat of plunderers and mis-
creants: "'Thou shalt not steal,' there is no time
limit to that," in huge letters stretched across the
street, challenged the cries from Liberal placards that
unless the people strangled the drink monopoly they
would be strangled by it. Yet it seemed that the
great mass of this astonishing multitude—the good-
tempered, short-sighted, happy-go-lucky London
citizen—regarded all such fiery invective with fortitude, if not with indifference. He was out for fun:
to hear a little politics, though not too much; speakers
who attempted argument or quotation were speedily
deserted; what he liked was noisy rhetoric and
denunciation. "Give it 'em hot!" was his favourite
advice to any orator of either colour. He delighted
in quick repartee, the ready scoring off an interrupter,
the good telling of some story with a very obvious
point at the end. He liked to see the coal-carts
wading through the crowded streets, with the big and
little sacks of coal; and the so-called procession of the
unemployed from Woolwich, actual, tangible figures,
visible before his very eyes; and the huge painted
donkey, half as high again as himself, bearing the
legend, "My brother is going to vote for Gautrey"
(the Government candidate); and the Suffragettes
there in person, the very women (some of them
agreeable to look at) who have been carried out
of Parliament by the police, and done their "time"
in Holloway Gaol. He sought, above all, a new
sensation: cheering, now a man who, from the
summit of a soap-box proclaimed the approaching
end of the world; now "Mr. Hunnable," as he sur-

mised that in the coming University boat race both
Oxford and Cambridge would be found among the
first three; now a sad-faced woman, whose contribution to the discussion consisted in ringing a huge
dinner-bell for half-an-hour without stopping; whose
thoughts, like the thoughts of the Turk who followed
Anacharsis Clootz in the French Convention, "remain
conjectural to this hour."

Upon such material clever men set themselves to
work with commendable zeal: knowing that the Crowd
may be stampeded by constant repetition of the same
thing, by pictorial illustration from which it cannot
escape, and by the excitement of the appeal
flashed upon it seemingly from a variety of different
sources that it should advance along a particular
road. So a "Coal Consumers' Defence League"
asserted, with monotonous insistence, that coal
would rise in price if the Government candidate
were elected; and attained the hypnotic success
which always recompenses a monotonous insistence
sufficiently prolonged. And the "Brewery Deben-
ture Shareholders' League" announced the approaching misery of the widow and the orphan. And long
lines of street bookmakers, in tall white hats and
genial, vacant, or bibulous faces, inquired of the
passing mob why they should not be allowed to
bet in the streets if they wished. And every public-
house became a Tory committee room, with all its
windows plastered with Tory bills and cartoons, and
the evidence of a brisk trade and many conversions
within its walls. Outside the Metropolitan Gasworks
at the dinner hour, and in Peckham High Street after

nightfall, a cloud of mingled, confused oratory and invective rose to the unconscious stars; as six or seven meetings, each within easy earshot of each other, shouted in hoarse accents for women's votes or cheaper food or the rights of the publican. Wagon-loads of pictorial illustration wedged their way through the coagulated masses of South London, now lit with fierce glare of torches, now disguised as an illuminated fire-engine pumping truth upon the Liberal mendacities; now loaded with slum children, looking, it must be confessed, exceedingly happy and healthy, but dolorously labelled "Victims of the Public-house Monopoly." Hysteria, as in all such deliriums, was never far away; women shrieked aloud at meetings, and had to be removed; madness fell upon a boy of twelve, and he stood on the top of a barrel, talking Tariff Reform. The extraordinary good-humour, the extraordinary stupidity, and the extraordinary latent forces, so concealed as to be unknown even to themselves, in these shabby, cheery, inefficient multitudes of bewildered and contented men and women, were the dominant impressions of this gigantic entertainment.

Do they care? Yes, undoubtedly, with, beneath all the love of fun and frolic, a really pathetic desire to know the truth: to understand what actually lies behind these fluent orations and facile statistics, and all the fury of illustration and argument which descended upon their inconspicuous abodes. Will they ever know? That is an unanswerable query. There are the knots and gatherings of convinced politicians, who will cheer for "Chamberlain" or denounce Protection, just as there are the knots and gatherings of convinced religious adherents, crystallised out of the huge aggregation of indifference, who worship in various forms a God who is unknown to the general. But the physical conditions of the city life are so novel to them, the bustle and violence of it all so insistent, the effect of the mechanical labour, the little leisure, mostly consumed in transit, the grey, similar streets of tiny houses so desolating, that it is hard to stimulate a high political, social, or religious aspiration. They will continue, for the most part, tacking from side to side in blind, uncertain fashion, firmly convinced at one moment that they have solved the secret, firmly convinced a few months afterwards that they have been mistaken. They will continue their hurried, uncertain lives with indomitable patience, courage, and hope always for "better times." They will be deluded, and after a time they will recognise their delusion, and after a further time be as readily deluded again. They will trust individuals with a fine generosity. They still believe that things are true because they see them in the newspapers. They exhibit an extraordinary absence of envy of those who are better off than themselves, an extraordinary patience in enduring unendurable things. The Crowd never revolts until the conditions have already become intolerable. It never complains unless its wrongs and disabilities have become themselves clamorous for redress; unless, if it ceased, the very stones would cry out. It is always being betrayed, cajoled, deceived, exploited: now stimulated to fury in warfares carefully engineered by the wealthier classes, in which it has no interest: now directed from those who are exploiting it into anger against "the foreigner," who is generally a crowd of similar persons being similarly inflamed against itself. It throws up occasional leaders who disappear from its horizon into other universes, from which come only rumours of justification or betrayal. It is being perpetually excited by words and phrases which mean little, which it repeats with an air of owlish wisdom: concerning the satisfactions of Imperial citizenship or the need for new ships, or the advantages of municipal reform. So it continues its patient subterranean life, staggering forward through time, bearing on its shoulders the vast edifice of modern industry: labouring, not without pride and pleasure, for advantage that other people shall enjoy.

And it possesses its own enjoyments also, and these not only those of which the moralist would disapprove: a too exuberant thirst for drink, or a passionate desire to obtain reward without labour. Charles Lamb would "often shed tears in the Strand for fulness of joy at so much life." His joy might be more keenly excited to-day, upon the days when the City crowd is out for a real holiday: something more agreeable than the Election carnival, and with no smudge of moral improvement on it. You may see it in the Saturday football crowds in all the manfacturing cities: see it in concentrated form when a selection of all the Saturday football crowds has poured into London for the "final contest" at the Crystal Palace for the "Cup,"

which is the goal of all earthly ambition. All the
long night overcrowded trains have been hurrying
southward along the great trunk lines, and dis-
charging unlimited cargoes of Lancashire and York-
shire artisans in the grey hours of early morning.
They sweep through the streets of the Metropolis,
boisterous, triumphant. They blink round historic
monuments, Westminster Abbey, St. Paul's Cathedral. They all wear grey cloth caps, they are all
decorated with coloured favours ; they are all small
men, with good-natured undistinguished faces. To
an Oriental visitor they would probably all appear
exactly alike, an endless reproduction of the same
essential type. In the afternoon the bulk of them
gather at the Crystal Palace, to see their carefully
labelled representatives compete for the highest prize
in the contest between various professional teams for
the football championship. They encourage these
hired persons with shrill cries. They follow the
various fortunes of the game with approval or discontent. At the end one half is kindled to elation,
the other sunk in disappointment. A crowd of
adult English citizens assembles round that arena,
in number some five times as great as the total
Boer commandoes which surrendered after the Peace
of Vereeniging, which had defended a country half
the size of Europe against all the armies of the
British Empire. And the irresistible query is sug-
gested by the sight of that congestion of grey, small
people with their facile excitements and their little
white faces inflamed by this artificial interest, whether,
in a day of trial, similar resources could be drawn

from them, of tenacity, courage, and an unwearying devotion to an impersonal ideal. "*If thou hast run with the footmen, and they have wearied thee, then how canst thou contend with horses? And if in the land of peace, wherein thou trustedst, they wearied thee, then how wilt thou do in the swelling of Jordan?*"

No one can question the revolution which has overtaken the industrial centres in the last two generations of their growth. Reading the records of the "hungry forties" in the life of the Northern cities is like passing through a series of evil dreams. Cellars have vanished into homes, wages have risen, hours of labour diminished, temperance and thrift increased, manners improved. The new civilisation of the Crowd has become possible, with some capacity of endurance, instead of (as before) an offence which was rank and smelling to heaven. But this life having been created and fixed in its development, the curious observer is immediately confronted with the inquiry: what of its future? Are the main lines set us at the present, and later development confined to variations in length and direction along these lines? In such a case progress will mean a further repetition of the type: two cotton factories where there is now one; five thousand small, grey-capped men where there are now three; perhaps, in some remote millennium, fourteen days of boisterous delight at Blackpool where now are only seven. A race can thus be discerned in the future, small, wiry, incredibly nimble and agile in splicing thread or adjusting machinery, earning high wages in the factories, slowly advancing (one may justly hope) in intelligence and sobriety, and the qualities which go to make the good citizen. These may at the last limit their hours of labour everywhere to the ideal of an eight hours day; everywhere raise their remuneration to a satisfactory minimum wage; everywhere find provision for insecurity, unemployment, old age. The "Crowd" is then complete. The City civilisation is established. Progress pauses—exhausted, satisfied. Man is made.

John Stuart Mill in early manhood was troubled with an inquiry that nearly compelled him to abandon the effort of reform. Suppose all the old wrongs righted, and the whole work of liberation accomplished, what then? He saw a vision of mankind in a kind of infinite boredom, an everlasting end of the world. The desolation of such a vision was only removed by study of the poems of Wordsworth. He found fresh inspiration for the work of progress in the vision of mankind, at last tranquil and satisfied, occupying its leisure in reading Wordsworth's poetry. The modern city crowd would allow scant tolerance to such visions as these. They demand excitement, adventure: the vision of that physical activity and control which is denied to themselves. To make two blades of grass grow where one grew before is the ideal of the lower, physical energies. To establish two football contests where only one existed is the translation of it into terms of the soul. A young workman from Sheffield, confronted with the prospect of certain and speedy death, journeys to London by the midnight train to see the final Cup Tie. On his return he takes to his bed. "In his last moments he asked his mother to so place the Wednesday colours that he might see them, exclaiming, 'I am glad I have lived to see good old Wednesday win the Cup.'" And so he died.

This reaching out of the crowd from its own drab life into the adventurous and coloured world of "make-believe" is not peculiar to these islands. Pallid young men collect outside the hotels in Madrid or Seville, where the bull-fighters are established before the contests, feeling a kind of satisfaction in the physical proximity to the heroes of their devotion; just as pallid young men collect outside the hotels in the English cities, happy in the conviction that only a thin wall of brick and stone separates them from those whom they contemplate with a kind of worship. In America, always more determined and fearless in pushing the new development to a logical conclusion, we find the actual schools of training for the baseball player, similar to the schools of the gladiators, whose ruins still survive in Pompeii and old Roman cities. Is this, after all, an artificial product of a time of tranquillity? Is its nature ephemeral? And will mankind ever again in these countries find physical exhaustion in the life of the fields, and mental excitement in the business of war and conquest? No one can answer. Certainly even that political activity in England, which is largely a great game, played with good humour and the element of uncertainty which gives spice to all adventure, for the majority does not count at all in comparison with these more obvious satisfactions. And of any other competitive attraction there is no trace at all. The intellectual profess contempt or despair. The " sporting " element exult in enthusiasm. The wisest at least will accept the fact, without too great exaggeration of praise or blame. For this is Democracy ; victorious ; unashamed.

The country has furnished these citizens, or their immediate ancestors. But now the country has been bled " white as veal." The cities will be compelled in the future to trust to inbreeding ; to rear, as best they may, in their own labyrinths children who will mate with children of a similar upbringing. What will be the effect of such inbreeding, in five generations, or in ten ? There can be no certain reply. Perhaps the cities themselves will not last long enough to ever furnish a certain reply. But the carefullest observers can already note some lines of definite change. Mr. Bray in his *Town Child* has indicated some of them. He is inclined to take a gloomy vision of the future.

Southey, seeing their variable beginnings, proclaimed that cities were the " graveyards of modern civilisation." Wordsworth found there the " soul of beauty and enduring life," amid the press " of self-destroying transitory things " diffused but " through meagre lines and colours." A long tradition, from Rousseau to Tolstoy, has denounced the growing multiplication of the town. Mr. Bray endeavours to see the town through the mind of the growing child : the child, not of the city splendour, but of the city squalor ; pent up within the elements there provided for the perceptive material of the developing mind. He finds the

keynote of it all in its self-destruction and its transitoriness.   The new forms of sickness from which
the body suffers are due "to the more malignant
because more concentrated contagion of man."   But
it is mind sickness which he most dreads ; in an en-
vironment where little makes for silence, permanence,
or repose ; where "all things, whether animate or in-
animate, change and change ceaselessly ; they seem
to emerge from the nowhere without rhyme or reason,
for a brief space form a portion of the child's universe,
and then, without rhyme or reason, pass out into the
nowhere again."   Excitement, noise, and a kind of
forlorn and desperate ugliness are the spirits watch-
ing round the cradle of too many children of the town ;
whose work, when fully accomplished, has created the
less reputable characteristics of the city crowd.   "The
human element, a very incarnation of the spirit of
unrest, encourages a temperament, shallow and without reserve, which passes in rapid alternation from
moods of torpor to moods of effervescent vivacity,
and nurtures a people eager for change and yet discontented with all that change brings ; impatient of
the old, but none the less intolerant of the new."
"Isn't the noise of the machines awful?" was the
question put to a young factory worker.   "Yes," he
replied, "not so much when they are going on as when
they stop."   The City-bred Race are going to find the
noise "awful" when it "stops."   Already in America
one can detect a kind of disease of activity, in a
people to whom "business" has become a necessary
part of life.   The general effect is of children of overstrung nerves, restless and aimless, now taking up a

book, now a plaything, now roaming round the room
in uncertain uneasiness.   The city-bred people, we
are confidently informed, will never go "back to the
land." In part this may mean that they will never return
to long hours of hopeless drudgery for shameful wage.
In part it may point to a certain condition of "nerves"
excited by city upbringing: a real disease of the soul.
Silence, solitariness, open spaces under a wide sky,
appear thus intolerable to a people never quite content
but in the shouts, the leagues of lights, and the roaring of the wheels.   And the scattering and separation
of man from man in a region still untamed and given
to large mysterious forces, the wind and weather
under huge spaces of the night, produces in a race
thus reared something of the impression of children
left alone in the dark.

Life thus developing, in lack of "the elements of
permanence, of significance, of idealistic imaginings,"
demands some special conscious and deliberate effort
to supply those elements.   The main interest of the
State (immortal and conservative) is to preserve its
own existence.   This preservation is impossible unless
it can guarantee to the next generation a healthy
start ; physical and mental efficiency, with the best
moral training at its disposal, to those who will be
the citizens of the future.   Changes which might
guarantee such preservation are denounced to-day as
involving a weakening or destruction of the family.
To many observers it is just the absence of such
changes which are ensuring the weaknesses and destruction of the family.   In the present confusion, on
the other hand, infantile mortality shows no decrease

in half a century, and the birth-rate steadily declines; on the other hand, where the mere pressure of animal and physical necessity has become too burdensome, the family is breaking to pieces under the strain.

"Few people," rightly says Mr. Bray, "seem to realise how nearly the lives of the poor reach the limits of human endurance." He believes that "the affections of the parents would increase, and the home duties be performed with greater success and animation," if "with a vigour less impaired by intolerable toil." He draws an arresting contrast between the long mechanical drudgery of the life of wife and mother in a poor family, and the life of a mother in those decent middle-class homes where perhaps the family tie is strongest to-day; not the rich and extravagant, but those who can afford some space and some leisure and the luxury of a servant. "The ties of family are stronger among the servant-keeping class than among the poorer class," is his conclusion, "and they are stronger because the stress of physical toil is weaker, and the pains of parenthood less insistent."

He utters grave warning to those well-meaning philanthropists who, in the name of Family Sanctity, are opposing the reforms which Social Reformers most ardently desire. "If it be a question of providing work for the unemployed, meals for the children, pensions for the old; if it be a matter of municipal trams, municipal wash-houses, municipal dwellings, in every instance," he protests, "they raise the cry that the independence of the family is threatened, and exhort their friends to fight the measure to the death.

Is it surprising that the word 'Family' has come to stink in the nostrils of those who are striving to improve the conditions of the poor? Is it any cause for wonder if they begin to attack the Family, and inquire what manner of monster that is which can only be preserved by bringing as offerings to its den hungry children and suffering mothers?" "The sanctity of the family," he boldly affirms, "is menaced at the present time by the austerity of the thoughtful rather than by the sentimentality of the thoughtless."[1]

However this may be, the Crowd consciousness and the city upbringing must of necessity act as a disintegrating force, tearing the family into pieces. If the Crowd condition, which, in part, is to supplement it, may be made a dignified and noble thing, there need be less regret over a change which, desirable or otherwise, would appear to be inevitable. The communal midday meal, for example, which the school children of the cities are coming to partake of altogether, should be something better than a squalid scramble for physical sustenance in soup or suet. The communal recreation, one would hope, may develop in something more desirable than the aimless activities of the Hampstead Heath bank holiday. The communal politics should be something more restrained than the stampeded "Swing of the Pendulum," first against one party in power, then against the other. The communal intellect might be directed towards other and more reputable ends than the devising of the last lines of "Limericks," or the search for true "tips" of horses, in the effort after

[1] *The Town Child.   R. A. Bray.*

unearned monetary gain. And the spirit of a collective mind, "the spirit of the hive," residing in the various industrial cities, may find expression and a conscious revelation of itself, in something more beautiful and also more intelligible than the chaotic squalor of uniformly mean streets and buildings which make up the centres of industrial England.

Certainly, unless the life of the Crowd can be redeemed, all other redemption is vain. Here is the battle-ground for the future of a race and national character. "Democracy," says Canon Barnett, the wisest of all living social reformers, "is now established. The working classes have the largest share in the government of the nation, and on them its progress depends." They possess, in his verdict, "the strenuousness and modesty which comes by contact with hardship, and the sympathy which comes by daily contact with suffering. They, as a class, are more unaffected, more generous, more capable of sacrifice, than members of other classes. They have solid sense and are good men of business, but they cannot be said to have the wide outlook which takes in a unity in which all classes are included. They are indifferent to knowledge and to beauty, so they do not recognise proportion in things, and their field of pleasure is very restricted between sentiment and comfort." "They suffer, as the great German socialist said, from 'wantlessness.' They prefer honest mediocrity to honest intellect, and would still vote for W. H. Smith rather than John Stuart Mill. Their actions are generous, but their philosophy of life is often of that shallow sort which says, 'Does Job serve God for naught?' and they are often, therefore, to be captured by 'a policy of blood and iron': they are easily taken by popular cries; they are fickle and easily made 'the puppets of Banks and Stock Exchanges.' They are sympathetic, but for want of knowledge their suspicions are soon roused, and they soon distrust their leaders." Yet his final conclusion is that " the working class is the hope of the nation, and their moral qualities justify the hope."[1]

III

Or, again, we may attempt to understand a particular class of society from knowledge of a typical member of it: from one life, to judge all. The difficulty in the case of the multitude is due to the fact that any person who has arisen into public fame possesses, from the very fact of such attainment, qualities which to the many are denied. The new Labour members in the House of Commons are often supposed to reveal the "working man" at last arrived: to be able to furnish a kind of selected sample of the English industrial populations. They may perhaps stand for the working man in opinion. The majority of them are certainly remote from him in characteristic. Many are Scotsmen; and there is no deeper gulf than that which yawns between the Scotch and the English proletariat. They are mostly men of laborious habits, teetotalers, of intellectual interests, with a belief in the reasonableness of mankind. The English

[1] *Towards Social Reform. Canon and Mrs. Barrett.*

working man is not a teetotaler, has little respect for intellectual interests, and does not in the least degree trouble himself about the reasonableness of mankind. He is much more allied in temperament and disposition to some of the occupants of the Conservative back benches, whose life, in its bodily exercises, enjoyment of eating and drinking, and excitement of "sport," he would himself undoubtedly pursue with extreme relish if similar opportunities were offered him. Figures like Mr. Snowden, with his passionate hunger for reform, like Mr. Henderson, with his preaching of religious and ethical ideals in Wesleyan Chapels, like Mr. George Barnes or Mr. Jowett, with their almost pathetic appeals to rational argument in the belief that reason directs the affairs of the world, are figures in whose disinterested service and devotion to the work of improvement any class might be proud. But in their excellences as in their defects they stand sharply distinct from the excellences and defects of the average English artisan. They care for things he cares nothing for: he cares for things which seem to them trivial and childish. In Mr. Grayson, again, a certain type has become articulate; the "Clarionette" with red tie, flannel shirt, and bicycle, who has been moved to continuous anger by the vision of trampled women and starving children in the cities of poverty. Such men see the world transfigured in the light of a great crusade. They are convinced that by demonstration and violence to-day, or (at latest) to-morrow, "the people" will rise in their millions and their might, pluck down the oppressors who are "sucking

their blood," and inaugurate the golden age of the
Socialistic millennium. But meantime the " people "
are thinking of almost everything but the Socialistic
millennium. They are thinking how to get steady
work ; of the iniquities of the "foreigner "; of the
possibility or desirability of war, now with the
Transvaal, now with Germany. They are thinking
which horse is going to win in some particular race, or
which football eleven will attain supremacy in some
particular league. They are thinking that wife or
child is ill or happy, of entertainment, of the pleasure
in reminiscence of one past holiday or the pleasure
in anticipation of another. They are thinking (in a
word) of all the variegated and complex joys and
sorrows which make up the common lot of humanity.

One figure, however, in this interesting and excellent party does directly exhibit the character of a
particular class. In Mr. "Will Crooks"—a kind of
East End superman—the proletariat of London has
found voice. He is the East End with all its qualities—with all its qualities intensified, but with the
same proportion kept between them. It is true Mr.
Crooks is a teetotaler, and never puts a penny on a
horse : and that, in part, distinguishes him from an
industrial population which finds the necessary relief
from a grey existence in the excitement of the
possibility of gain, or in the convivial glass of an
evening. He would probably affirm that in the
excitement and conviviality of Parliament and a
political career he finds sufficient substitute for such
milder intoxicants. But reading him you are reading
the East End working man, and learning much that

was before inexplicable: why the East End exists,
and why it continues to exist: why no sudden flame
of violence consumes these crowded streets and
tenements: of its cheerfulness, its energy, its humour,
its unquenchable patience. You are learning also
some of its weaknesses: its willingness to think well
of others, its readiness to make allowances and to
forgive—so fatal to the austere work of Government;
its reckless, whole-hearted charity, which is the
despair of the Provident Visitor and the Charity
Organisation Society; its perpetual search for short
cuts, and the summary severing of the knot of old
problems.

He stands to-day born of these people and part
of them—the very child of the crowd. Most of his
life has been spent there. He has plumbed the
height and depth of human experience in this
smoky and bewildering universe. As a child he
has known hunger and the unsatisfied demand for
bread. He has been an inmate of the workhouse,
and the ruler of it; a forlorn waif in a Barrack
School with unforgettable memories of its polished
impersonal cruelty; and again the great man who
comes down as visitor to the Barrack School of a
later generation. He has tramped its streets in the
vain search for work, and been glad to accept twopence from a friend. He has travelled on the upper
half of a boot, tied on to the foot with string; and
he has organised schemes for the unemployed which
have been stimulated by that adventure into hell.
He has obtained education as so many quick and
intelligent East End boys are still obtaining it: from

10

the riotous revel of the "penny dreadful," through the *British Workman*, and the *Sunday at Home*, and similar literature which good people scatter gratuit-ously amongst the working classes; to the *Pilgrim's Progress* and Shakespeare "Recitations," and those social appeals of John Ruskin which have become the sacred writings of the new Labour revival. He hates charity organisation, the adventurous slum chronicler, officialdom, and institutions, just as the poor hate them to-day. He loves a joke, born of extravagance and a kind of boisterous humour, the salt which keeps this starved life from putre-faction. He understands his own people, amongst whom he has lived all his days. He is a living example—one of the few living examples—which offer hope that Democracy may still become a real thing.

I have seen "Will Crooks" addressing an open-air meeting outside the Arsenal Gates at Woolwich, in a wonderful bye-election which startled many political pundits with a vision of new things. It was the working man of London for a moment self-conscious: hearing itself for the first time speak. Picture an enormous sea of drab persons, a multitude of cloth caps and shapeless clothing, and little white faces. On a kind of rock, standing out of the sea—a humble carrier's cart—a short man with a black beard and long arm is addressing this great crowd. To many observers the vision is a vision of foreboding; the proletariat rising at last in the mere might of its incalculable numbers, to demand its share of life's good things, and brutally trample down all opposition. What is he saying to them? He is playing on this vast gathering as on an instrument of music, and he is making it discourse most excellent harmonies. At one moment he is stringing together the stories it delights in, and you can see the ripple of laughter running amongst the listeners like the wind through the cornfields. He is recounting the difficulties of the Imperialist Missionary down in Poplar: to the first woman: "Don't you know you belong to an Empire on which the sun never sets?" And the reply: "Wot's the good of talkin' like that? Why, the sun never rises on our court." To the second: "You've got to learn to make sacrifices for the Empire."— "Wot's the good of talkin' about sacrifices when we can't make both ends meet as it is? Both ends meet! We think we're lucky if we get one end meat and the other end bread." To a third: "If you don't agree, you're Little Englanders."—"If I'm to pay another twopence a pound for meat, my children will soon be Little Englanders!"

Then in a moment he will change the note, and now he is telling them of a day in the life of the unemployed: the monotonous search for work, the kindness or insult at each application, the alternation of revolt and wretchedness, fury and apathy, the unwillingness to face the wife again in the evening with nothing with bad news. They all know it, they have mostly been through it; it is a shadow which hangs over them all. And a strange, impressive hush falls over the vast assembly, and men cough or rub their eyes, or turn away from each other's faces.

" Give 'em a chance," he will suddenly cry, with uplifted arm, and the tension thus released finds relief in thunderous volleys of applause.

Such is " Will Crooks " in his own home, addressing his own people, a natural orator commanding to the full the humour and pathos of work-a-day life, whose influence is directed towards wholesome things, with never an unworthy appeal. And such, in its essential soundness, in its perplexity before complicated issues, in its acceptance of all established things, even in its distrust of itself, its almost exaggerated willingness to receive guidance from others, is the million-peopled constituency who through this man has found voice —the Multitude which forms the people of England.

The spread of " Socialism " amongst these, the voters who can decide elections, has been causing anxiety to many observers, especially to those who find a difficulty in discovering what function they would be called upon to fulfil in the Socialistic State. " Socialism," however, up to the present, has been mainly a movement amongst the intellectuals and the Middle Classes: almost the male members of a type whose female representatives find the cause necessary to their energies and devotions in the agitation for women's vote. The " Socialists " who assail each other so fiercely in queer, violent little newspapers, the writers of tracts, pamphlets, and appeals, the young men and women at the Universities who a generation ago would all have called themselves " Radicals," and now all call themselves " Socialists," are principally drawn from that " intellectual prole- tariat " which to-day is finding a growing gulf between

possibility and desire. The stiff pictures of recon-
structed worlds—a Bellamy's "Utopia," a Morris's
"Nowhere"—offer little attraction to the ordinary
working man; whose idea of a Utopia is something
far removed from these scenes of severe toil and
voluntary or compulsory virtue. Mr. Wells has
described, in brilliant, bitter sentences, the kind of
Socialism thus propagated, and the classes to which
it appeals. Academic, uncompromising Marxian
Socialism appears as "the dusky largeness of a great
meeting at the Queen's Hall," with the back of Mr.
Hyndman's head moving quickly, and the place "thick
but by no means overcrowded with dingy, earnest
people," and in the chair "Lady Warwick, that
remarkable intruder into the class conflict, a blonde
lady, rather expensively dressed, so far as I could
judge, about which the atmosphere of class consciousness seemed to thicken." The impression was of
"the gathering of village trades-people about the
lady patroness. And at the end of the proceedings,
after the red flag had been waved, after the 'Red
Flag' had been sung by the choir and damply echoed
by the audience, some one moved a vote of thanks to
the Countess, in terms of familiar respect that completed the illusion." And the Fabian Society, the
laboratory in which intellectual Socialism is matured,
with whose policy Mr. Wells is, on the whole, in
agreement, appears to him incarnate in a "small,
active, unpretending figure with the finely-shaped
head, the little imperial under the lip, the glasses,
the slightly lisping, insinuating voice"; with a following of "Webbites to caricature Webb" with excessive

bureaucratic notions, and a belief that everything can be done without any one wishing to do it; the disciple "who dreams of the most foxy and wonderful digging by means of box-lids, table-spoons, dish-covers—anything but spades designed and made for the jobs in hand—just as he dreams of an extensive expropriation of landlords by a Legislature that includes the present unreformed House of Lords."[1]

In face of such realities as these—the few with their enthusiasm for a new gospel or with ingenious devices for effecting the millennium by back-door entrances, the many with their occasional gusts of interest, their normal lassitude and contempt for those who disprove God or attack Society—the observer is often discouraged in the work of reform. "Socialists," says one of their most brilliant younger writers, "cannot look with full confidence upon the English electorate. It is hardly disputable that millions of electors in the greater cities have reached a point of personal decadence—physical, mental, and moral—to which no continental country furnishes a parallel on any comparable scale. Time is steadily multiplying these millions; and for English Socialism there is therefore a race against Time which it is very likely not to win."[2]   Mr. Ensor's testimony is in part endorsed by the very remarkable evidence of various popular elections; that "Socialism" amongst the working peoples propagates and triumphs in times of plenty, withers up and vanishes in times of depression. This is exactly the reverse of the accepted belief,

[1] *New Worlds for Old.   H. G. Wells.*
[2] *Socialism.   R. C. Ensor.*

which thought that the poor are stung into Socialism by suffering, as poets are stung into poetry by wrong.

Yet, paradoxical as it may appear, the assertion is probably true that "bad times"—especially in connection with unemployment—are enemies rather than friends of the Socialist cause. It is quite a mistake to suppose that Socialism gains its firmest grip first upon the poorest ; that its chief allies are hunger and cold. In England the poorest are often impervious to a direct political or social appeal ; they are sunk below the level of consciousness which can respond to any hope of change. The skilled artisans of Colne Valley and Jarrow vote Socialist when trade is good and all the factories are working overtime. The slums of Southwark or Ancoats fail to respond to the vision of a new good time coming, although their present state is beyond measure deplorable. What they are looking for is a relief of the immediate necessities of the moment, for food and drink for the day. Given these, they are content until the next scarcity arrives. More especially is this true of unemployment. When the artisan or labourer is in work, he will find leisure to interest himself in various social gospels, study the exhortation of the street corners, inquire the meaning of capital value and class war and the exploitation of the working man. When he is out of work, he is naturally filled with but one impulse, which passes quickly from a terror into an obsession—an impulse to obtain work again. That impulse operates even amongst the men who remain in the factory. They see their companions turned away, tramping the streets in search of a job,

undergoing all the privations which they themselves
have experienced in similar vicissitudes in the past.
They know that they have no security but one week's
notice: that any Saturday the announcement will be
made to them that their services will no longer be
required.   Under such circumstances the whole social
problem narrows itself down to the one problem
of maintenance; or rather, the problem of maintenance enlarges itself to fill the whole horizon.   Yesterday or to-morrow men may cherish the dream of
a transformed society.   To-day the question is merely
the continuance of such work as will provide for
immediate food and shelter.   That is why Socialism
has grown in times of prosperity, and withered in
times of decline.   It is the " Tariff Reformer," and
not the Socialist, who seems likely to gain in days of
trade depression.   In those days " work for all " is a
more persuasive appeal than " Justice to the worker,"
or " State ownership of all the means of production."
Man, fallen to bedrock and fighting for his life, has
little inclination to turn to visions of universal justice
in a redeemed Society.

To expect men and women to become " Socialists "
in times of trade depression, is to expect the survivors
of Messina, stricken by earthquake and famine, to
meditate with enthusiasm upon the future of the race.
Socialism, founded on Poverty and Social Discontent,
and finding there its argument for change, does not
flourish in the heart of that poverty and hungry
wretchedness.   The Socialist uses the sweated women
and starving children as material for inflaming to pity
and anger.   But he rarely obtains adherents from the

husbands of the women or the fathers of the children thus broken at the basis of society. The unemployed leaders are a different class and type from the unemployed whom they shepherd and control. And the average citizen has not yet come entirely to trust the new gospel; is not yet convinced that its adherents will make a better job of it than the "boodlers" and "blood suckers" whom they denounce so fervently. No Socialist councillor has ever been convicted of municipal corruption : and Socialists are sometimes surprised that a party so pure in aim and disinterested in service should be so often rejected by the electorate. But purity of purpose and incorruptibility of standard are not yet regarded by the average citizen as being the most essential qualifications for local or national government. The "man in the street," here and in America, would seem to be content—except in sudden hurricanes of revolt against too flagrant corruption—with a not too ostentatious standard of civic purity, if the men who are running the machine are men of substance, energy, and position. Miss Addams, from Hull House, has described the failure of the reform party to carry an election even against the most offensive "boodlers." The people acknowledged the corruption, but were convinced that all the aldermen do it, and that the alderman of their particular ward was unique in being so generous to his clients. "To their simple minds he gets it from the rich, and so long as he gives some of it out to the poor, and, as a true Robin Hood, with open hand, they have no objection to offer." The people are found to be

ashamed to be represented by a bricklayer — the
intelligent, clean-handed nominee of the reforming
party. The "boodler" is elected "because he is a
good friend and neighbour. He exemplifies and
exaggerates the popular type of a good man. He
has attained what his constituents secretly long for."
They become generally convinced that "the lec-
turers who were talking against corruption were only
the cranks, not the solid business men who had
discovered and built up Chicago." The same difficulty faces all those reformers to-day, who, in a
settled, orderly, and on the whole comfortable, society,
exhibit a too violent agitation for reform. The
"comrades" propagate the cause with a splendid
devotion, arguing at street corners, descending like
locusts at bye-elections, organising themselves cheerily
into missionary bands with particular buttons and
badges and neckties. Men listen to their eloquence ;
but the citizen with a stake in the community shrinks
from entrusting to them control of the ratepayers'
money, and the rank and file of the working people
turn away from a type so different to their own
boisterous, happy-go-lucky, acquiescent existence.
An appeal for "Labour representation" can fill the
working man with enthusiasm—the enthusiasm of
Mr. Crooks's first sensational victory at Woolwich.
An appeal for "Socialism" attracts him when his
own position is secure : when that is precarious he
is fearful, unless his trouble is prolonged until it
threatens a revolution. And an England with permanently declining trade, with the cream of its
artisan population permanently out of employment, is

an England which this generation has never known:
something which, if it occurs in the future, will tear
to pieces all our accepted standards, and render all
prophecy vain.

Yet there is danger perhaps in exaggerating this
complacency, acquiescence, and absorption in such
passing pleasures as are possible upon a limited
weekly wage, which at present keep so many of
the working people in this country aloof from political and social discontent.   Those who in similar
situation have counted upon a boundless patience
have often found that patience rudely exhausted,
and all their calculations brought to nought.   No one
can pretend that a condition of stable equilibrium
exists, in which as to-day, with the removal of supernatural sanctions and promises of future redress, the
working people find a political freedom accompanying an economic servitude.   We have carried out to
the full on the one side, says M. Viviani, in France
—and the same is true, though in less universal
degree, in England—the promise of the Revolution.
We have advanced from the affirmation of Equality of
Citizenship to universal suffrage, and from universal
suffrage to universal education.   There has vanished
the hope that once kept the labourer docile—hope of
the attainment of better times beyond the grave.
" *Ensemble, et d'un geste magnifique, nous avons eteint
dans le ciel des lumières qu'on ne rallumera plus.*"
Are we able to believe, he inquires, that the work
has ended ?   No, is the reply, it is only beginning.
Political liberation has to find expression for itself
in the economic sphere : must inevitably work itself

CHAPTER V

PRISONERS

THE surface view of society is always satisfactory. You may walk to-day through the streets of a Russian city, and watch the people at their business and their pleasure, with no revelation of the unseen hunger for change which is tearing at the heart of it. You may traverse England from north to south and east to west, admiring the beauty of its garden landscape, the refined kindly life of its country houses, the opulence and contentment of its middle class, the evidence everywhere of security and repose. Only at intervals, and through challenges which (after all) are easily forgotten, is there thrust before the attention of the observer some manifestation of the life of the underworld. The sea shines and sparkles in the sunshine beneath an unclouded sky. Why excite disquietude concerning the twisted, distorted life which lives and grows and dies in the darkness of the unplumbed deep?

To investigate the life there, it is no longer necessary to follow the romantic novelist or even the private statistician. All these may be under the charge of sensationalism, of writing to a purpose. They excite impatience amongst outside critics, who are convinced that the poor could all be prosperous if they would only work industriously, exercise thought, and avoid alcoholic refreshment. It would be well, therefore, to keep to the safe sobriety of official publications, to all those series of Commissions, Committees, Reports, and Inquiries which, outwardly forbidding, are found on examination to be filled with a rich human interest. Any one familiar with the reports of the Government Inspectors appointed to control the forces of greed and of degeneration in the obscurer regions of modern life, need never be accused of hysteria if he finds the thing henceforth a perpetual companion.

In the annual Reports of the Factory Inspectors, for example, he can see the result of occasional complaints, of sporadic surprise visits; with imagination he can extend these revelations over widening areas of submerged life. These summaries appear as the letting down of dredges into the depth and the bringing to light of the things which exist far below the surface. They are records of the daily and hourly warfare of the embodied conscience of the community against human fear and human greed. That conscience, working through a great machinery of protected law, is endeavouring to guard the men and women and children of the nation against the more outrageous forms of destruction: against the readiness with which the Fear of Destitution is pressing them into all forms of distorted, intolerable, poisonous pursuits. The laws are passed, the inspectors appointed, then the nation turns to other interests in confidence that all is well. Such confidence is based upon an altogether inadequate estimate of the two strongest impulses in the life of man. Avarice can usually overcome terror. Fear acting against greed is occasionally triumphant. But when the two are operating in unison, the result is as the letting out of water. In every trade there are those who will supplant their neighbours by the cheapening of the cost, the lengthening of hours, the avoidance of appliances. In every city there is the unlimited supply of disorganised women's and children's labour, which sees before it no alternative but of a quick or of a prolonged decay. The will-to-live still resists all efforts to render human desire impossible. The apathy of the East, accumulated through centuries of oppression, has not yet infected the industrial life of the West. So the unequal strife continues, between the attempt to raise these broken people into some semblance of rational and humane existence, and the pressure which drives them to choke themselves with dust, and poison themselves with noxious vapour, and ravage into collapse and ruin the bodies and souls of women and children.

They never complain until things have become intolerable. The anonymous complaints show the same percentage of justification as the signed. They work in unventilated workrooms. They are stinted of holidays. They are compelled to work overtime. They endure accident and disease. They are fined and cheated in innumerable ways. Their life is often confined to a mere routine of work and sleep. Yet they endure; and even at the heart of foul and impossible conditions retain always some rags of decency and honour. Some break loose from the accepted drudgery for a brief period of pleasure and idleness; to be found afterwards in the silent, stern discipline of the Rescue Home; where, says a Report, "the extreme youth of many of the inmates is a very distressing feature of many of the homes, and it is grievous that the sins of others should be so heavily visited upon these poor children, to whom the simple natural joys of home life are now denied."   Here austere virtue encourages "in some of the Scotch institutions," where the hours of work are from eight to seven, "a poor dietary," although "many of the inmates were young undeveloped girls."   But most are still resisting; as in the non-penitential laundries where "as a rule complaints are amply justified," although "the workers still find it very difficult to summon up courage enough to speak the truth as to irregularities, from fear of the loss of employment, and consequent shortage of the necessities of life"; or in the "millinery workshop, with a large shop attached, in North London," which ingeniously evades the factory law by combining operations of millinery apprentice with that of shop assistant, and "on my visiting one of the mothers of the girls she told me her young daughter still arrived home worn-out and crying with exhaustion"; or in the outworker's home in the City of London, where a "young girl" is "making and elaborately trimming babies' white silk bonnets beneath a ceiling black as ink, and walls with black and different coloured patches, looking as if some madman had found a pastime in scratching them," and the girl spares "½d. for potash, and to the best of her ability washed and scraped the vermin from the walls." Noting how clean and tidy she is in her own person, says the inspector, "I am not surprised to see the shudder with which she speaks of the struggle with dirt and filth."

They die like flies directly they are born. The tender-hearted may perhaps rejoice in this extravagant mortality. To some the waste of it will appear most apparent. In the Pottery Towns, for example, the infantile mortality is well up to 200 in the 1000: due, says the report, "to the employment of married women in the earthenware and china works." A regular slaughter of innocents every year in Longton, says the Medical Officer of Health, "is due to this and premature births." But the waste of death is the least element in this extravagance. "The damage done," says another Medical Officer, "cannot entirely be measured by mortality figures, for these take no account of the impaired vitality of the infants who manage to survive to swell the ranks of the degenerate." Stunted, inefficient, overworked, underfed, they struggle towards maturity. Quaint and grotesque occupations are found for them ; as for the "forty little girls, twenty-one of whom were half-timers," who are found licking adhesive labels by the mouth at the rate of thirty gross a day, "whose tongues had the polished tip characteristic of label lickers, and the rest of the tongue coated with brown gum." Or there are the girls who carry heavy wedges of clay and boxes of scrap (forbidden to such labour by the French Factory Laws of fourteen

11

years ago); as in the "complaint awaiting investigation" from a mother of her daughter who has out-
grown her strength, and is now ill with what she
believes is consumption; "who when working complained much of pain in the shoulder on which she
carried the clay and scrap, and of pain in the collar
bone on the same side." Or the children in the
Nottingham lace trade, whose eyesight is impaired
or destroyed by the double work of school and employment; and the half-time school at Dundee, where
"narrow-chested children sit on backless benches";
or the half-timers at Belfast, "undersized, round-
shouldered, delicate in appearance," where the head
teacher testifies, "these children seem always tired;
during the recreation period they prefer sitting down
in the playground to running about, and in this
matter they are especially noticeable in comparison
with the children who do not work." They struggle
towards maturity, unorganised, unprotected; fined in
one dressmaking workshop in West London in fines
which were supposed to be sent to the Fresh Air
Fund—a statement which, says the inspector, "had
no foundation in fact"; or "verbally promised
2s. 6d." for making a sample silk blouse, for which
"when Saturday came, the occupier, instead of giving
the agreed price, refused to pay more 1s. 3d." Most
of them will die under thirty, is the testimony of the
teacher concerning her half-time pupils; but if they
live it out, in old age they will be once more dragged
in by fear and bewilderment to compete against the
coming generations, and make the life of those
coming generations more difficult to endure.

"God help the poor!" concludes one half-unintelligible complaint of swindling deductions, where, on investigation, "the workers were at first terrified to give me information," says the inspector, "and I was met with entirely false statements." "God help the poor!" is written over all this haunting and dolorous record. It is the record of prisoners: *sedentes in tenebris et umbra mortis.*[1]

Gentility, again, is desirable. So is the supervision of the morals of young men and women. Both are enjoyed—in abundance it would seem—by the shop assistants, half a million of whom "live-in," or are affected by the living-in system. Some twenty thousand of them, organised in a Trades Union, are endeavouring to climb into citizenship: with less moral supervision it may be, but with the individual development that comes from self-ordered life and some suggestion of freedom. The necessity for the receipt of wages of something like a pound a week, if these people are to choose their own lodgings and dwell at ease, is a necessity which offers a considerable barrier to reform. And with the prospect of financial disability laid upon them if the present system is abolished, there is small wonder that a number of employers are enthusiastic over its advantages. The "discontented" Unionists—discontented in the opinion of many of their employers, like the dog who went mad in Goldsmith's elegy in order "to gain some private ends"—keep up the agitation bravely. On occasional bank holidays, when their less vigorous brethren are enjoying their four days

[1] *Report of H.M. Factory Inspectors, 1907.*

a year of statutory idleness in the open air, they suddenly appear like fish attaining sunshine from deep waters: hold their "conferences," pass their resolutions, then vanish again into the neat, obsequious serviceable men and women who attend to the whims of customers and encourage their tentative efforts towards purchase. Meetings of shop assistants are held in the big cities after darkness has fallen. A crowded company of unknown persons assembles to pass resolutions against "living-in" or in favour of short hours, then vanishes again, into the barracks or pleasant commercial "hotels" in which they reside. Evidence is obtained with difficulty even when a Government consents to interfere, and appoints a Commission to investigate. "Miss X——" does not wish to give her name. "If my name is published I get the swap," she says, "and I have to go at a minute's notice; and my employer would not mind spoiling my reference. He does not know that I have come here to-day." "I was summoned to come yesterday," says Mr. Y—— wearily, "and I asked for a day off; but I suppose I shall be dismissed when I go back for taking two days, so that I do not suppose it will matter a great deal whether my name appears or not." There are plenty of specific cases of ill-treatment and niggardly treatment against which no inspection can guard: of poor food and monotonous food, overcrowding in bedroom, squalor of accommodation, lack of suitable sanitary and washing arrangements, and the like. But the emphasis of those who resist is not upon specific complaints. It is directed against a general system which herds men and women together, all of one class and one occupation, in unnatural contiguity, and leave them there, under regulations rather humiliating to adult persons, to make the best of life seen through distorted glasses, and from the inside of a regulated home. There are testimonies, indeed, of the excellence of the best, in perpetual care for the welfare of the employees. It is perhaps a misfortune that the comfort and kindliness of these best should throw an ægis of justification over a system which is the worst, and even in the average, stands on so many counts condemned.

"Living-in," declares the Report, in certain retail trades, is generally made a condition of employment, either express or implied. The board and lodging accommodation is often inferior and inadequate. Sleeping and other accommodation is frequently bad. On the moral side the system has often not only no advantage, but is actually harmful. The daily rush from counter to dining-room and back, the unappetising food, the wearying sameness of the menu, the insufficiency of the food, often supplemented by "extras" sold by the firm, like the "tuck shop" system of the English public school, are all described by actual sufferers, in experience which seems to have stepped clean out of the pages of *Kipps* or *Vivian*. Five beds "invested with bugs in one room," an attic in which three men sleep "that in the heat of summer smelt like a fowl-house," beds with four clean sheets in six months, rooms with rats plentiful, bedrooms which open into corridors, the light being obtainable through a pane of glass in the wooden partitions—these and other similar experiences testify to the price which often has to be paid for the "moral supervision" which the young shopman or shop girl enjoys. The Report declares that in a number of cases at least this claim of moral supervision is cant—the old cant of cheapness; the cant in its revived form of the "moral supervision" of the workhouse children which were bought up in batches for the factories eighty years ago. An employer "would place no obstacle in the way of his male assistants marrying," is the confession of one, "though," he adds, "he certainly does not like his assistants to marry on an inadequate wage." "Male and female created He them," says Mr. Lewisham's friend in a well-known novel, "which was d—d rough luck on assistant masters." It would seem to be rough luck also on shop assistants who have the bad taste to prefer matrimony to moral guidance.

Such well-known employers like Mr. Debenham and Mr. Derry in London, who have changed from the living-in to the natural system, brush all this cant and vapour away with a healthy breath of fresh air. "The character of some employers," says the latter, "I would not trust from their own housekeepers. I do not think that drapers are worse than any other commercial men, but all commercial men are the same." He sees "no difficulty in finding proper apartments outside," with people "in whom we should have every confidence to put our own children." "I am quite out of touch with excuses which have been made by employers at conferences

I have been at, with regard to the moral side of the question. I think it is sheer nonsense."

The system is sometimes enforced by a system of "fines": the substitute, in a humanitarian age, for more drastic disciplinary measures of the older servitudes. Fines for smoking or reading in bed-rooms, fines for sleeping out without permission or for arriving after locking-up time, fines for taking supper away, for burning candles after the gas is turned out, for heating water on the gas, exhibit the method by which adjustment has to be effected and the smoothness of the communal existence main-tained. "The system," says Miss Bonfield, "robs the assistant, whether men or women, of the sense of personal responsibility which is developed by ordering and controlling one's own life. The herding together of large numbers of either sex, restricted as to the most ordinary intercourse with the opposite sex, creates an unnatural and vicious atmosphere which is morally dangerous to both men and women." She repudiates the idea that there is "any kind of home life, any kind of home consideration"—at least in her personal experience. The dinner-hour she found "the most disagreeable interval of the day." "In a long business experience I have never yet had a properly made cup of tea." "The sitting-room of a business house is usually a most dreary place, very much like the waiting-room of a railway station." In many shops the hours worked are seventy per week: the atmosphere in one experience "particularly vitiated, and the assistants chronically overtired." The work is peculiarly stimulating to nervous strain: fretful customers, sometimes friendly, sometimes bullying, often merely tiresome—for hour after hour of the day. Even when the catering is excellent, is another experience, the girls "have no appetite for food." "What they need is fresh air and more outdoor exercise. The factory girl who eats her unscientific meal in the street, does so with a greater relish and with more profit to health than does her sister of the shop extract from the choice meals eaten in the atmosphere of the shop dining-room." "I have frequently gone to my dinner feeling faint for want of food, and on entering the dining-room have been nauseated to such an extent as to be unable to eat anything except dry bread." Compensations appear, however, in some cases to exist. In the report of one establishment—only men living-in—after "washing accommodation inadequate, food badly cooked, table service not clean, men's sitting-room, three chairs and broken table for the use of twenty men," it is encouraging to read that "every apprentice is required to attend a place of worship at least once on a Sunday." So is fostered the traditional religion of the people. There is a suggestion that the feverish competition in retail trade, and the general willingness to obtain a maximum of profit, has even here produced a change in spirit and temper. "I have been able to watch the change," says Miss Bonfield, "since first I went into the distributing trade. The old system of trying to build up an establishment on the value of your goods, and on giving real work for money, has been steadily changing, and the assistant now who is considered the smartest assistant is the one who can sell to customers worthless goods, goods that yield a very large profit, goods that look fairly showy on the surface but are not really wearable, and are not satisfactory in other ways." From both sides—men and women—comes personal testimony to an "immorality of the mind" which is "worse than immorality of the body"—an "over-sexed" condition due to the herding together of young men or young women of a certain age in an atmosphere of nerve stimulation and little physical exercise and limited external interests. One male assistant protests against "the daily rush from counter to dining-room and back to counter without even a breath of fresh air. Often the food provided is unappetising, cooked and served very roughly, served in dining-rooms situated in the basement, artificially lighted and without proper ventilation." "The sameness of the menu becomes positively wearying." "In a large number of cases the food provided is insufficient for the physical need of the employee." Mr. Tilley, once a shop assistant in the town, now a draper on his own account in a small way in the country, roundly asserts that "the good conditions are the exception, bad conditions the rule." "Celibacy is a condition of employment. Here we are faced by the greatest of the many evils which arise from this," as he calls it, "pernicious system." "It is absolutely essential," is his summary, "for the physical and moral welfare of the assistants that 'living-in' should be abolished." The old order of things has changed. The personal element between employer and employee is steadily vanishing. And the assistant of to-day finds himself bound and fettered with this legacy of feudal days which his employer is often using for all it is worth to exploit the labour of the employees in this and kindred trades. The emancipation of the shop workers of this country can never come until they are rid of this "living-in" system, is the announcement which is robbing them of freedom of action, individuality of character, and the "political and social rights of an Englishman."[1]

"The political and social rights of an Englishman." We are fortunate in the possession of a man of genius who has also had personal experience of this particular life, and has left in literature a sharp-cut picture of the "political and social rights" interpreted into terms of daily experience. "'By Jove,' said Buggins, 'it won't do to give these here Blacks votes.' 'No fear,' said Kipps. 'They're different altogether,' said Buggins. 'They 'aven't the sound sense of Englishmen, and they 'aven't the character. There's a sort of tricky dishonesty about 'em. . . . They're too timid to be honest. Too slavish. They aren't used to being free, like we are; and if you gave 'em freedom, they wouldn't make a proper use of it. Now *we*—Oh, *damn*!' For the gas had suddenly gone out, and Buggins had the whole column of Society Club Chat still to read."

"What becomes of the good shop assistant when he grows old?" is a question almost as difficult to answer as the question, "What becomes of good Americans when they die?" The Government Com-

[1] *Report of the Committee on Truck, 1909.*

mittee could obtain no certain evidence. " I cannot
say what does become of them. Some start in
business on their own account; but now that the
conditions are so changed, that is very difficult.
They leave the drapery trade. Some get inferior
situations. You may find old drapers' assistants
driving cabs to-day." In South Wales, says one,
" amongst the miners, I myself have come across
an enormous number of old shop assistants." The
majority, like the majority of assistant masters in a
slightly more exalted station of life, seem to slide out
into all sorts of bypaths—in the one Empire building, tomato growing, or running preparatory schools
whose competition and fate seems generally similar
to that of the small retail drapery stores; in the
other, " insurance agents, booksellers, and things of
that kind." But the work is genteel; sharply distinguished from that of the artisan: it is supposed to
be especially suitable to boys and girls of delicate
physique : and there are many who, from the beginning, would wish no otherwise than to be shepherded, tended, taken in and provided for, without the
pains and risks of outside adventure. "We're in a
blessed drainpipe," says Mr. Minton to Kipps cheerfully, "and we've got to crawl along it till we die."
Only to a percentage, at first, and then in effort,
which every year diminishes, does the conviction come,
as to " Kipps " in the night watches, when "all others
in the dormitory are asleep and snoring," that "the
great stupid machine of retail trade had caught his life
into its wheels, a vast irresistible force which he had
neither strength of will nor knowledge to escape."

"Night after night he would resolve to enlist, to run away to sea, to set fire to the warehouse, or drown himself, and morning after morning he rose up and hurried downstairs in fear of a sixpenny fine."[1]

And the alternatives—especially for the women— are not all so promising that they can afford lightly to forego the advantage here offered of assured food and shelter. Far below is a vision of pitiful poverty, into which, at any time, any unfortunate worker may be precipitated; rarely, henceforth, ever to rise into the clear air of intelligible life. Somewhere festering at the basis, round the foundations of the great mansion of England's economic supremacy, are to be discovered the workers of the "Sweated Trades." At intervals of ten, fifteen, or twenty years the dredger is let down, to scrape up samples of the material of the ocean floor: in Royal Commissions, Committees of the House of Commons, or the House of Lords. It is always the same there, whatever tides and tempests trouble the surface far above: a settled mass of congested poverty shivering through life upon the margin below which life ceases to endure. The sensational novelist utters his study in fiction, the cause and the remedy; the public conscience is stirred by the exhibitions of "sweated" goods and "sweated" women: after a time distraction intervenes, a war, a colonial football or cricket tour, ecclesiastical dispute over posture of praying, or colour of garment. The sweated workers, for one moment indecently revealed in the sunshine, return again to the welcome

[1] *Kipps. By H. G. Wells.*

obscurity of their twilight world. A recent House of Commons Committee has once more raked over the bottom; examined, with blinking eyes, the strange things found there; reported in favour of Government action. The evidence is of the monotonous simplicity familiar to all similar investigations. "My attention," says Mr. Holmes, the police court missionary, "was drawn to the home workers first about ten years ago. I met two or three widows at the police court, charged with attempted suicide, and I naturally took interest in them. I visited their homes, and became aware of the conditions under which they lived; the prices paid for their work, the hours they generally worked, the amount of rent they paid, the kind of food they ate, and everything of that description. On one occasion I took three widows for a holiday. Each of them had attempted suicide, and was broken down in health of mind and body through hard work and poor food. The story of their lives, their manner, their appearance, and their broken spirit was a revelation." The broken spirit, indeed, so characteristic of those who, from the beginning, have enlisted in the service of fourteen hours' work a day, does not appear entirely to have brought the felicity which—in orthodox views —accompanies a docile and grateful working-class population. Nor does the complete absence of Trades Unions—those "cruel organisations"—appear to have effected that "economic liberty" which the supporters of "Free Labour" endeavour to obtain by the smashing of these instruments of tyranny. "My experience of ten years is this," says Mr. Holmes, "that I have found them to be the most industrious, sober, and honest class of the community that it has been my lot ever to meet with; in fact, their goodness appals me." Here, indeed, are the examples, at length realised in the flesh, of the workings of the "laws" of the older political economy: the "iron law of wages" driving, through the frantic competition for employment by the workers against each other, those wages down to the minimum of existence. "I know one widow," is the testimony, "who is working, and has done nothing else than work, at these little things at her own home in Bethnal Green for forty years, and her payment for that work now is practically the same as it was at the beginning of that period. Her fingers have got stiffer, and she cannot earn quite so much now." "It is the apathy of the people"—after forty years of it—one witness complains, "engaged in all these things, and their helplessness which forms the greatest obstacle to their advancement." These apathetic classes, indeed, appear largely as those for whom petitions are presented in the Christian Church for special and peculiar mercies—"women labouring with child; sick persons; young children." And the reply to the petition is this Home work, falling as the gentle dew from heaven upon the place beneath, and blessing him that gives and him that takes: obtained "by sending boy or girl to the city for the stuff with a more or less dilapidated, cast-off perambulator, which they push home full up with shirts or mantles or skirts, which are taken back to the warehouse when finished." The actual workers appear before the

Committee in kindly anonymity, having little violence of protest against Providence, the employers, or themselves. The tendency of payments, they are compelled to confess on examination, have steadily gone down; that is because "women are always applying for work, and they have no work to give them; and therefore they cut the prices down, because the women go and beg for work." The "expenses" of each of two workers sharing a room, "without the rent," are one shilling and three-pence a week. "Do you have a fire in this room?" is asked. "No," is the reply; "we light a lamp to warm ourselves." The difficulty of the Committee, in examination of wages budgets, was to find any margin at all for food and firing; a difficulty which the witnesses were unable to remove. Prices, confesses one, "have come down ever so much; they have come down in the last four years so that I cannot keep myself now." "It is almost a mystery," is the challenge to another, "how you manage to live at all." Yet others do well, earning (in one case) ten shillings a week—for work between "fifteen and sixteen hours a day"—sometimes up at six o'clock, and "I work till ten at night." These, however, are the limited hours of a "very quick" worker. "Can you suggest anything," is the forlorn inquiry to one of them, "that anybody could do for you which would induce your master, or perhaps compel your master, to give you a fairer or a larger wage?" "If he would only time an article," is the doubtful reply; "state how long the article would take to make, and give you a certain wage of so much an hour, it would be fair, if it was only a living wage; we only want to live."

This "want to live" is the endurance, not of the "unemployables," but of those who are engaged night and day in an insect-like activity: uncomplaining, with an Eastern endurance, in the dark. Investigation amongst the "sample" witnesses who appeared before the Committee exhibited no contradiction of their veracity. "I wanted to say about the girl C——," says the investigator, "whose father is out of work, that her home was visited, and that practically everything in it has been pawned: they are owing money, of course, and are expecting the bailiffs in, so that she is at a crisis in her affairs. The girl C—— has hardly any clothes, and when we found her she was almost starving. She is really in a very bad position. She has her old father, who hawks her goods sometimes in the evening, and that is how she makes some extra money." Of another G——. "I cannot find out myself," is the testimony, "how she can subsist at all." "How she manages to support herself and her child is an 'absolute mystery.'" "She looks rather starved herself at present." Even where some kind of organisation exists, it is found almost impossible to arouse these industrious persons to any visions or hopes of permanent betterment. "In going about among them," says one witness, concerning the Nottingham lace makers, "I have found that the first difficulty you had to overcome was the abject apathy that existed among them. You see they are most of them, very many of them, working for the next meal, and nothing you say about the meal for to-morrow affects them: they are not concerned about that. After you have aroused some interest in them, you have also to arouse some sort of courage."[1]

So, while the white hotels rise on all the shores of England, and the apparatus of pleasure is developing into ever new and ingenious forms of entertainment, continues through the nights and days the grey struggle of the Abyss. It is the indomitable will to live, resisting always that press of circumstance which would squeeze out the life of the disinherited, and leave a solitude where once was industry and action. The question how long such will survive, in the depths, the absence of all that life should mean, is as unanswerable as the question how long the will to live will survive the satiety at the summit which comes from superfluity of pleasure. For a society fissured into an unnatural plentitude on the one hand finds as its inevitable consummation a society fissured into an unnatural privation on the other. Here is the "price of prosperity" as interpreted at the dim foundations of the social order; a menace to the future, less in the fury of its revolt than through the infection of its despair.

II

So appears — at the base — the regular hive of industry: the life of those who, uncomplaining, maintain the work of the world. This fixity of tenure in a house which may be termed a home is

[1] *Report of Parliamentary Committee on Home Work, 1908.* To-day in Parliament a "Trades' Boards Bill" seems at last to offer a way towards remedy.

the ideal of the Social Reformer. To such a goal of human endeavour he would always direct the errant impulses of those who fail to appreciate its full satisfactions: who shirk with indifference, who revolt in open rebellion against the accepted standards of civilisation. These latter form no negligible company. They include women who, uncheered by the remuneration of the factory girl or the domestic servant, have embraced unrecognised careers and professions offering more immediate monetary returns, if less guaranteed security of livelihood. They include a prison population of habitual thieves and outcasts who have definitely declared war against their neighbours, and whose life consists of adventure varied by long periods of compulsory silence. They include the "unemployable," the vagrants, the people born tired and the people who have grown tired; the army of broken persons, weak in body or in mind, which choke up the workhouses and asylums: an aggregation of human failure which represents a "bye-product" of the industrial organisation whose worth in the market has not yet been adequately demonstrated.

The Tramp Life, the underside of the world, generally appears in writing in exaggerated sunshine or gloom. Some who have lived through it—notably Mr. Bart Kennedy and Mr. W. H. Davies—have written sincere and truthful reminiscences of adventure in England and America. They set themselves, in union with a great company, to "cheat Admetus": to live on the industrial populations, just as the idle rich live on the industrial populations, without giving back adequate return. They perform this feat, partly by begging, partly by stealing, partly by grudging spells of special and not unenjoyable labour highly paid at certain seasons of the year—such as fruit-picking, cotton-gathering, clam-fishing, and the like. When they grow tired of the open road, they take to the railway, accepting free passage hidden in the goods van or riding upon the front of the engine. They have their experiences, also, of society's reprisals, in occasional spells of imprisonment, not altogether disagreeable in the more humane cities of America. The general impression conveyed is of a life of adventure and considerable physical satisfactions, of health in the open air, of a variegated and coloured experience along the great ways of the world which is denied to the assiduous and driven labourer of machine and factory. That is one side of the picture. The other is given by Government reports and personal investigations by such observers as Miss Higgs and Mr. Ensor, of the casual ward, the common lodging-house, and all the race who have eluded or been squeezed out of the meshes of regular toil. And here there is impression of degradation and permanent discomfort, dirt, squalor, and misery, a shambling, discouraged rabble of creatures that once were men and women. Those who have scrutinised the wreckage of humanity which collects in the so-called "able-bodied" workhouses, or can be seen drawn up on cold nights in ragged regiments on the Embankment waiting for the midnight dole of soup, will be more inclined to believe in the degradation than in the adventure. Yet the few persons who have gone forth without prejudice to know these despised and broken persons—tramps, criminals, prostitutes, unemployed, unemployable—who wander through the darkened ways of the City, have no such experience of universal collapse to record. Those who come as learners rather than teachers—with a sense of humour, of friendliness, an ultimate reverence for anything human, above all, with acceptance rather than with criticism—are perpetually astonished at the resistance which humanity is able to present to the most calamitous of outward circumstance.

The revelation of the authentic witnesses—those in whom this queer universe has become articulate—is of a complete overturning of the accepted standards. In *Slavery*, Mr. Kennedy has traced the whole process of escape: from upbringing in a cellar dwelling at Manchester, through revolt against the tyranny of monotonous toil, to an enlisting in a kind of buccaneering expedition against all the world. It is the normal civilised universe seen (as it were) from the reverse side in which the grey has become blue and the blue grey. The inhabitants are at war upon the working world; using its charity and its clumsy legislation in order to suck from that world no small advantage. They have eluded, like the inheriting wealthy, the obligations of labour; like the inheriting wealthy they possess their own exacting moral codes, differing from the moral codes of working humanity, which supports them, if not with equanimity, at least with fortitude. Mr. W. H. Davies, in his *Autobiography of a Super-tramp*, offers a similar and more amazing life history. "I was born thirty-five years ago, in a public-house called the Church House, in the town of N——," is the commencement of a story not altogether unworthy of Defoe's *Robinson Crusoe*. Without his sincere, if somewhat intrusive, moral determinations, this voyager is also living amongst the aborigines on the desert island of this "floating, transitory world." In the final chapter he sums up the philosophical advice which he would bequeath to similar sojourners. The most important dogma of it is "contained in the simple words: 'Never live in a house next door to your landlord or landlady'; which," he declares, "deserves to become a proverb." "Many people might not consider this warning necessary," he concludes, "but the hint may be useful to poor travellers like myself, who, sick of wandering, would settle down to the peace and quiet of after days."

It is the normal world, in England and America, turned inside out, seen from the other side of Looking Glass country. From this side are examined the benevolence of the rich and the benevolence of the poor, the Salvation Army shelter, the common gaol, the Charity Organisation Society, the various efforts of Society to protect itself against the locust and the caterpillar. The locust, it must be confessed, especially in new countries, generally has the best of it. The artless and somewhat clumsy organisations of State and city and private persons spread their simple traps of cheese or delicacies for the mouse. The mouse annexes the cheese and leaves the trap scatheless. Especially is this true in

America, where wealth, easily and carelessly heaped
together, is as easily and carelessly scattered.   Many
of Mr. Davies' confessions of American begging
experiences are almost incredible in their suggestion
of opulence.   An hour or two in streets of modest
comfort will yield, to the experienced workman, a
profusion of good things—money, clothes, rich and
pleasant food.   Free rides by "beating" the various
trains, transformation with changing climate of
summer and winter from the north to the south,
occasional interludes in local gaols, where the officials,
being paid by the number of their captives, offer
increasing attractions to those who will condescend
to accept such hospitalities, yield a healthful and
variable existence of adventure and repose.   The
companions of the road offer no despicable advantages.   There is, indeed, no "honour among
thieves"; they rob each other with effrontery, and
make no assertion of chivalry or fine and decent
living.   But they are generous in their sharing of
the booty with their companions, and possess a ready
sociability which leads them to partnerships and
associations of some enduring value.   The two un-
forgivable crimes are work and thrift.   Effort and
Accumulation—the gods of the working world—have
become idols to be trampled on.   Yet, in the underworld, the appeal to compassion is still irresistible.
The cattlemen who bring the living food of England
across the Atlantic to Liverpool "are recognised as
the scum of America, a wild, lawless class of people,
on whom," says Mr. Davies, "the scum of Europe
unscrupulously impose."   Mr. Davies had frequently

made the journey, and tells horrible tales of the indifferent cruelty to the beasts. Habitually the cattlemen arrive, fresh from such degrading experience, upon a city of poverty. Habitually they part with their scanty earnings in gifts to that poverty when they arrive. "Having kind hearts, they are soon rendered penniless by the importunities of beggars." "These wild but kind-hearted men," is the testimony, "grown exceedingly proud by a comparison of the comfortable homes of America with these scenes of extreme poverty in Liverpool and other large seaports, give and give of their few shillings, until they are themselves reduced to the utmost want."

In America, under the expert advice of "Brum," the young novice learnt the valuable secrets of the trade. On entering any town, look out for a church steeple with a cross, which denotes a Catholic church and therefore a Catholic community. "If I fail in that portion of the town I shall certainly not succeed elsewhere." Fat women are the best to beg from. "How can you expect these skinny creatures to sympathise with another," is the unanswerable argument, "when they half - starve their own bodies?" In begging in England, avoid every town that has not either a mill, a factory, or a brewery. But in America the gold mines are the watering-places and haunts of the idle rich: perhaps because they recognise natural allies in the other class of Anarchist, perhaps because they satisfy a slumbering responsibility and compassion in a careless scattering of uncalculated charity. Amongst the New York watering-places "the people catered for us as though we were the only tramps in the whole world, and as if they considered it providential that we should call at their houses for assistance." In such providential plenty the standards are well maintained: otherwise this inverted world might right itself and become normal once again. The travellers are received with disfavour by a stranger, who later is smitten with remorse. "Excuse me, boys, for not giving you a more hearty welcome," is the apology; "but really, I thought you were working men, but I see you are true beggars." In a cottage an aged labourer, who had amassed a modest fortune after a life of toil, hangs on the wall the shovel which he had used in early days. To these wanderers the vision is as distasteful as an image of a saint to a Covenanting assembly: a symbol of false gods.

Here is the voice of the Tramp as he appears to himself: full of complacency as he looks back upon his past successes: naked before his audience, and entirely unashamed. In the revelation of the sub-merged as they appear to others—to those friends of theirs who possess sympathy and humour and a wide acceptance — this subterranean existence appears also full of excellent things: comradeship, kindliness, laughter, and tears. Such vivid and truthful writing as that of Mr. Neil Lyons in *Arthurs* throws no unfriendly light upon the waste places of the city. He has taken for the scene of his inquiry a London coffee-stall "somewhere between Brixton and the obelisk in South London." "This is an ambiguous direction," he declares. "But then we night-seekers are jealous of our ill-fame, and the fear of the Oxford movement is strong upon us." Round this coffee-stall, attracted like moths to a candle, gather in the heart of the sleeping city those to whom sleep is denied. Night-workers seeking refreshment mingled here with women of the streets; an occasional drunken sailor, a thief making a rendez-vous with a thief, tramps and wastrels, foregather for a moment within the circle of light before drifting out into the darkness again. There are some who are regular customers, who develop a kind of comradeship, exchanging tales of misfortune; and from these the author weaves a tragic or pitiful or romantic story of human lives. For all the permanent elements of romance are in this underworld, only with the values distorted and modified. Here, also, are sudden vicissitudes of fortune, passionate human affections, love of woman and of child, fear of violence and of death. It is life lived close to the margin, in perpetual familiarity with the reality of common things; darkness and cold, hunger and despair. It is life lived, that is to say, as perhaps the majority of mankind are living it to-day; never so far removed from the possibility of privation and of danger as to be able to settle down tranquil in a universe of security. The common impression, amongst those who do not dwell in such a universe, is that existence under such conditions must reel back into savagery or apathy—into a kind of numbness before all the slings and arrows of outrageous fortune, or into the fierce fight for existence upon the sinking ship or in the crumbling earthquake city. But experience is quite otherwise. Comradeship, desire, human affection, kindliness, and pity, all here survive amongst men so shabby and twisted as to appear scarcely human, and women with painted faces not pleasant to look upon. Nay more, a certain attitude of cheeriness and enjoyment seems to be bred out of the very extremity of fortune. There is a rich humour in all Mr. Lyons's sketches, for much of which, indeed, the onlooker and recorder may be responsible, but some of which is native to the original character. Sometimes it assumes the form of verbal exaggeration and comments in which all working-class London is so ready, the most reputable product of the industrial metropolis. Sometimes it finds satisfaction in the jollity excited by drink, as in the experience of the drunken sailor who uplifts his voice in blood-thirsty ballads. Sometimes it has the peculiar reckless insolence of the defiance, out of extremity, of all time's revenges ; the reckless insolence of the " seven men out of hell " in the story of the " Bolivar " who have " euchred God's almighty storm " and " bluffed the eternal sea."

There is here, however, none of the idealisation, the roseate visions of sordid and ugly things suddenly seen through a mist of make-believe, which fills with an intolerable sentimentality the works of many popular writers of fiction. " Arthur's " clients, having plumbed the bedrock of life, are suffering no illusions concerning it. They are emphatically convinced that dust is dust and mud is mud, and that a spade may justly be called a spade. Outside the coffee-stall itself, in the small hours of the morning, there is continual necessity for the suppression of rowdies and marauders and those who exhibit anarchic tendencies in a civilisation remote from our own, but with very definite standards. In that civilisation kindliness and good fellowship stand at the summit of the hierarchy of virtues, and a large tolerance replaces the negative prohibitions of the accepted commandments. And in all that company of children, bewildered and confused in a world which they have never learned to understand, the acceptance of a certain level of honour and of order is more clearly recognised than amongst those who, reaching towards the enforcement of austerer limitations, are, perhaps, less successful in attainment. " Sometimes," says Mr. Lyons, " a sailorman in the throes of a fever may form our circle. Arthur will then arise in his might, peer over his spectacles, and lifting a withered forefinger say, ' George, I'm surprised at you. Be'ave yeself.' And George, if he be not very drunk, will subside instantly, saying, ' Righto, Guv'nor,' or he will ask respectfully for another cup of coffee and a thick 'un, at the same time challenging the company to deny that Arthur is a gentleman, or he himself a Briton."

So that amongst incidents seemingly trivial—a crying baby, a meeting of a tramp and his pal, the attempt of Arthur's soldier son to choose between two rival candidates for his affection—there is revealed a whole depth of human helpfulness, and of human sympathy which is not helpful but is exceedingly desirous to be so. In one of Mr. Lyons's exuberant evenings a man with a baby in his arms wearily drifts to the coffee-stall, waiting for the belated all-night tram. And at once this company of nightbirds and homeless populace become absorbed in one overwhelming problem—how to stop the baby crying. "Arthur" himself starts the enterprise. "I ain't no amatoor at this business," he cheerily remarks. "Soothin' down babies is one of my specialities." So he makes grimaces, shouts "Oy! oy! oy!" at the unfortunate infant, emits shrieks to imitate a locomotive in "a performance very unusual and distressing," bays like a bloodhound ("trying the dawg on him," he calls it), imitates various other animals —with disastrous effect. Arthur's "man" then steps into the breach, "I know a dodge about babies," he remarks. "First of all," explained the specialist, "you turn 'im over on 'is chest. Then you say, 'Hups a daisy! *There's* a little man!' and thumps him on his back. Then you give 'im a fork or sich like to play with. Then you say, 'Did 'e 'ave a dirty blackguard of a father then?' (no offence to *you*, sir, only it's the custom), and then you jerk 'im up an' down, and 'old your breath till 'e falls asleep." This also fails. The owner of the infant meanwhile imparts reminiscences of his life, his sister and the baby, full of intimate detail, to the friendly company. A "certain old drab," half-starved, is stuffed with coffee and sardines and promised "tuppence" to stop the child's "'ollering." She immediately succeeds. The tram arrives; the father and child vanish in the night. It is twenty minutes past one o'clock—in a submerged, undistinguished corner of six millions of sleeping people. But all

modern life is in it—the stupidity, the gravity, the
generosity, the ready companionship and sympathy
under misfortune which may be common to all, of
half-lost, undistinguished people who normally travel
through mean streets to no profitable end.

They quote poetry—sentimental maunderings, the
humorous ditties of the lower-class music-halls, or
bloodthirsty, recounting how "Joe Golightly"
"stabbed 'im in the spine." They crack their little
jokes, and score off each other and off themselves,
when in the lowest depth of poverty—with nothing
between them and ultimate destitution. When
prosperity comes they share with each other, standing
"treat" in "cawfee" and sardines and hard-boiled
eggs. There fall down to them occasionally visitants
from another world. Now it is a "gentleman" killing
himself as speedily as possible with drink and sordid
adventure, on the way between prosperity and death.
Now it is a "benevolent idiot" desiring to see the
"darker side of London life," whose comments are received with marked disfavour by the normal members
of the street. Now it is a revivalist or philanthropist
seeking passionately to persuade them to return to
the accepted ways of men. His efforts are useless.
They have chosen their portion, and in that portion
they will abide: drifting with all surrounding human
lives, through their narrow space of being, towards
whatever fate or fortune may offer them in that day
when all days will have become as one day, and
to-morrow joined with yesterday's seven thousand
years.

CHAPTER VI

THE COUNTRYSIDE

OUTSIDE this exuberant life of the cities, standing aloof from it, and with but little share in its prosperity, stands the countryside. Rural England, beyond the radius of certain favoured neighbourhoods, and apart from the specialised population which serves the necessities of the country house, is everywhere hastening to decay. No one stays there who can possibly find employment elsewhere. All the boys and girls with energy and enterprise forsake at the commencement of maturity the life of the fields for the life of the town. A peasantry, unique in Europe in its complete divorce from the land, lacking ownership of cottage or tiniest plot of ground, finds no longer any attraction in the cheerless toil of the agricultural labourer upon scant weekly wages. In scattered feudal districts a liberal distribution of alms and of charity masquerading as employment may serve to retain a subservient population in a "model village." When these hierarchies and generosities are absent the cottages crumble to pieces and are never repaired; no new cottages are constructed: the labourer loses not only intimacy with the land, but even all desire for the land; that longing for a particular position of his own which is the strongest animating force in the peasantry of every other country in the world. The villages are left to old men and to children, to the inert, unenterprising, and intellectually feeble. Whole ancient skilled occupations—hedging and ditching, the traditional treatment of beasts and growing things—are becoming lost arts in rural England. Behind the appearance of a feverish prosperity and adventure—motors along all the main roads, golf-courses, game-keepers, gardeners, armies of industrious servants, excursionists, hospitable entertainment of country house-parties—we can discern the passing of a race of men.

From every region of southern England comes the same testimony. "There is no social life at all," writes a Somerset clergyman. "A village which once fed, clothed, policed, and regulated itself cannot now dig its own wells or build its own barns. Still less can it act its own dramas, build its own church, or organise its own work and play. It is pathetically helpless in everything." He sees no forces in being adequate to arrest this prolonged secular decline. "As things go on now," is his forecast, "we shall have empty fields, except for a few shepherds and herdsmen, in all the green of England. Nomadic herds will sweep over the country, sowing, shearing, grass-cutting, reaping and binding with machines : a system which does not make for health, peace, discipline, nobleness of life." "England is bleeding at the arteries, and it is her reddest blood which is flowing away."[1]

In rural Essex another observer finds the land

[1] *C. L. Marson in The " Commonwealth."*

becoming "one vast wilderness," "a retreat for foxes and a shelter for conies": with the houses tumbling into decay, no new houses built, apathy settling down like a grey cloud over all. "The sturdy sons of the village have fled; they have left behind the old men, the lame, the mentally deficient, the vicious, the born tired." Farm buildings and cottages are rapidly going to pieces. He notes the steady increase in the agricultural returns of "Land laid down to grass." "It would be better described," he declares, "as land which has laid itself down to twitch and thistle." He heaps scorn upon "those glowing patriots who, in their anxiety to build up an Empire, have been grabbing at continents and lost their own land."[1]

And in Wiltshire, again, another observer can show the two great wants of the labourer still unsatisfied—Hope and a Home. He laments the passing of the old village gentry, who still had some sympathy and channels of communication with the labourer; and the substitution for them of the large farmer, who utterly hates and despises the class beneath him. "'As long as a man stays on the land, he can't call his soul his own,' is an expression often heard among the poor." He exhibits the striking contrast between the brother and sister: the sister who has "gone into service," and found a demand for her work, and acquired under such conditions hope, independence, and a vigour of mind; the brother left on the fields, with the prospect before him of unchanging manual labour, at unchanging, scanty wages, until the workhouse absorbs him at the end. He shows th tra-

[1] *The Ruin of Rural England.*

gedy of the mere material collapse in the material conditions; village after village, in which no new cottages have been built for a hundred years; crumbling walls, falling into decay; crowded families, with all the starved life and degradation inevitably associated with such overcrowding; the whole presenting an aspect of fatigue and of decline. " To outsiders, who live in country villages, the wonder is not why many leave, but why any stay." He will not agree that this is merely the normal condition of the rural population, as seen through jaundiced eyes. Once there was life in rural England. That life is vanishing like a dream. " ' Still as a slave before his lord,' represents the attitude of the farm hand in the presence of his employer, No sheep before her shearers was ever more dumb than the milkers and carters and ploughmen at the village meetings to which their masters choose to summon them. They are cowed. It is to this that the race has come whom Froissart has described as ' *le plus périlleux peuple qui soit au monde, et plus outrageux et orgueilleux.*' Pride is dead in their souls." [1]

This writer does not despair of revival as a result of large and drastic changes. "The monopoly of great farmers must be broken up," he boldly declares, "before the dawn of hope can rise upon the English peasant." He has discovered deep in the heart of the country labourer that " Love of the Land" which has survived through all the generations of hopeless drudgery. He recognises it as "a survival from the days when an able-bodied

[1] *D. C. Pedder. Where Men Decay.*

Englishman, bred on and to the land, might cherish the hope of one day calling a corner of it his own, at least as the tenant of a landlord without personal interest in the degradation of his dependants." Here is the sole asset we possess in the work of rural revival. Parliament has been attempting by legislation to give to some select persons in the villages direct access to the land. The labourer to-day is slowly and doubtfully realising that a law has been passed which is designed to work for his benefit. The whole conception is new to him. "Law" he has hitherto regarded as something remote or inimical, symbolised by the village policeman, or the magistrates who penalise poaching and petty larceny. Those who made themselves missionaries of the new Act in the villages found everywhere this first incredulity. They announced the decree of Government that henceforth the first charge on the land should be the allotment or small holding; that nothing was to stand in the way of the provision of such holding when it was desired; that, if necessary by compulsion, the claims of sport, the claims of pleasure, the ambitions of the large farmer adding field to field, the prejudice or caprice of those who dislike the creation of these small plots and gardens, were to be made to yield to the primary necessity of finding land for the landless. The labourer was silent, astonished, doubtful, wondering if this was a new trick designed for his disadvantage. There were meetings at night, to which men came furtively; suggestions that one is a "spy," and dogged silence until he has departed; doubt as to what Mr. A. (the landlord) would think of it, or whether Mr. B. (the farmer) would dispossess all those who apply for land, or if Mr. C. (the vicar) would be inclined to look favourably on the affair. The stirring and the movement for a time seemed real; far more real than many had ventured to hope for when the Act was passing through Parliament. But the rather cumbrous machinery is difficult to put into operation, and the future is still uncertain. If the Parish Councils and County Councils and Central Commissioners prove adequate to the situation, they may yet reveal life where there now is little but death, and a transformation of England's deserted countryside. If the difficulties are insuperable or action too long delayed, with Councils embarking upon one experiment chosen from ten applications, postponing for months or years any energetic action; there will be no vocal protest, and few who cannot look beneath the surface will realise what has happened. The serene life of rural England, viewed from the country house or city observatory, will continue undisturbed. There will be no revolution, red flags, open riots, rick-burning. But the people will quietly melt away, into the cities, beyond the sea. The last of the Sibylline Books will have been flung into the flames.

What this vanishing life signifies, in its strength and in its weaknesses, can only be revealed to those who through months and years have made it the subject of sympathetic study. The landlord, the farmer, the clergyman, the newspaper correspondent primed with casual conversation in the village inn, think that they know the labourer. They probably know nothing whatever about him. With his limited vocabulary, with his racial distrust of the stranger, and all of another class, with a mind which maintains such reticence except in moments of overpowering emotion, that labourer stands, a perplexing enigmatic figure alone in a voluble, self-analysing world. In certain sympathetic studies he is revealed in his strength and his weakness, by those who are able to get behind much that is superficially unattractive to the solid endurance and courage and helpfulness beneath it all.

In his *Memoirs of a Surrey Labourer*, Mr. " George Bourne" has presented an illuminating picture of an old man who himself stands for the last relic of a vanishing race. He has collected and treasured the sayings of "Bettesworth" as he passes slowly downward in the day's decline; remarks trivial or commonplace, worldly wisdom, strange superstitions, acceptance of the sunshine, bewilderment before the hostile forces of the world. There are years passed in almost daily intercourse before his master discovers that Bettesworth had once fought through the Crimean war. That experience had made no permanent impression of horror or of pride. The events of the day, which influence men's passions in some mobile, distant universe, filter down into this quiet country like the noise of something far away. And the South African War, and the death of the Queen, and a General Election scarcely do more than ripple the surface of these deep waters. Of more importance is the untimely summer rain which ruins the harvest, dispossession from a cottage, the illness of a wife, the calamity of advancing age. The heroic patience and endurance of the labourer is here revealed, in face

of accepted and inevitable change. He resists the
embraces of the workhouse with that dogged
despair with which the English rural poor have
resisted the "Bastilles" since their foundation. He
clings to life and its possible activities, continuing
his work, suffering and half blind, meeting death when
it comes as the poor have usually met it, without hope
and without fear ; his mind at the end with the past
rather than with the future. The Pagan remains, and
refuses to be silenced by the long centuries of Christian tradition.   There is scepticism concerning " these
here places nobody ever bin to an' come back again
to tell we." "Nobody don't know nothin' about it.
'Tain't as if they come back to tell ye. There's
my father what bin dead this forty year, what a crool
man he must be not to've come back in all that time,
if he was able, an' tell me about it. That's what I
said to Colonel Sadler. 'Oh,' he says, 'you had
better talk to the Vicar.' 'Vicar?' I says; 'he won't
talk to me. Besides, what do he know about it
more'n anybody else?'"
He is seen moving into his squalid cottage, and
refusing to be dislodged from his lair : resisting, to the
death, the services of the efficient poor law infirmary
or the suggestion of Hospital kindliness.   He had a
theory that "bread never ought to be no less than a
shillin' a gallon" if farmers were to prosper : but on
hearing of the new "fiscal reform," "Oh dear !" is
his comment, "we don't want no taxes on food."   In
war-time he is on the side of "our country," and has
a subtle explanation of the report of "missing" in the
newspapers.   "Prisoners—or else burnt."   "They

burns 'em, some says." He enjoys his life to the end; despising, so long as is possible, the forces of ill-health, advancing old age, weariness; exhibiting in circumstances of bereavement and squalid misery the astonishing endurance and clinging to life which is found amongst the rural poor of England. "During the last year or two of his life he was seldom without pain. He could joke about his passing indispositions as he could defy his landlord. A neighbour looking in upon him, and seeing his serious condition, said genially, ' You ben't goin' to die, be ye, Freddy ? ' And he answered, ' I dunno. Shouldn't care if I do. 'Tis a poor feller as can't make up his mind to die once. If we had to die two or three times, then there might be something to fret about.' " Later, he adds more seriously, "But nobody dunno *when*, that's the best of it."

The author recounts, with a poignant simplicity, the incidents of the old man's death: in hot July weather, with the year at the summit of riotous life, and every element in nature taunting the impotence of humanity before the triumphant forces of destruction. "He is dying," was the thought at the end, "without any suspicion that any one could think of him with admiration and reverence." His race is perishing in similar ignorance, unhonoured and unsung: without a suspicion that "any one could think of it with admiration and reverence." The agricultural labourer survived the intolerable conditions of the early century when his life was one impossible struggle against penury and starvation. He stands to-day for a moment, an old man in a crumbling home, the last of a long line of high tradition and heritage.

He stands to-day without successors: occupying the region of his ancestors, which they had peopled since England first was: which they had maintained, with no ignoble life, through the transitory centuries.

He is vanishing from the world, and there are few that regret his departure. "Progress" has effected a destruction where penury and starvation had failed. He endured through all the lean years, somehow obtaining nourishment and rearing his children, clinging tenaciously to the earth, within the earth-bound horizon. At length appears the end; a rather squalid and mournful end—to a life which had once stood for the bedrock life of England. The peasant's resources, the peasant's vigour and resistance, the peasant's slow-moving, deliberate mind, had borne the burden of war and change. From his villages came the old folk-songs of the nation; he built the village churches, which are the treasures of rural England, and once took a pride in them. His secret wisdom, his fragments of half-heathen, half-Christian philosophy, his standards of bitterness and enjoyment, once made up the temper and mettle of the common people of England. The period of his greatest degradation coincided with the period of a sudden offer of escape. As the common land passed from his occupation, and he sank steadily to the landless depth of day labour, the cities, with their unlimited demands for the peasant energy and vigour, open to him welcoming arms. The few that remain are coming more and more to present the appearance of a declining race: a race which has lost the secrets of the arts which once flourished in the region in which it dwells.

The English countryside to-day, still a thing of beauty, with its thatched cottages and old high-timbered roofs and glory of village churches, presents a picture similar to those in which races of dulled intelligence blink and creep within cities of magnificent architecture once raised by their ancestors, the secrets of whose construction they have neither energy nor intelligence to regain.   "The evidence is abundant and positive," writes Dr. Jessop, as a result of most careful examination of first-hand authority, "that the work done upon the fabrics of our churches and the other work done in the beautifying of the interior of our churches, such as the wood carving of our screens, the painting of the lovely figures in the panels of those screens, the embroidery of the banners and vestments, the frescoes on the walls, the engraving of the monumental brasses, the stained glass in the windows, and all that vast aggregate of artistic achievements which existed in immense profusion in our village churches till the frightful spoliation of those who in the sixteenth century stripped them bare—all this was executed by local artists."   He will not listen to the tradition of indebtedness to monk and squire.   "In the thirteenth and fourteenth centuries," he declares, "there were no squires—that is the naked truth."   The property belonged to the parish : it was always growing.   It was of a richness and variety almost incredible to those who to-day see but the last guttering flame of parochial life, the attempt by parish councils, guilds of village players, and all the enterprise of occasional vigorous resistance, to combat the spreading atrophy of decay.   Here are "ornaments and church furniture, bells and candlesticks, crosses and organs, and tapestry and banners: vestments which were miracles of splendour in their colours and materials and incomparable artistic finish of needlework: not to speak of the fine linen and the veils, the carpets and the hangings."[1] It is a treasury of wealth, not so much in its direct suggestion of opulence, of services and bequests freely given, as in its indication of a life which can take pride in itself and its labour: a life, however difficult and limited, yet finding occasion for a handicraft in which men and women may delight, and some interests other than that of concentration upon dull and trivial things.

Such were the beginnings of this long sorrowful progress: in villages which could create these things and take a pride in them. The end reveals an England vulgarised by the clamour and vigour of the newer wealthy, racing each other down on motor cars from the noise of the town, into the heart of a great silence: the silence that broods over a doomed and passing race. There remains at the summit a joyful aborption in physical exercises and pleasures: in the midst of which, almost unnoticed amid the new gaiety, " Bettesworth " is shambling to a pauper grave, and his children vanishing from the life of open sky into the mazes of the lamplit city.

" In England alone, among all modern countries, the English people are imprisoned between hedges, and driven along rights of way." The beauty of continental landscape—of the Touraine and the Midi, the little Norman orchards, the extraordinarily

[1] *Before the Great Pillage. Dr. Jessop.*

fruitful fields of Southern Germany, the rude plenty
of the Balkan principalities—is the beauty of "peasants'
country": the beauty that is provided by security and
close cultivation, excited wherever the peasant is
assured that he will reap what he has sown. The
beauty of English landscape is the beauty of
"landlords' country"—the open woods, the large
grass fields and wide hedges, the ample demesnes,
which signify a country given up less to industry than
to opulence and dignified ease. The one is a park:
the other, a source of food supply and the breeding-
place of men. The typical English countryside is
that of great avenues leading to residences which lack
no comfort, broad parks, stretches of private land,
sparsely cultivated, but convenient for hunting,
shooting, and a kind of stately splendour. The
typical continental countryside is that of tiny white-
washed or wooden broad-eaved cottages, freely
scattered over a region of fruit and flowers and
close-tilled coveted land, which, in fact, is one large
garden. The record of the great landowners of this
country is of vast accumulations of acres: aggregations
of whole counties, or estates dotted over many
counties, each organised on the same plan of inherited
feudal tradition. Where the money can still be
obtained from external sources—the new wealth
of the towns, or tribute from new nations abroad—
some semblance of that feudal tradition still remain.
Cottages are let at less than their market prices, old
men and women on the estate are comfortably
pensioned, there are almshouses and model villages
and "Church" schools, a deferential and grateful

population, and all the apparatus of the model village, guided and controlled by the occupant of the great house. Yet even from these well-favoured regions the census returns reveal the population fleeing from the neighbourhood as if from some raging pestilence: making what haste they can to be gone. The smaller "landed gentry" have been most hardly hit by agricultural depressions, the general fall in prices, and the obligations of a growing standard of luxury, confronting a falling income. Here the estates are encumbered or falling into decay. The physical aspect of comfort and pleasant non-economic industry is far less apparent. There is evidence, even in the outward scene, of the malady within. In the case of some of the larger estates, and a great number of the smaller, the land is being transferred to those who, having made fortunes in trade, business, or financial speculation, have desire of settling down into the life of the country gentleman. In many of the home counties, for example, the bulk of the older estates have passed into the hands of the owners of the "new wealth," the Plutocracy which looks for its consummation in ownership of a portion of the land of England. Many of them are assiduous in rural welfare: some have taken over what remain of the feudal tradition as a "going concern," and delight in the fresh air, the opportunities for "sport" and exercise, the ample bestowal of patronage, and all the manifold energies and charities which flow from the great house into the surrounding countryside. There are some also who introduce a breath of fresh air—even an unashamed Democratic spirit—into the somewhat

heavy atmosphere of the remoter regions of rural
England. To others, however, all this is frankly a
toy and a plaything. They have purchased an
estate, as they would purchase food or raiment, for
the purposes of enjoyment. They convert the house
into a tiny piece of the city, transplanted to the
healthier air of the fields. They entertain themselves
and their friends in the heart of an England, for
whose vanishing traditions and enthusiasms they care
not at all. In that England, indeed, everything seems
to arrive too late. Men only awaken to the necessity
of doing something after the opportunity for that
particular something has already gone. The rural
Labourers' Union succeeded and collapsed just before
the great fall in prices : instead of effecting its objects
at the time when wages could easily have been raised
out of the natural profits of the land. To-day land
is being slowly and laboriously offered to the people,
a generation after the people who once hungered for
that offer have flung themselves into the cities or
beyond the sea. In another period of years, progress
may have compelled the breaking up of the big estates ;
once again, after the population who would avail
themselves to-day of such offers, to-morrow will have
passed from the scene. In exercise and enjoyment,
in parties and pleasant gardens, amid a playing at
the ancient rural traditions, and through the newer
mechanisms of locomotion, the decay passes almost
unnoticed. The few who lift up their voices in
warning are openly despised as agitators, or
condemned as political pessimists. The rural
reformer finds himself not so much opposed as

ridiculed. What remains of the system, fortified by
the city wealth, is so evidently unassailable by what
remains of any resistent forces, that it can afford to
contemplate all efforts towards revolt with a good-
tempered disdain. Occasionally a village learns of
some legislation designed for its benefit, of "Small
Holdings" which a benignant Government designs
for the advantage of the adventurous, of the apparatus
of rural Self-Government, which can give to the
poorest some right of control of the village commercial activities. It cautiously or boldly essays the
paths of progress. The inhabitants apply for land
to the great landowners who constitute the County
Council, or organise themselves into a tiny village
caucus for the capture of the Parish Meeting. Then,
in quiet and effectual action, the movement of revolt
is scattered and suppressed. It is explained to the
applicants how unsuitable they are for the position of
independent agricultural industry: or the leaders of
the democratic upheaval are informed that it is not in
the least convenient to their owners that they should
concern themselves with the intricacies of local self-
government. In a few months, or, at most, a few
years, order reigns—at Auburn, as at Warsaw. And
those who had been galvanised into some semblance
of life have, for the most part, disappeared: to
London, to the nearest city, to the British dominions
beyond the sea. Such pitiful uprising, with its
consequent disasters, evokes no resentment against the
dominant power. It rather evokes resentment against
those who had stirred up the forces of disturbance.
In a certain village in Oxfordshire an unwary Liberal

member of Parliament recently stimulated resistance to the enclosure by the landlord of a right-of-way. The resistance was sustained, and the village preserved in its ancient privilege. But all six witnesses who had testified to the ancient customs were dismissed from their occupations, and driven from the district. And indignation fell, not on the landlord who thus revealed his power, but on the member of Parliament who revealed his impotence. It was the Liberal, not the Conservative organisation, which henceforth found a united opposition to its energies : as the population, worshipping always only the strongest, discovered its leaders deported over so unsatisfying a controversy as the vindication of a public right. There was a general village uprising in the Election of 1885, when the newly enfranchised labourers turned eagerly to the promise of independence upon the land. There was another village uprising in 1906, when the labourers turned sullenly away from the proposal to tax their food. But the one was an uprising of Hope: the other, of Fear. In the intervening period there had vanished, from large areas of rural England, the possibility of the reconstruction of a rural civilisation.

"The human wealth of a populous countryside, in which all classes lived, and could live, at peace for centuries—that," says Mr. Ensor, "is our achievement as a nation, the source and condition of our other greatnesses, the bark on whose fragments, 'majestic though in ruin,' we can still found, if not our loudest, at least our most legitimate fame."[1]

[1] *England a Nation.*

All that is over. It would appear to be over for ever. A few old men, gathered round the hearthstone of the village inn, testify in the nights of winter to the passing of a whole people. Already the manifestations of resistance and of aspiration, associated with the democratic victories of the last election, are sinking back into the older acquiescence: as the rulers of the countryside exhibit, by a combination of kindliness and austerity, how undesirable is such an overthrow of the accepted ways. Villas and country houses establish themselves in the heart of this departing race: in it, but not of it, as alien from its ancient ways as if dropped from the clouds into another world. Wandering machines, travelling with an incredible rate of speed, scramble and smash and shriek along all the rural ways. You can see them on a Sunday afternoon, piled twenty or thirty deep outside the new popular inns, while their occupants regale themselves within. You can see the evidence of their activity in the dust-laden hedges of the south country roads, a grey mud colour, with no evidence of green; in the ruined cottage gardens of the south country villages. From those villages themselves not only the evidence of activity has departed, but the very memories of it. They cannot, to-day, make the folklore popular songs. They cannot even cherish the folklore songs which were made by their fathers. And "few sadder or more thought-begetting experiences can be undergone," is the testimony of a lover of this land, "than to sit in an inn in a remote country village, and hear rustics troll tin-kettle ditties about Seven Dials or the Old Kent Road."

Over all which vision of a secular decay Nature still flings the splendour of her dawns and sunsets upon a land of radiant beauty. Here are deep rivers flowing beneath old mills and churches; high-roofed red barns and large thatched houses; with still unsullied expanses of cornland and wind - swept moor and heather, and pine woods looking down valleys upon green gardens; and long stretches of quiet down standing white and clean from the blue surrounding sea. Never, perhaps, in the memorable and spacious story of this island's history has the land beyond the city offered so fair an inheritance to the children of its people, as to-day, under the visible shadow of the end.

CHAPTER VII

SCIENCE AND PROGRESS

SUCH appear some, at least, of the characteristics of the various classes of Society to-day in England. In general material condition there is little to excite foreboding. A proportion of the population is raised well above the privations of poverty larger than ever before in history. Extravagance and a longing for pleasure and excitement are common to all classes. The aggregation of plenty is such as the Old World has never before seen. The vision, as a whole, is of a laborious energetic race, deserting the countryside for the cities, and there heaping up wealth, which is shared, in some degree, by all but the poorest. If anything is wrong in material conditions it is in the apparatus, not of accumulation, but of distribution. An altogether inadequate proportion of this accumulation is the absolute possession of a tiny class which sits secure upon the summit. In heavy tolls levied upon labour in the form of royalties and the monopoly rents of land, in inherited fortune which reaps its interest from remote regions and foreign kingdoms, in unusual profit of industrial investment through times of trade "boom," in financial speculation and all the various special advantage of business, commerce, and manufacture in this free market of England, there is being concentrated in few hands vast and ever-increasing fortune.   Security accepted as normal, comfort more widely spread than ever before, and a standard of extravagance and display which would have astonished all previous ages, characterise the heart of the Empire at the height of its material greatness.   " Situate at the entering of the sea," with a population exceeding Scotland or Ireland, and the revenues of many European States, the greatest city of that Empire is taking toll from the industry of all the world.   In the midst of which outward evidence of attainment sounds almost unnoticed the complaining of a poverty more degraded and intolerable than in many less successful lands : whose misery is intensified by its conjunction in adjacent cities with a people evidently given up to the arts of enjoyment, and finding an ever-increasing plenty inadequate to its ever-increasing demand.

And always the hope is latent that " something will turn up " which will solve all the unfortunate social problems, and make every one happy and content. Sometimes it is to be the advance of mechanical discovery, sometimes a new spirit of kindliness and patience : sometimes fuller conquests of trade or commerce or Imperial dominion ; but always the bringing in from outside of a *Deus ex machina* which will supplement nobody's loss with everybody's gain. The advance in acquisition during a century of invention has been so astonishing, the progress of whole classes from a low-grade, comfortless, ignorant life into a highly-paid, skilled, intelligent working-people so remarkable, that to many the continuance of such a process seems inevitable. Amelioration is to come as a legitimate child of the forces of change, and without effort or sacrifice is to reveal a continuous process of uplifting. Certainly by all material and tangible tests — income, prices, security, comfort, addition to leisure and wages—the bulk of the people of this country have advanced so incredibly since the "Hungry Forties" that the reality of those days would appear to the present generation but as bad dreams. They cannot believe that these things were actually enacted upon these islands less than eighty years ago. The Report of the Royal Commission on Children's Labour in the Factories,—the most sensational blue-book of the century,—for example, would seem rather to refer to the Spaniards in the West Indies or the administration of King Leopold in the Congo than to the solid ground and pleasant airs of England. And in every kind of material test—fall of pauperism, fall of the death-rate, decline of infectious and poverty diseases—or increase of wages, shortening of hours of labour, fall in prices ; or, again, spread of education and of means of recreation, improvement in houses and in the sanitation of cities, the offering of opportunities of advancement : in all these the advance has been so amazing that there would seem to be no place for the pessimist who would prophesy coming disaster.

It is rather in the region of the spirit that the doubts are still disturbing. Fulness of bread in the past has been accompanied with leanness of soul. And the modern prophet is still undecided whether this enormous increase of life's comforts and material satisfactions has revealed an equal and parallel advance in courage and compassion and kindly understandings. The nations, equipped with ever more complicated instruments of warfare, face each other as armed camps across frontiers mined and tortured with the apparatus of destruction. A scared wealthy and middle class confronts a cosmopolitan uprising of the "proletariat," whose discontent it can neither appease nor forget. The industrious populations which have been swept into masses and congestions by the new industry has not yet found an existence serene, and intelligible, and human. No one, to-day, looking out upon a disturbed and sullen Europe, a disturbed and confident America, but is conscious of a world in motion: whither, no man knows. "The people of our Christian world," so runs the cry of the first of living prophets—"the people of our Christian world live like animals, guided in their lives merely by personal interests and by their struggle with one another: differing from animals only in that the animals, from time immemorial, have kept the same stomachs, claws, and fangs, while people move with ever-increasing rapidity from roads to railroads, from horses to steam, from spoken sermons and letters to printing, to telegraphs and telephones, and from sailing boats to ocean steamers, from swords to gunpowder, cannons, quick-firing guns, bombs, and war aeroplanes. And life, with telegraphs, telephones, electricity, bombs, and aeroplanes, and with hatred of all for all: directed, not by some uniting spiritual principle, but, on the contrary, by animal instincts which divide, and which employ mental powers for their own satisfaction, becomes even more and more insane and wretched." [1]

What mechanical invention, what mechanical skill, have any promise to offer of immediate and large improvement? Will the cunning ingenuity of men, which embarked on the path of scientific exploration with such large hopes of service to humanity as well as attainment of truth, be able, even at this last, through the multiplication of machinery to eliminate poverty, through the development of the arts of healing to eliminate pain? Or if this be unattainable and delusive, can we find through these and other progressive agencies a permanent healing for the sick soul of humanity? Is the twentieth century to advocate a scheme of life which will itself provide a consolation in the loss of the older faiths, and redeem mankind from a mere animal struggle for the apparatus of material pleasure?

The "Bankruptcy of Science" is a term which has become common to European literature since M. Brunetiere first scandalised the naive ingenuous persons who accepted empiricism as a new religion. And, in a large movement of popular opinion, mankind has turned with some indignation and some regret from a method which has proved altogether inadequate to the immense hopes that it once excited amongst its first admirers. The greatness of the disappointment is proportioned to the greatness of the promise. The accusation—in its popular form—is an unfair one. Natural science,

[1] Tolstoy, *Fortnightly Review*, February 1909.

as such, makes no claim to remedy human ills; makes no claim, indeed, to exercise any kind of influence upon human life at all. It does not reveal, and it does not profess to reveal, the secret and meaning of the Universe. That is the function of a metaphysic. It does not labour in aid of religion, art, economic equality, or social comfort. It does not labour against them. It leaves them alone. These are outside its province. There is no possibility through investigations in the higher mathematics, of solving the problem of the injustices of human fortune. There is no prospect through examination of the brains of dead animals to discover or disprove the existence of the human soul. There is no promise, by however subtle elaboration of mechanical invention, permanently to better the lot of those poor who in every variation of human society are always living near the margin of what is humanly endurable. Such disabilities are no charge against human reason, concentrated upon investigation of the nature of the material Universe. They are a charge, if charge at all, against the somewhat too sanguine dreamers who asserted that through human reason, in investigation of the nature of the material Universe, mankind would finally achieve secrets which would make them rivals of the older gods. The large hopes and dreams of the Early Victorian time have vanished: never, at least in the immediate future, to return. The science which was to allay all diseases, the commerce which was to abolish war, and weave all nations into one human family, the research which was to establish ethics and religion on a secure and positive foundation, the invention which was to enable all humanity, with a few hours of not disagreeable work every day, to live for the remainder of their time in ease and sunshine—all these have become recognised as remote and fairy visions. One man now produces—by the aid of machinery—what a thousand could but hardly produce a century ago. "Argosies of commerce" post over land and ocean without rest. Not two but two hundred blades of grass grow where one blade grew before. Factories and furnaces, in never-ceasing activity, vomit forth ever more elaborate products, clothing, furniture, houses, implements of brass and steel, by methods which would have excited wonder and worship in earlier, simpler ages. Yet ten millions, disinherited, out of a doubtful forty, shiver through their lives on the verge of hunger: to the bulk of the remainder existence presents no certain joys, either in a guaranteed prosperity or in any serviceable and illuminating purpose of being. Civilisation, in the early twentieth century in England, suffers no illusions as to the control of natural forces, or the exploration of natural secrets furnishing a cure either for the diseases from which it suffers in the body, or the more deep-seated maladies of the soul.

It is making life noisier: is it making life—to the general—a richer, a better thing: existence more worth the living? Once more, here is no charge against invention, against the persistent labours of select and powerful minds to ascertain what knowledge is obtainable by the method of experiment and observation. They might justly reply that it is not in their province to make life a richer and better thing: existence more worth the living. Their function—in so far as it touches human life at all—is to increase the aggregate control of "mind over matter"; to release man from the mere impotent cowering before the brute forces of Chance and Necessity, which can deal with him as a plaything, or overwhelm him, casually and indifferently, without praise and without blame. They have no function to determine what distribution of this increase in human wealth and control will most make for the happiness and development of the human family, or to adjust whatever affirmations they may be able to advance with some certitude to historical religions, moralities, or customary courses of conduct. "The changing conditions of history," says a great modern philosopher, "touch only the surface of the show. The altered equilibriums and redistributions only diversify our opportunities, and open chances to us for new ideals. But with each new ideal that comes into life, the chance for a life based on the old ideal will vanish: and he would needs be a presumptuous calculator who should with confidence say that the total sum of significance is positively and absolutely greater at any one epoch than at any other of the world."

As the mechanical discoveries swing forward there will always be those buoyant persons to whom the newer inventions are most welcome, contrasted with the more conservative elements who ask for quiet, and some position secure from the cyclic disturbances of change. In the next generation, any particular change has become the normal, and excites neither satisfaction nor disgust. So it has been with improved locomotion, with telegraphs and telephones, with all the outward apparatus which has set the unchanged human spirit in a world of marvel and miracle. The most obvious scientific advance which is already visible upon the horizon, is the invention of flying: which may be accepted, almost before these words are in print, as something no longer so astonishing as to excite enthusiasm or foreboding. It may exercise the profoundest influence upon the possibilities of war, of land frontiers, of divisions between contending nations. It has no real power either of infecting with disease a civilisation that is healthy, or of healing a civilisation that is sick and tired. For many years, perhaps, aerial navigation may be the sport and plaything of rich and adventurous spirits, like the first motor-cars; creating occasional sensations by circling round St. Paul's Cathedral, or descending unexpectedly in other people's back gardens. That is the stage when mankind will rejoice in the ingenuity of its inventors, heedless of the tremendous changes which such inventors must ultimately originate. Then the airship will find itself utilised for military purposes, perhaps with startling result. Then for locomotion and the transfer of people and merchandise from place to place above the recognised boundaries of ocean or territory. Finally, it will appear as a normal factor of man's life, transfiguring the world as much as the steamship or the railway; occupied in the service of the poor as well as of the rich, under private as well as public control. It may eliminate natural boundaries which have exercised a dominant influence upon human life since human life first was. The "precious stone set in a silver sea," with its moat defensive "against the envy of less happier lands," may find itself suddenly helpless and vulnerable before armies dropping from the skies. War itself may become impossible or utterly destructive. Protective barriers disappear, and the ingenuities of the construction of a scientific tariff melt into thin air. Man, whether he will or no, is drawn inevitably nearer to man. He must federate, or perish in homicidal mania and blind impulse of hatred and revenge.

On the other hand, quite apart from the question of national rivalries or the old impelling causes of the madness of war, there is the further consideration of the influence of such achievements upon the delicate fabric of the body and soul of mankind. At best, any large accomplishment of flying must mean an increased hustling and speeding up of human life; more hurry, more bustle, more breathlessness, more triumphant supremacy of material things. In all our mechanical ingenuities we have constructed masters for us, rather than servants; being compelled, immediately such ingenuities have found fruit in invention, to adjust our lives to the new conditions which these, and not we ourselves, henceforth dictate and impose. We are compelled, for example, to avail ourselves of the telegraph and the telephone; we are driven to the express train, the motor omnibus, the various expedients which are adapted to acceleration, rather than to happiness. If we do not adjust our lives to such accelerations, we are swept aside or trodden under by the crowds which press behind; like those who fail in the daily leap for the Brooklyn cars at New York, and are swept aside or trodden under almost unheeded. Has all this violence and tumult made life richer, fairer, more desirable for the children of men? Or is man losing in the mere blind effort of acceleration some of those experiences which once transfigured and glorified his little span of days? "Can you really turn a ray of light by magnetism?" shouted Carlyle scornfully. "And if you can, what should I care?" Matthew Arnold complained that the modern Englishman "thinks it the highest pitch of development and civilisation when his letters are carried twelve times a day from Islington to Camberwell and from Camberwell to Islington, and when railway trains run between them every quarter of an hour. He thinks it nothing that the trains only carry him from an illiberal dismal life at Camberwell to an illiberal dismal life at Islington, and the letters only tell him that such is the life there." Airships journeying daily from Paris to Pekin might excite exultation in a humanity which has emulated the exploits of Icarus, without exciting, like Icarus, the wrath of the jealous gods. Of what profit if they be found merely to transfer to Paris an existence which has become intolerable at Pekin, and to Pekin an existence which has become intolerable at Paris? It is a remarkable fact in the history of European development, that all the recent success of scientific and mechanical invention has been accompanied by an ever profounder questioning of the advantage of it all; so that to-day, when we seem on the verge of such discoveries as would have made our ancestors shout for joy in the mere triumph of creative energy, great writers are inquiring, with more bitterness and uncertainty than ever before, whether a verdict of bankruptcy has not been passed upon the whole of this complicated and baffled society. Mr. Wells has exhibited the old potato digger, "a greengrocer by trade, a gardener by disposition," confronting with a deepening disgust the restlessness of being. "Heaven had planned him for a peaceful world. Unfortunately, Heaven had not planned a peaceful world for him. He lived in a world of obstinate and incessant change." He is revealed in his little garden; gas-works and electric power stations rising up to heaven beside him, mono-rails running across his head, flocks of balloons and aeroplanes clouding the horizon; everywhere on earth and sky the impression of a hustling, distorted, dissatisfied energy, writhing into fresh forms of grotesque invention. "This here Progress," is his dull conviction; "it keeps on. You'd hardly think it *could* keep on." It is not only Mr. Tom Smallways who is bothered with doubts of an uncertain future. The vision of all poverty and sweat of labour vanishing by the occasional pressing of a button, while mankind lies at ease on the hillside like the Olympian gods, has joined the vision of all disease abolished by scientific ingenuity in the kingdom of the shades. Flying will bring men together, abolish boundaries, multiply the facilities of exchange, increase the wealth of a few. Can it offer satisfaction for one of the necessities of the soul? There will always be those who find a bracing and tonic in the roar and exultation of riotous life, the mingling of the machine with the inspiration of the crowd. There will always be others who will seek satisfaction in quietness and common things — the untroubled horizon, the secure possession of the heart of humanity. Between which two extremes the mass of mankind will go forward, sometimes indifferent, not without courage and patience, towards a life increasing in complexity, and making ever more difficult demands on body and soul.

And as with flying, so with all similar advances in mechanical discovery. Man creates and man consumes; no happier for a provision which merely feeds a restless, hungry impulse towards change. So many houses, so many clothes, so many elaborate meals, so many holidays to-day. The number is doubled to-morrow. The many acquiesce: the few, on the one extreme, accept and rejoice; the few, on the other, push aside the banquet untasted, or spurn the feast with bitter gibe at the futility of it all. "The barrenness and ignobleness of the labourer's life," says a modern philosopher, "consists in the fact that it is moved by no ideal inner springs." But the labourer has no monopoly in such a loss and deficiency. The whole of modern life has the accusation resting upon it, that it is moved by no ideal inner springs. Some find satisfaction in political

energies, others in religious ardours; others, again,
—in the mere play and triviality of wealth accumulation,—card games, or ingenious children's diversions
carried into the larger universe of human affairs.
Pursuit of knowledge claims a tiny "remnant,"
with a high intellectual hunger; or enthusiasm for
the future of the race, as they see always, luminous
and clear on the horizon, the shining of the star of
a new dawn. But to the general these "ideal inner
springs" are wanting. They feel confused in a world
of confusion. Social unrest affects large masses
of them whose restlessness finds no clear fruit in
action. Literature proclaims a disenchantment.
Man wanders unsatisfied in the spacious palaces of
his new material splendour. Many, after a rebellion
at the time of adolescence, settle down into acceptance; into making the "best of it" in a world hard
to understand, but, on the whole, easy to endure.
Others still refuse to relinquish the past for the in-
tangible, elusive promises of the future. "Enlightened
persons," wrote Chateaubriand, "cannot understand
how a Catholic like myself can persist in sitting in
the shadow of what they call ruins. Tell me, for
pity's sake, in the individual and philosophical
society which you offer me, where shall I find a
family and a God?"

In the abolition of poverty by mechanical ap-
pliance, in the provision of ethical and moral satisfactions for the human spirit which desires richer gifts
than material supremacy, this empirical method
would seem hitherto to have failed. They would

appear, however, to be on surer ground who prophesy its success in the war against disease. Here at least discovery can have none but beneficial results; and the competition is one of absolute human advantage. Yet the progress of the modern campaign against diseases, distinguished as it has been by triumphs which appear almost miraculous, still suffers resistance which baffle and frustrate its purpose. There appears a kind of unseen antagonist, who will rally in one region forces which have been beaten elsewhere, and is determined never to allow mankind the full fruits of victory. That all diseases will be slain by science, and all slain speedily, was one of the accepted anticipations of the earlier nineteenth century. In the great outburst of a triumphant optimism which inspired the Early Victorian literature, the present, whose discontents were clearly diagnosed, was sharply contrasted with a future where such discontents would be no more. Here, on the solid ground, a new race should arise, whose life, if limited, should be at least secure. On one side, it may be confessed, there are evidences of an almost exultant advance. The surest ground for optimism, for faith in the " beneficent processes of the unseen time," is provided by examination of how many human scourges have been rendered innocuous within living memory. We have eliminated from Europe the menace of those sweeping cyclones of pestilence, whose terrors brood like a grey cloud over all the brightness of the Middle Ages. One-third of Christendom perished in the few months' agony of the Black Death. The sound of its

lamentation, the madness caused by its apparently
irresistible destruction, still remains revealed in
those "Dances of Death" which absorbed the later
medieval time, and in the literature of protest and
despair of a similar age. The Plague still ravages
the East, but science has succeeded, and apparently
will succeed, in protecting Europe against it. Other
malignant fevers we seem on a fair road to stamp
out altogether. Smallpox has almost disappeared,
under the combined effects of sanitation and vaccination. Diphtheria has lost its terrors since the arrival
of the antitoxin treatment. Hydrophobia has become merely a dread memory of the past. Even
tuberculosis, the special and terrible scourge of the
northern races, is likely to become in the future but
as an evil memory of old years. Science again,
through the devotion and intelligence of a long roll
of volunteers, has boldy sallied out from the limited
abodes of men into the wild and shaggy regions
of Nature, in the determination to strike its enemy
boldly at the centre of its empire. It is not content
with mere preventives and prophylactics, dosing men
with drugs or covering them with veils and protec-
tions. It is setting itself to extirpate the very
instruments of the propagation of the disease. Its
enemy is the insect. That extraordinary populous
and intelligent kingdom might have once attained
the supremacy of the world, but for some inexplicable limitations in size which has prevented any
of its denizens from challenging the forces of mankind. Michelet has described the kind of horror
with which the head of an ant inspired him, as first

seen under the microscope ; with its vast and complicated eyes, its evidence of incalculable brain power, but with the utter absence of any of those human qualities which are revealed even in the vertebrate animals. Yet those ants can exhibit inexplicable powers of communication, and a social organisation which has been the envy of many a philosopher, as he contrasts it with the chaos of human life. Ants charged with "Boom food," ant communities of many thousands, all six feet high, might provide a considerable obstacle to the accepted supremacy of mankind. But the insect, however tiny, is becoming more and more to be recognised as one of the enemies of the human race. There is here no possibility of compromise. We can be sentimental over the horse, the cat, the dog. If we are sentimental over the insect, we are lost. "Why should I harm thee, little fly?" was Uncle Toby's famous inquiry. "Is there not room enough in the world for me and thee?" Science is unhesitatingly pronouncing a grim negative to the question. There is not sufficient room in the world for "me and thee." This is probably true of the common house-fly, who more and more is coming to be branded as a propagator of disease. It is already accepted of his cousin, the mosquito, against whom the whole of the world is turning with a set purpose of extermination. The alleged unhealthiness of marshes and tropical regions, formerly ascribed to heat and noxious vapours, is now declared to be entirely explicable by the spread of a definite bacterium through the bites of insects. Where the insects are destroyed the white man flourishes.

Panama, in the early days of the Canal building, was converted into a visible hell, in which a population rioted and rotted and died, as they rioted and rotted and died in the days of the plague. The Americans to-day have descended there with all scientific resources. They burn the insect, they choke its offspring with oil, they drain the stagnant pools where it can breed, they consume it in clouds of evil-smelling smoke. They are rapidly making Panama a healthier place than New York or Chicago. All down the coast of South America, yellow fever has decimated mankind for centuries. To-day it is well on its way to becoming a thing of the past. Six years ago an international campaign was inaugurated against the *Stegomya fasciata*, the "white-ribbed mosquito," which spreads the disease. At Rio Janeiro, Dr. Cruz, "Cruz the mosquito killer," has practically removed its menace. Repairing choked-up gutters, draining stagnant marshes, fumigating and isolating, scattering oil on the still waters, he is speedily and relentlessly exterminating this enemy of mankind. Yellow fever and malarias will become shortly things of the past, as the warfare, at present of necessity limited to the neighbourhood of the cities, is extended through all the waste places of the world.

And if the discussion passes from the prevention to the cure, here also the sanguine dream of our fathers might seem in process of realisation. We can treat the tortured human body as Brutus wished to treat the condemned Cæsar—"Carve it as a dish fit for the gods," and still preserve life and ensure recovery. First in antiseptic, then in aseptic surgery, we have discovered a method of safe operation, under which death would have been inevitable a few years ago. Gambetta perished in early manhood, because the doctors were afraid of an operation from which to-day over ninety per cent. of the patients recover. Opiates and anæsthetics, combined with the agile use of the knife, have eliminated on the one hand an almost inconceivable burden of pain, on the other have rendered possible a tearing and lacerating of the frail physical human body which would have seemed incredible to our predecessors. Nor can any one imagine that we are anywhere but in infancy in this particular progress. If, as eminent physiologists assert, the nerves of pain are distinct from the nerves of sensation or volition, it may be found possible to compound some subtle drug which will blockade these particular channels of communication, and render mankind henceforth completely immune from the pangs of physical suffering.

But then thought turns to the other side of the picture, and is immediately faced with a challenge to its optimism. As soon as one disease is eliminated, another steps into its place to continue the old tragic function of scourging mankind with pity and terror. Science is always discovering new maladies, which baffle its exultant energies. Medical, as distinct from surgical effort, is still largely in the condition of alchemy: stretching blind hands in the darkness towards a secret not yet revealed. A great man of science recently asserted that there were only two medicines whose beneficial effect—in application to specific disorders—could be guaranteed—quinine and mercury; and that the operations of both of them were completely mysterious. We drain our cities, we use our knives and our medicines, we maintain armies of doctors, huge hospitals, and halls of research. And the result is that in the factory centres one-fifth of the children born perish within the year. Consumption, plague, malaria disappear. Their places are readily assumed by cancer, which is steadily increasing; by appendicitis, which had not even a name twenty years ago; by meningitis, which is excited by the ordinary harmless cold in the head. One woman in every twelve dies of cancer, and the cure still remains altogether unknown. The human body in increase of prevention, seems also to lose the power of resistance. Carefully shielded from the rough forces of the world, it falls a prey to injuries born out of the very conditions of safety which it has so laboriously constructed. "He who has ordained all things in measure, number, and weight," said Mansel, "has also given to the reason of man, as to his life, its boundaries, which it cannot pass." Some unknown Power seems with these "boundaries" still to defy man's determination to push them back or fling them down. In ten thousand years mankind has not added a cubit to his stature. The Greek vision of bodily perfection has shown no advance in succeeding time. In the Middle Age, with its outward squalor and frequent pestilences— so operative in men's minds that to some observers the whole appears as a kind of physical delirium—

there are figures of Popes and Emperors taking the field at eighty years of age, and an ineffaceable impression of an enormous physical vitality. It would appear that, at least as far as one can look ahead, uncertainty, sorrow, pain, and longing are to be accepted as companions of the life of men. From these, indeed, have been born men's highest achievements. Metchnikoff still proclaims unfaltering faith in the triumph of human intelligence, and sees a vision of humanity sustained on a diet of soured milk, to well beyond a normally secure centenarianism. The cry of such might still be the cry of Tithonus—"Release me, and restore me to the ground," in a desire for the return to the fate of "happy men that have the power to die." For, however successful we may find ourselves in curing the maladies of the body, such efforts are of little use if there remains unhealed the deeper malady of the soul.

CHAPTER VIII

LITERATURE AND PROGRESS

LET us turn, then, from science to literature: to the attempt made by this age, or a certain section of it, to find self-conscious expression for its praise or blame. I spoke at the beginning of the impeachment of the nineteenth-century civilisation by its greater writers: their conviction of a mortal disease. We have few great writers and far less violence in denunciation. The change is becoming manifest as comfort increases and wealth accumulates, which has been manifest in all similar transformations. Literature loses its ardour and its inspiration. It becomes critical rather than invigorating: sceptical, questioning, sometimes with an appearance of frivolity, sometimes torturing itself with angers and despairs. The note to-day is that of a time of disenchantment. Here is reaction after the fashion of high hopes: indignation at the bankruptcy of things which promised much and accomplished so little; a conviction that the zest and sparkle has gone from a society which suddenly feels itself growing old.

" The great evil of our age," is the summary of one clear-sighted critic, " is that we are constantly and terribly aware of evil." With wealth accumulated to the astonishment of mankind, tribute sucked from all subject races, opulence which makes poorer nations envious, literature reveals no content, no deliberate acceptances, no high inspiration. "Our science, philosophies, and inventions and manufactures and infinite complexities have conspired to make us more discontented, even if we have not actually more cause for misery."[1] The verdict of the sceptic from the heart of a civilisation advancing in material triumph and more comfortable in the world than ever before, is a verdict of weariness and vanity.

The "ache of modernism" and the turmoil of Whitman's "growing arrogance of realism" confront the demands of the human spirit for adventure and of the human heart for triumph over time and change. Science in its buoyant beginnings had provided great inspiration, of wonderful gifts for man's enjoyment, of wonderful knowledge of the universal secret. Sixty years ago it seemed to be offering humanity not only control of material forces and cunning invention, but also the interpretation of the secret of life and destiny. But science to-day— in the critic's examination—protests in literature the affirmation of a bankrupt creed. The revelation of the secret has become the assertion of Haeckel, that "consciousness, thought, and speculation are functions of the ganglionic cells of the cortex of the brain." And the inspiration of the discovery sinks back into the declaration that "Democracy is an

---

[1] *Modernism and Romance. By R. A. Scott James.* The whole book forms a very interesting study of the possibilities of the survival of "Romance" in the modern world.

expression of the constant desire for change, due to a hope that change will bring some remedy for the really incurable ills of human nature." In such a critic as Mr. Hardy, reaction against this failure, the bankruptcy of the creed of science, passes into an almost savage revolt against the blind purposes of life ; its clumsy cruelties, its lack of guidance or intelligible meaning. "Hardy goes so far as to suggest that God is either a defeated God or that He is indifferent, if not actually hostile, to men." "Human beings are for him worthy of praise and pity because they have been laden with sorrows which they did not deserve, and are kinder to one another than God is kind to them."[1] This great writer sees in vision the tragedy of "the modern vice of unrest," of "the view of life as a thing to be put up with, replacing that zest for existence which was so intense in early civilisation." "It is the beginning of the coming universal wish not to live."

In face of such disallusionment the men who attempt literature attempt escape in various ways. And "escape" is the prominent aspect of to-day's art, in a deliberate turning away from the realities of the present, which only a few accept as substance for artistic interpretation. Some fling themselves out of the main stream of life like the "Decadents," finding satisfaction in sense-given impression, repudiating ultimate purposes. To these the present is already in Autumn, and its noises and tumults but the jarrings of a machine running down ; worn with the dust of its own grinding. Others, like the psycho-

[1] *Modernism and Romance.*

logical novelists, attempt analysis without affirmation or denial. They exhibit the world as they see it, or a particular select portion of it. They dissect a character or a situation in all its implications and aspects. They would be the first to repudiate either approval or criticism of this subject - matter of delicate and refined writing. At the opposite pole are the apostles of protest—a Gorky, a Wells, a Mark Rutherford, who stab and slash at a life so remote from the ideal, in furious revolt against its complacencies and cruelties. Some fall back on dreams and memories, finding, either in a transfigured past or in the kingdom of fantasy which never was upon the solid ground, satisfaction denied in a world which has become "so unworthy." And others seek refuge in dreams of a transfigured humanity from the implacable defiance of present things; with pictures of that new world which yet shall rise when "every life shall be a song." Beyond these are the fugitives who frankly take to flight; like Lafcadio Hearn, turning first to the south, then to the east, "to the unexplored Eastern mind which may yet afford a refuge from 'modernism,'" and finding his latter days saddened by the aggressive entrance of "modernism" even into these remote fastnesses, and civilisation ravaging the simplicities of old Japan. In the near East, Mr. Scott James found the challenge frankly flung down, and the two forces—romanticism and "modernism"—joined at death grips. "'Time!' ejaculates the Montenegrin. 'What is time? Time is nothing. You live, and then you die.'" The same resistance, the same overthrow is being revealed here as Mr. Fielding Hall discovered in a far East, and so unforgetably stamped into literature, in his picture of the passing of the soul of Burma before a conquering imperialism and a vigorous commercial development. "I know what it means, this civilisation," says the priest of "Our Lady of the Rocks" in the remote mountain fastness of the Balkans. "My poor people. They have no idea what life is, out in the great world, and it is coming to them." "Till now they have lived with God and the mountains. It is so very little that one needs in this life. We have so short a time here."

A few years ago I selected for criticism and for praise certain contemporary writers who were refusing to take "opium."[1] These set themselves definitely in the heart of present affairs to endeavour to understand and to interpret the meaning of their day and generation. In almost every case the progress of things since that estimate has taken them into darker and more ominous outlook upon the future of the modern world. To Mr. Wells it is all a "spectacle of forces running to waste, of people who use and do not replace; the story of a country hectic with a wasting, aimless fever of trade and money-making and pleasure-seeking." The hero of his greatest novel reveals an experience fragmentary and disconnected in a tumultuous world. Mr. Wells can show that world in its rockings and upheavals, until beneath the seeming calm and conventionality of the surface view, is heard the very sound of the fractures and fallings; an age in

[1] In a volume of essays, *In Peril of Change*.

the headlong rush of change. George Ponderevo is at one time floating immense financial companies, a king of speculation, courted by the great, one of England's "Conquerors." At another he is quarrelling and forgiving and quarrelling again with a little commonplace uncomprehending wife down in a commonplace villa at Ealing. He is learning to fly, absorbed in the work of scientific invention—the one real thing of solid resistance in a universe of slush and mud and make-believe. He is engaged in random, fantastic sociabilities at Beckenham or Chislehurst, discussing, under the conflagrations of sun and star, the respective merits, as domestic pets, of cat or dog. He is plunging, in disconnected adventure, into a piratical raid into West Africa after "quap," a poisonous radio-active product of enormous value; and again, emerging from that terrific battle with unclean and tenacious forces, he is balancing toast on a tea-cup in a London drawing-room. He tumbles into love, driven forward by blind, tyrannous forces which overthrow reason and conventional restraint, against which he has never been warned, in whose service he can find no meaning. And in problems of sex which appear simple to the orthodox upholders of the existing moral standards, and simple, again, to the orthodox revolters from the existing moral standards, he can find nothing but perplexity and confusion—no certain guidance at all.

At the beginning the child is reared under the shadow of Bladesover, under the dominance of the great house, in the feudal tradition seen from the underside. And here was a civilisation which could be approved or condemned, but which at least stood as a coherent thing—a rule of life, a code of conduct, an organic society. But as he grows to manhood, Bladesover is sinking into decay, perishing, not knowing that it is perishing, thinking that it will endure for ever. The man who is living amid that long-drawn decline is wandering between two worlds, one dead, the other powerless to be born. It is an age in passing. What is coming to replace it? No one knows. The religion, the moral affirmations and denials of Bladesover are vanishing with it. Like the great house, the outward seeming still maintains an appearance of life; still church steeple and feudal tower together dominate the countryside. But the inner heart of it has gone. Man, as he achieves maturity, as he achieves sincerity from the rubbish heap of dead and dying assertions and denials in which he is being upreared, finds himself naked and alone in the midst of all the clamour and violence of encompassing hordes of his fellows. No pillar of cloud by day, no pillar of fire by night, directs his onward journey. And the irony of the experience is provided by the fact that the moment of the apprehension of this loneliness is the moment also of the apprehension of magnificence in material achievement—when civilisation, intoxicated with the attainment of comfort, is crowning itself with flowers and calling itself immortal. The effect is similar to that of the splendour of a palace which is found to be designed by a madman.

It is a "new hotel population" revealed as the ascendant race: the "multitude of economically ascendant people who are learning how to spend money." They are "running the world, practically, running it faster and faster." Of the fate of such an Age the hero here makes no prophecy. The sadness of his frustrated life, the denial of the only thing in life that he passionately desires, fills the whole scene with the sense of baffled purposes, of a striving that ends in nothing. " It may be," he confesses at the end, " I see decay all about me because I am, in a sense, decay. To others it may be a scene of achievement and construction radiant with hope. I, too, have a sort of hope, but it is a remote hope, a hope that finds no promise in this Empire or in any of the great things of our time. How they will look in history I do not know."[1]

And here speaks the ordinary man in his moment of introspection: in that rare moment when standing aside from the hurry and dust of it all he asks himself whence? why? and to what end? The other qualified critics of the time are scarcely less discomforting. Mr. Bernard Shaw, after devoting half his lifetime to the satirising of the advocates of order, seems determined to devote the other half to the satirising of the advocates of change. Ridicule of the hypocrisy and self-deceptions which are the permanent accompaniments of reform, is a task not only easy in itself, but exceedingly agreeable to all those to whom Reform itself is tiresome. The satirist enjoys, therefore, a widespread popularity. The portrait of the blatent Liberal phrasemonger in *John Bull's Other Island*, the failure of philanthropy and the triumph of efficiency in *Major Barbara*, the universal confusion which falls upon the new moralists

[1] *Tono-Bungay. By H. G. Wells.*

in the conversation in *Getting Married*, seems extraordinarily pleasant to all those to whom Liberal ideas
and philanthropic ardours and new moralities are
undesirable intruders in a well-regulated existence.
Only occasionally, and then through the intervention
of a " madman," does the voice of the prophet declare
" woe " to a world of blindness and illusion.   Little
Rosscullen, the Irish parallel to the remote Mon-
tenegran village, invaded by the representatives of
" Progress " is found far from any condition of idyllic
innocence.   Amid the splendour of the natural scene,
the granite rock and heather in the setting sun,
poverty, selfishness, superstition, ignorance, indifferent
cruelty compete for mastery.   The priest tyrannises
and bullies, the farmer cheats the labourer ; furtive
cunning and idleness and revengeful memories occupy
the place of the simple devotion and pastoral rejoic-
ings of the popular picture.   But the new world which
is to civilise this dreary swamp of humanity out of
existence offers to the observer food no more satisfying to the hungry heart of man.   The " Progress "
which modern life here unfolds to the medieval is a
" progress " which terminates in blind endings—the
product of the Town of Vanity.   " I shall bring
money here," is the twentieth-century promise to all
Rosscullens.   " I shall raise wages.   I shall found
public institutions, a library, a polytechnic (un-
denominational, of course), a gymnasium, a cricket
club, perhaps an art school.   I shall make a garden
city of Rosscullen.   The round tower shall be thor-
oughly repaired and restored."   To which the twelfth
century replies in an epitaph written over the graves

of many kings. " Believe me, I do every justice to
the efficiency of you and your syndicate. Mr.
Broadbent will get into Parliament most efficiently ;
which is more than St. Patrick could do if he were
alive now. You may even build the hotel efficiently,
if you can find enough efficient masons, carpenters,
and plumbers, which I rather doubt. When the
hotel becomes insolvent your English business habits
will secure the thorough efficiency of the liquidation.
You will reorganise the scheme efficiently. You
will legislate its second bankruptcy efficiently. You
will get rid of its original shareholders efficiently,
after efficiently ruining them. And you will finally
profit very efficiently by getting that hotel for a
few shillings in the pound. Besides these efficient
operations, you will foreclose your mortgages most
efficiently. You will drive Haffigan to America very
efficiently. You will find a use for Barney Doran's
foul mouth and bullying temper by employing him
to slave-drive your labourers very efficiently. And
when at last this poor desolate countryside becomes a
busy mint in which we shall all slave to make money
for you, with our Polytechnic to teach us how to do it
efficiently, and our library to fuddle the few imagina-
tions your distilleries will spare, and our repaired
Round Tower, with admission sixpence, and refresh-
ments and penny-in-the-slot mutoscopes to make it interesting, then no doubt your English and American
shareholders will spend all the money we make for
them very efficiently in shooting and hunting, in operations for cancer and appendicitis, in gluttony and
gambling ; and you will devote what they save to fresh

land-development schemes.   For four wicked centuries
the world has dreamt this foolish dream of efficiency.
And the end is not yet.   But the end will come." [1]

Which outburst, like the denunciation of the
American millionaires by the preacher whom they
pay for such services, excites no resentment, but
rather applause.   "Too true," replies Mr. Broadbent,
"only too true, and most eloquently put."   "He has
made me feel a better man," is the grateful verdict.
"I feel now as I never did before, that I am right in
devoting my life to the cause of Ireland.   Come along
and help me to choose the site for the new hotel."

Nor are the younger writers of to-day entirely free
from this infection of fatigue and of revolt against the
triumphant forces of the modern world.   In the days
of the Reaction in politics, a few were conspicuous
both for the vigour of their attacks against its falsities
and cowardices, and also for their undismayed assertion of another ideal.   Yet after that Reaction's
overthrow they seem to find little satisfaction: and
reveal in their criticism a rejection, not merely of
systems of government or worship of false gods in
modern life, but of the whole soul of a civilisation
visibly—as it appears to them—sick unto death.
Mr. Belloc—one of our few living masters of irony
—has advanced from the limited survey of "Mr.
Burden" an attack, with some kindliness and some
good nature, upon a particular phase of financial
manipulation, to the bitter and mirthless impeachment of "Mr. Clutterbuck"—an attack on modern
life itself as fundamentally a thing unclean.   Rich

[1] *John Bull's Other Island.   G. Bernard Shaw.*

men struggle for money or worldly honour as dogs fight over offal. Middle classes, vacuous in intelligence, humourless in daily existence, reveal as sole ambition, longing for wealth and rank and social advancement. Behind is a shadowy background of inert, vacant " populace," ignorant, violent, despicable, only appearing in the scene to be cajoled and deluded in popular elections. The general result is the picture of a Society afflicted with an incurable decay, a carcase eaten of maggots and worms. Mr. Chesterton, again, first entered the arena of controversy in another spirit : crashing upon the stage sword in hand, and with a breath of jolly fresh air offering to lead all humanity to the downfall of Doubting Castle. His challenge and defiance were to all pessimisms and life denials, to all who refused to affirm that to-day was the first of days, and every dawn a miracle. The slums of the cities were stupendous, the suburbs sublime. Each fat red pillar-box was a symbol of enchantment. Dragons' eyes glared from the lights of engines, and the lamp-posts shouted, like the sons of God, for joy that they were made. But to-day in our solitary and splendid optimist the rejoicing has already become sickled o'er with the pale cast of doubt. The music of his rustic flute has kept not for long its happy country tone, and has taken a stormier note from the tempest-tossed children of mankind. So the sunlight fades in the vision of a people which has abandoned Liberty, Equality, and Fraternity, of political parties bought for ignoble ends, a nation which has turned its back upon the clean ways of progress, and lies deferential and prostrate before an

16

oligarchy of rich men; who only cannot be bought because they have sold themselves already.

And in a thousand lesser ways in various efforts through industrious novelists and essayists, in the newspaper and the pulpit, there is made manifest this bewilderment, doubt, and uncertainty of the future. " Neither hast Thou saved Thy people at all," is the summary of many who hoped so much from the discoveries and progresses of the last century, and now find their hopes unexpectedly baffled. The majority of writers are in revolt against the organisation of present-day society. Some call themselves Socialists. But by " Socialist " they mean little but an impeachment of the present. With some that impeachment is definitely of certain specific and economic evils. Poverty in the midst of plenty, extravagance of wealth helpless before extravagance of penury, a growing absorption in pleasure, lack of simplicity, of patriotism, or of impersonal ideals, are the subjects which fill their pages with lamentation. There are others, however, in whom the criticism goes deeper, with whom complaint against life's ironies and injustices has passed into complaint against life itself. They can see present wrongs, but if all these wrongs were righted, they can see no rational or satisfying ideal. Level the poor to the rich, convert Poplar or Wapping into Belgravia or Mayfair, make every labourer's cottage, as by the waving of a fairy wand, into the security and splendour of the country house. What after all, they declare, have you accomplished but the conversion of a society scourged with hunger and cold into a society afflicted with a great weariness. Humanity, at last self-conscious, has understood the meaning of the World Process and will be no longer fooled by its futile, irrational demands.

What can be discovered, in this evidence of wasting and decay, of another character : of a literature which accepts the present with rejoicing, or looks through the present to a transfigured future, or sees the present itself transfigured by a perpetual benediction? Can there still be descried, under grey skies and in an age of comfort rather than of inspiration, those who still assert the reality of the Vision Splendid, and essay adventure down all the great ways of the world.

Still two voyages are being accepted : a voyage without, in the actual encounter with primitive and hostile forces, and in a universe of salt and bracing challenges ; and a voyage within, across distant horizons and to stranger countries than any visible to the actual senses. In the latter there is revealed a continuous tradition through the older mystics, of those who are secure in whatever wild whirlpools or stretches of sullen marsh the river of time may flow, because their goods are gathered

> " Where change is not, nor parting any more,
>   Nor revolution of the moon and sun."

The Reverend Thomas Treherne, in a quiet corner of seventeenth-century England, could declare that "all Time was Eternity and a perpetual Sabbath." "The corn was orient, and immortal wheat which never should be reaped, nor was ever sown. The dust and stones of the streets were as precious as

gold : the gates were at first the end of the world."
"Everything was at rest, free and immortal. I know
nothing of sickness or death, or rents or exactions,
either for tribute or bread. In the absence of these
I was entertained like an Angel with the works of
God in their splendour and glory. I saw all in the
peace of Eden."[1] A hundred years later Blake in
the dusty byways of dead cities could carry on the
tradition of those who accept and yet rejoice—perpetually charging themselves in Whitman's cheerful
proclamation with "contentment and triumph." Seeing God visibly with the naked eye, angels "with
bright angelic wings bespangling every bough with
stars" in the trees of Peckham Rye, and the sun not
as a golden guinea hung in the sky, but as a multitude of the heavenly host singing "Holy, Holy, Holy,"
this master mystic could defiantly proclaim that
"though on earth things seem permanent, they are
less permanent than a shadow, as we all know too
well." A century afterwards the tradition still abides,
and life is still illuminated by an adventure through
and beyond the sense-given impression of the outward
show, into a universe of fire and splendour. To some
it is effort towards a secret, a refusal to accept the
knowledge which is given as the last word on the
matter : an attempt to get once more behind both
science and revelation to the Quiet which lies beyond
all the noises of the world. To others it is a spiritual
pilgrimage, not so much towards knowledge as towards attainment ; an attempt through the will, in the
business of life, to identify life as a journey : along a

[1] *A Century of Meditations. Thomas Treherne.*

"road which leads to a light on the far horizon and beyond to the presence of God." In each there is an escape from a tyranny of a present offering grey streets encompassing grey people, evolving itself into a future which offers more grey streets encompassing more grey people. Against so desolate a prospect sounds the summons of high enterprise, in the affirmation of a splendour not yet revealed, of shadowy presences and casements opening upon the perilous seas of fairyland.

In the other voyage, that enterprise is offered in no shadowy region of dreams, but amid the hard and tangible materials of to-day: in that "Romance" whose habitation is everlasting, and kingdom without end. It is the inspiration of Stevenson and his successors: accepting all things, delighting in all things with the solemn engrossing play of children; living in "make-believe," knowing it make-believe, and yet not desiring to have it otherwise. "He seems to be marching through a land and atmosphere," says a critic, "where the men are strange men, and the lights are garish, and there is a queer noise of music borne upon the wind. And yet this land, for all its strangeness, is found to be the land we knew before, but seen under a new perspective, upon a more imaginative plane." He has never lacked successors: some finding in the actual adventure of so-called settled and orderly life all the amazing romance of the vicissitudes of fortune: some, like Mr. Rudyard Kipling, exhibiting just outside the ordered garden the riotous forces of natural and untameable things — the hills and the sea—calling upon man joyfully to an encounter which may be ruinous but is never dull. So there is inspiration in such a great writer as Mr. Joseph Conrad, with his sense of companionship, laughter, and fury in the defiance of wind and tempest: in a lesser example, in that "Beloved Vagabond" who discovered "why I was sent into the world. It was to play the fiddle up and down the sunny land of France."

II

But this, after all, is "make-believe" — the play of children; and children grow tired of their toys. Dressed up in gorgeous garments, marching through the world with helmet and tin sword, they may pretend that tremendous events accompany every day. If, to the majority, these tremendous events do not accompany every day, they are destined sooner or later to be found out. Lives insurgent and confined may take delight in the vision of strange countries and far horizons, just as Dick Heldar at his window looking over the lights of the enormous city is roused into a sickness of longing by the song of the "Men of the Sea." But to the general such emotions must remain a passion vicariously experienced. We must seek elsewhere for a spirit, expressing itself through literature, to which any large proportion of the citizens of the twentieth century can respond. It must be a spirit which will reveal the present as itself satisfying, apart from unknown to-morrows and dead yesterdays. It must stand independent of all attainments of political and social changes, as something by which human life will find itself ennobled, when all the old wrongs are righted and an economic basis of possible existence secured for all. It must be a spirit of joy as well as of reason: yielding exultant satisfaction in a delight which is beyond the mere momentary enjoyment of the senses in the dull instincts of thrift and gain. And it must be independent for the immediate future of supernatural securities and definite theories as to the meaning and purpose of the world. Such theories will continue, indeed, to be maintained with greater or less allegiances by large sections and organisations of the new race. These are not likely at any reckonable time to unite upon any single dominant philosophy of life, or, in union, to impose that dominant philosophy upon the people outside. For a large and probably an increasing proportion, relief from a kind of life-weariness must come from some element in the world as it is given; from renewed expression, either in response to the life of the earth, or in the fulfilment of artistic and creative powers, or in new forms of enthusiasm for their fellow-men, of the possibilities before a people which sees existence less as a pilgrimage than as a present boon.

Indications towards such a new inspiration are not lacking in Europe and America. They are found in the works of such a writer as Whitman, with his ecstasy at the "ever-returning miracle of the sunrise," the love of ferries and crowds, cities and men, and all the beauty of the world. A more exotic but still hopeful creed is that of Maeterlinck, with his delight in the white road, and the silence of the night, and the splendour of the sunset; his vision of a humanity whose hearts will grow more gentle with the weather, absorbed in persuading the earth to bring forth ever more marvellous treasures of fruit and flowers. And in England also, in such writings as those of William Morris and Richard Jefferies, there would appear a kind of foretaste of a spirit which in its acceptance and its rejoicing, may be found to build up behind the deserts of life-weariness a triumphant affirmation of the greatness of Present Things.

This exultant optimism would often seem to be entirely independent of narrow circumstance or present discouragement. "You never enjoy the world aright," says Mr. Thomas Treherne, "till you so love the beauty of enjoying it that you are covetous and earnest to persuade others to enjoy it." Most of those who in latter years of depression and grey skies have revealed themselves as "covetous and earnest to persuade others to enjoy it," have been great physical sufferers. From a life of physical torment, perhaps intensified and heightened by that torment, they have been engaged in "corroborating for ever the triumph of things." Stevenson and Henley, Whitman and Jefferies, all those who have "made to-day the first of days and this field Eden," have learnt the intoxication of present pleasure from association with present pain. "He was a very marked case of hysteria in man," was one medical verdict upon Jefferies. In the long years of torture which terminated in premature death, "in some way not yet to be explained," says his latest biographer, "the mortal pining of his body was related to the intense vivacity of his last years." "Some of my best work," he wrote, "was done in this intense agony." In the midst of which agonies he stands as typical of the company of "Life Worshippers" who, awakening while other men were asleep, could behold something of the splendour of the world, the magic of each moment as it passes, vindicating its existence before it dies.

This "Life Worship" becomes revealed as a gluttonous grasping at the present, the sucking of the rind and core of its delights; a response to the consciousness of the crowd; a refusal to accept any standard but the standard of Life, before which many impulses and all inhibitions stand judged and condemned. "I believe in the Body," is the beginning of the Creed. "I believe all manner of asceticism to be the vilest blasphemy; blasphemy towards the whole of the human race. I believe in the flesh and the body, which is worthy of worship. . . . The ascetics are the only persons that are impure." In Jefferies worship of natural things became a kind of physical avidity; intensified by a sense of touch and vision exceedingly delicate and violent. He devoured colour, finding "every spot of it a sort of food." In the later spring "the ears listen and want more," he writes: "the eyes are gratified with gazing, and desire yet further; the nostrils are filled with sweet odours of flower and sap. The touch, too, had its pleasures, dallying with leaf and flower." "Can you not almost grasp the odour-laden air," he asks, "and hold it in the hollow of the hand?" It is a riot of sense-given impression, accepting, without questioning, very content. These men are of the company who find the world "more to man since he is fallen than it was before," accepting the challenge of the mystic—"you never enjoy the world aright till the Sea itself floweth in your veins, till you are clothed with the Heavens and crowned with the Stars."

It is a pageant, the pageant of the moment which passes and yet abides, ever old and ever young. It delights in "the old road, the same flowers." It accepts the wind's whispering that "there never was a yesterday, and never will be a to-morrow." It finds "always hope in the hills." "All the grasses of the meadow were my pets," wrote Jefferies of his childhood's days. "I loved them all." Of poppies, "there is genius in them," he proclaims, "the genius of colour, and they are saved." With Thoreau he will abandon all for which most men labour to hear one cricket sing. "I found from the dandelion," he cries, "that there were no books." "The sunlight puts out the words of the printed books as it puts out the fire; the very grass blades confound the wise." To that sunlight he brings as a testing instrument all clamorous and appealing things: the hopes and dreams and perplexing ways of men. He is a worshipper of the sun, falling in the afternoon in Trafalgar Square, on the crowded Brighton promenade, in the woods of high June, or under a cold November day. He applauds it stored in the gold of the wheat or woven into the petals of the rose. "More sunshine; more flowers" is a perpetual hope for the future of mankind. For this sunshine is

life—riotous, confident, unashamed; life congruous
to and illuminating all the physical beauty of the
human body, of the world of out of doors; the life
which made him almost intoxicated with the marbles
in the British Museum, which drew him, resisting,
to the unknown city multitudes; which left him in
childhood on the downs, "utterly alone with the sun
and the earth," lost in an ecstasy, an inflatus at "the
inexpressible beauty of it all."

And as "Life Worship" approves, it also condemns;
all energies directed towards blind alleys, burrowings
underground; all that is unable to encounter with
exultation the test of that strong stimulus and fever.
It rebels always against the mechanic pacing to and
fro; the set grey life; the apathetic end.   Its vision
of modern England is of the man with the muck-
rake, ever being offered the golden crown, ever
assiduously and with downcast eyes raking together
the sticks and small stones and the dust of the floor.
"The pageantry of power," says Jefferies, "the still
more foolish pageantry of wealth; the senseless
precedence of place; words fail me to express my
utter contempt for such pleasure or such ambitions."
He is dissatisfied that life for the general is "so little
and so mean." "Back to the sun" he is always
preaching, from "house life"—"house life" which he
denounces as the creed of the half-alive. "Remain;
be content; go round and round in one barren path,
a little money, a little food and sleep, some ancient
fables, old age, and death."   As a mystic he belongs
to the class of those who aspire, rather than of those
who acquiesce. These are never in danger of becom-

ing quietists. Rejoicing in the moment, they are never content with the moment, demanding always that which the moment, with all its rich benefits, can never bestow. They ask "for a larger frame, a longer day, more sunshine, a longer sleep." They rise from the banquet of life never satisfied, encouraging illimitable desires. Longing—an invalid —for "the unwearied strength of Ninus to hunt unceasingly in the fierce sun," "still I should desire greater strength and a stouter bow," cries Jefferies; "wilder creatures to combat." "The intense life of the senses," he asserts, "there is never enough of them." "I should like to be loved by every beautiful woman on earth." Meat and bread he finds pleasant and wine refreshing, but "these are the least of all." He has never had enough of the vehemence of exertion, the vehemence of sunlight and life, the insatiate desire of love, divine and beautiful, the uncontrollable desire of beauty. "Give me these in greater abundance," he prays, "than was ever known to man or woman." It is the prayer of a cripple, in poverty and pain, stricken down ere the journey has well-nigh begun; so soon to pass to where all journeys end.[1]

And what they desire for themselves they come to desire also for all companions, as they march singing down the great roads of the universe. It is a life which will transfer no affections to some problematical future, but here and now will riot and rejoice in the glory of the sum of things. Jefferies was perplexed and saddened by the confusion that man has made of his world. "In twelve thousand written years the

[1] See *The Story of My Heart. By Richard Jefferies.*

world has not yet built itself a House, nor filled a Granary, nor organised itself for its own comfort. It is so marvellous I cannot express the wonder with which it fills me." Yet he believes that there would be enough for all, if only all were willing to share it. He brushes aside the ordinary ambitions which inflame mankind: "money, furniture, affected show, and the pageantry of wealth." He longs for the coming of a day when the ambition of the multitude will be fixed on the idea of form and beauty. "I would submit to a severe discipline," he declares, "and to go without many things cheerfully, for the good and happiness of the human race in the future." "The labour of our predecessors in this country, in all other countries of the earth, is entirely wasted. We live—that is, we snatch an existence—and our works become nothing. The piling up of fortunes, the building of cities, the establishment of immense commerce, end in a cipher. These objects are so outside my idea that I cannot understand them, and look upon the struggle in amazement. Not even the pressure of poverty can force upon me an understanding of, and sympathy with, these things." But he does not despair of the future. "Earth," he asserts in *The Pageant of Summer*, "holds secrets enough to give them the life of the favoured immortals." His heart was fixed firm and stable in the belief that "ultimately the sunshine and the summer, the flowers and the azure sky, shall become, as it were, interwoven into man's existence." "There is so much for us yet to come," he believes, "so much to be gathered and enjoyed."

So these writers can look towards the future with hope. Their visions and Utopias do not end in a sense of dust and ashes—an infinite weariness. The cities ever growing higher of M. Anatole France, in the heart of which men pile up wealth on a diet of sour milk and digestive tablets, the fat, settled comfort of Mr. Bellamy, the roofed-in labyrinthine airless ant-heaps of Mr. Wells's nightmare all leave an impression of emptiness and fatigue. But here is the sense of an inspiration and splendour which could become part of the common life of humanity. Nor does this splendour require, as in former appeals in literature, assumptions which the modern world is finding impossible. Wordsworth offered an escape from the tyrannies of a mechanical civilisation, in an exaltation of the appeal of Nature and of the life of the poor. But he demanded for his acceptance assumptions concerning both Nature and the Poor which men to-day are by no means prepared to give. He found the one charged with a spiritual presence, the other transformed by unusual tranquillity and piety. Not through such assumptions will society, in the immediate years to come, find the satisfaction which is the goal of all its wandering. There is more hope in the way of the Life Worshippers like Jefferies than of the Nature Worshippers like Wordsworth. Wordsworth assumes a Nature benignant and responsive, a spirit whose dwelling is the light of setting suns and in the mind of man. The result is a kind of refined and sometimes too rarefied Pantheism, which is compelled often to shut its eyes to the Nature which is "red in tooth and claw,"

and equally bestows increase and destruction.
Jefferies wove from his dawns and sunsets no roseate
scheme of natural religion. He acknowledged the
"blunt cruelty" of natural things. He always confessed no intelligence in human affairs : outside, a
Nature not so much hostile as utterly indifferent to
all the ardours of mankind. " The sea, the earth, the
sun, the trees, the hills, care nothing for human life."
He had no specific "humanitarian" teaching, and in
early days delighted in the work of devastation and
of slaughter. He was bored by the claims of science,
and thought nothing of the jargon of " Evolution."
The strength of his position rests in his association
of these realities with the overmastering "passion of
life." To him it was an adventure always, into a
region of fairyland, occupied as to another modern
mystic with "dust like the wreck of temples and
thistle-down like the ruin of stars." His strength
was in himself. It was from that hidden, mysterious
source of vitality that the colours appeared which he
sought in field and flower, that rain of fairy gold
which flung itself over the common things until every
bush was burning with fire. He did not find a
Presence which disturbed with the joy of elevating
thoughts. He found a Glamour—inimitable, inexplicable — which excited to passionate emotion.
Others have demanded Order, Understanding,
evidence of Purpose or Compassion. He asked only
for Beauty. And that Beauty is not denied to the
supplicant. The Seasons pass in their procession ;
Birth and Death weave their webs of being ; men are
seeking, and in vain, for sympathy and pity behind

the veil of visible things. Enough for him that here the sunlight flickering on the stems of old trees, the sap creeping up through a million tiny stems, the changes of expanding petals and of withered autumn leaves, can reveal a magic and a mystery which time shall never dim nor age destroy.

This unquestioning love of the Earth and the children of it is perhaps the most hopeful element for future progress. In a century of doubts and scepticisms it may serve to bridge the gulf between the old and the new. Whilst men are still confused concerning the purposes of Nature, and still doubtful concerning any definite or intelligent progress towards a final end, it is much that inspiration and contentment can be found in its present beauty and appeal. The "glory of the sum of things" may thus come to be interpreted in some particular sense-given experience, untroubled—in that present—by inquiry concerning a past that is dead or a future that is not yet born. Forgetful of the cold of a vanished winter, and of the inevitable fading of the flowers, man can accept the summer day, from dawn to sunset, as an "Eternal moment," something that is good in itself apart from remembrance of what has been or anticipation of what shall be. And if this acquiescence and enjoyment be supplemented by the recreation of a creative energy, in that special happiness which comes from the fashioning by human handiwork of things of delight, the possibilities of an inspiration can be discerned which even for a time, putting aside occupation in ultimate mysteries, may "bring satisfaction to the ways of men."

The demand for more and fuller life, which attempts in empty effort, in acceleration, in sense-given pleasure, in the mere blind and laborious effort at the attainment of wealth, may be here pictured as realising itself in no material or brutal fashion, through an experience which itself is its own justification. In such a life as that of William Morris there is the suggestion of a possibility of progress, more satisfying and at the same time more hopeful than Mill's refuge in transcendental poetry.   It is an advance on Jefferies because more determined and alive: more positive in its proclamation of life's good things.   It is the artist as craftsman on the one hand, as lover of the earth on the other, who appears typical of the best that can be expected in a world which has abandoned adventure beyond the sense - given universe.   His Socialism indeed led him amongst strange companions and into mean unlovely regions of the Newer England. But this Socialism was just the emotional revolt against all the multitudinous ugliness and captivity and starved limited life of those whose life could have been a thing so different.   The very thing that seemed to be intolerable, in a society which called itself a civilisation, was that the variable, fascinating aspects of a changing year should proclaim its appeal on wall and garden, and mankind pass by, with blind uncomprehending gaze, in a pursuit after irrelevant things; and that in the industry of a whole race of men engaged in extravagant toil, there should be absent from that toil the delight in inventiveness and original handwork which alone can convert labour into a joy.   His first allies had

17

been absorbed in the effort at escape: through Rossetti's exotic twilight, or Burne Jones's radiant visions of a world beyond the world. He also had sought the consolation which comes from far-off places, in a medieval England seen under a light which never was on sea or land. He drew from this passion of the past the best that the past could give; a sharp sense of the good things which are still offered to a world of children living always in fairyland: untroubled by present doubts and future fears. "With him," says his biographer, "the love of things had all the romance and passion that is generally associated with the love of persons only." "It has come to be to me," he wrote in 1882, of the Manor House at Kelmscott, "the type of the pleasant places of the earth, and of the homes of harmless, simple people, not overburdened with the intricacies of life. And as others love the race of men through their lovers, so I love the earth through that small space of it."

"Children we twain are," he could write of himself and his book, "late made wise in love, but in all else most childish still." Loving the earth and the joy of it, seeking still the pleasure of the eyes, exulting in its visible beauty, the waters gliding through the Hollow Land where the hills are blue, a walled garden in the happy poplar land, with old grey stones over which red apples shone "at the right time of the year" he could always cherish the hope that "our small corner of the world may once again become beautiful and dramatic withal": because the red apples and grey

stones and blue hills were possessions which required for their acceptance no impossible extension
of present human achievement.   In his vision of
satisfaction "now it is a picture of some great room
full of merriment," says a critic, "now of the wine-
press, now of the golden threshing-floor, now of an
old mill among apple trees, now of cool water after
heat of the sun, now of some well-sheltered, well-
tilled place among woods or mountains, where men
and women live happily, knowing of nothing that
is too far off or too great for the affections."   The
one cloud in the landscape comes from the knowledge that it will change and vanish: that, behind,
are always the hurrying of the inexorable hours
and the beating of the great wings of Death.   But
if the transitoriness of love and beauty causes some
pang of sadness, the intensity of it is deepened
by this conviction of its passing.   The shadow
creeping slowly over the dial, the vision of bare
November with its ruined choirs in the splendour
of the August afternoon, can excite a longing wild
with all regret.   But they can excite also an ever-
deepening exultation in Beauty all the more desirable
because it is "Beauty that must die"; and a passion
for the love and labour of the day because so soon "the
night cometh," when all love and labour are done.

Such are indications of a possible escape from a
literature that appears in the bulk in active warfare
against "progress," as the word is understood in
twentieth - century England.   The critics and the
novelists, no less than the poets, would seem to

have deserved Plato's rigorous sentence of expulsion from a civilisation against which they are openly at war. They cry pitifully or passionately over the huge ant-heap of modern industry, "What shall it profit?" Those who listen to their crying will probably drop under in the struggle, from mere inability—when the choice is offered—to fashion any intelligible goal of attainment. They exhibit progress making inevitable more men, but by no means better men. They demonstrate, as with the physical accuracy of the dissector's scalpel, the same selfishnesses and superstitions and weaknesses and impulses of lust and cowardice and greed, multiplying to-day as yesterday. They reveal in the few, as conspicuously as in the many, life directed by prejudice rather than by reason, arrogance and avarice and blindness exercising their ancient empire. They ask sometimes with impatience, sometimes with deliberation, if this be the final word in the matter: if the desirable things which are possible to human experience are always to be sacrificed to Accumulation or Acceleration, or a joyless extravagance, or (at the bottom) a mere animal struggle for food and shelter. And Civilisation, in reply to these "Anarchists," speaks with voice less certain than in former days; being itself perplexed why, after the long journey has been attempted and all the miracle achieved, it cannot at last see clearly on the horizon the walls and towers of the Golden City of men's dreams.

CHAPTER IX

RELIGION AND PROGRESS

LITERATURE—at its highest estimate—is, however, only the luxury of the few. It influences a strictly limited class. It is produced by a still more limited class. It is so little operative upon the general life of the nation that its very claim to be considered in a survey of the "Condition of England" is doubtful. The published writings which in the least degree influence the life and opinion of the majority are the published writings not of the present but of the past. In so far as such existence occupies itself with anything beyond the newspapers or the sensational and generally excellent cheap fiction of the day, it is with the "World's Classics," or the reprints of established authors, which now are so plentifully provided in portable form by the various contemporary publishers. Whatever evidence of weariness or revolt may be exhibited by the tiny group of practising authors makes no impression upon the contented, boisterous spirit of Middle Class England; which is inclined to attribute all such criticism to a temper soured by disappointment or a disordered digestion. And below such classes lie the huge and

inarticulate multitudes of the city people, who find
what spiritual and emotional satisfactions " literature "
can bring in the journals and popular writings
which they consume with ever-increasing avidity.
They seek romance—and find it—in a complex
murder case, in stories of crime which seem to
the fastidious sordid and disgusting, in stories
dependent in their appeal upon sudden vicissitudes
of fortune, in which chance or resolution are always
breaking down the insupportable sequences of
cause and effect.   That a man shall reap as he
has sown, that to-morrow shall be as yesterday,
that inevitable law shall bind and control the
revolt of human passion against circumstance—
these are the affirmations of moralist and philosopher against which the popular spirit is in
continual rebellion.   Rebellion will endure so
long as the human will affirms itself free, and
passion can draw its inspiration from some fire
beyond the boundaries of the world.   That fire
descends in the Divine fury of all revolutions;
which burn up and suddenly consume the civilisation which has become orderly and comfortable and
weary of it all.   It descends also when to some
remote obscure human being, set in the enormous
city, life suddenly acquires significance and high meaning, in utter devotion to a person or a cause.

To such the optimism and rejoicing of Jefferies
or Morris is as much an enigma as the questionings
and denials of Mr. Thomas Hardy or Mr. Bernard
Shaw.   They experience no exultation in Nature
because they are cut off from the experience of

Nature. They are untroubled by the question of
the goal of the industrial process because their
own particular part in it—the daily labour, the
maintenance of the home, the occasional recreation
of Saturday Sport or Sunday Excursion—absorbs
all their available energies. " In June 1902," says
Mr. Ensor, " the writer piloted four crippled workmen from a working-class district in Manchester
about some grounds on the edge of the suburbs,
and put to them a practical flower catechism.
Three of them, be it noted, had, before the events
which left them cripples, enjoyed high wages and
relative prosperity. None of them knew or could
name forget-me-nots, daisies, dandelions, clover,
pansies, or lilies of the valley, three of them were
baffled by a poppy, the fourth felt confident that
it was 'a rose.'"[1] Of what avail, to such a company,
to proclaim the exultation of the pageant of
Summer, or the joy in old walled gardens under
the apple trees "at the right time of the year."
And the crowd which grows delirious over the
spectacle of the football contests, and frankly sets
itself to enjoyment, in its own jolly fashion, in the
Election scrimmage or on an August Bank
Holiday, is not likely to find either inspiration or
sadness in the problem of what is to be the fate
of the human race when economic stability is finally
secured.

Among all of these—and they comprise in all
classes the overwhelming majority—the place of a
Philosophy or a Literature must be taken by a Religion.

[1] *England a Nation.*

And the question of the survival of a Religion—in the most liberal interpretation of the term—is the question of the survival of any extra-material ideal in the civilisation of the twentieth century. In this, the last of our researches into "the Condition of England," generalisation is more than ever difficult. Religions which appear dead are so often discovered to be only sleeping, variations in faiths and devotions are so frequent between youth and age, a dark fortune and a bright, that it is quite impossible to accept any mere superficial demonstration of development or decay. Statistics of church-going, varying from generation to generation, such as those of a recent census in London, may indicate a fluctuation in faith, or an alteration in social custom. Impressions of individual observers, such as the researches of Mr. Charles Booth and his assistants into the religious life of the Capital, may at the best be the impressions gathered from various separated workers set in the midst of silent untestifying millions. In every age the sterner moralist has proclaimed a national apostasy, and witnessed with astonishment a world repudiating its ancient pieties. In every age the prophecy of immediate collapse has been falsified by the events of history. More than a hundred and fifty years ago the least sensational of all great Christian apologists declared that in England "it is come, I know not how, to be taken for granted that Christianity is not so much a subject for inquiry, but that it is now at length discovered to be fictitious." "And accordingly," he continues in famous words, "they treat it as if, in the present age, this was an agreed point amongst all people of discernment; and

nothing remained but to set it up as a principal subject of mirth and ridicule as it were, by way of reprisals
for its having so long interrupted the pleasures of
the world." Yet the "pleasures of the world" find
themselves still interrupted by a faith which, with
its grave dug and its epitaph set up, unexpectedly
refuses to expire. Any variation or section of it,
whose end has been confidently predicted, will
suddenly flare up again into violent life and upset all
the calculations of its undertakers. In 1830 "the
acutest characters of the time," says Mr. Wilfred
Ward, "considered that the Church of England was
on its death-bed." "It was folding its robes," was
Mozley's verdict, "to die with what decency it could."
"The Church as it now stands," wrote Arnold, "no
human power could save." But to-day on any impartial judgment the "Established Church" whatever
gains or losses it may have received in the long struggle
with indifference and unbelief, would never be
threatened with any such suggestions of immediate
destruction. Sidney Smith in 1827 could plead for
toleration to Roman Catholics not because they were
strong but because they were weak. The power
of the Papacy was obviously a dead thing, in the
future so conspicuously to become impotent, that
he could exhort his fellow-countrymen to some
charity towards a forlorn and piteous supplicant.
"There is no Court of Rome," he could assert,
"and no Pope. There is a waxwork Pope and a
waxwork Court of Rome. Popes of flesh and blood
have long since disappeared. The follies of one
century," he proclaimed, "are scarcely credible to

that which succeeds it ; what will be said of all the intolerable trash which is issued forth at public meetings of ' No Popery ' ?   If the world lasts till 1927, this childish nonsense will have got out of the drawing-room and passed through the butler's pantry into the kitchen."   " If the world lasts till 1927," there will probably be still orators of " No Popery," and scornful critics of the same.   But he would be a rash prophet to-day who would endorse Sidney Smith's argument for toleration of a Pope and Court of Rome as being " waxworks," when these " waxworks " have revealed themselves, in the interval, so amazingly alive.

Yet I think there can be no doubt that apart from any questions of future revival, present belief in religion, as a conception of life dependent upon supernatural sanctions or as a revelation of a purpose and meaning beyond the actual business of the day, is slowly but steadily fading from the modern city race. Tolerance, kindliness, sympathy, civilisation continually improve.   Affirmation of any responsibility, beyond that to self and to humanity, continually declines.   Life therefore gradually ceases to be influenced or coloured by any atmosphere of " other worldliness."   Present disabilities find no compensation in the hope of a future redress, which makes the present endurable.   The general standard of humanitarian sentiment is probably higher in the cities than ever before, certainly exhibiting immense advance from that in the rude squalid barbarism of the submerged eighteenth-century life, or the vast penury and discontent of the early nineteenth.   But a " background " was implied or assumed practically by the

whole population, in these troublous days. Men
lived as the beasts, and as the beasts perished. Yet
few of them would have definitely denied that there
existed a Creator and there awaited for them a
judgment. The " Atheist " was as unpopular a figure
as the Republican ; and the sacking of the house of
a " Unitarian " as congenial an occupation as a " No
Popery" riot. To-day that " background" has vanished.
The Churches are extraordinarily active, endeavouring in this way and in that to influence the lives of
the people. Their humanitarian and social efforts are
widely appreciated. Their definite dogmatic teach-
ings seem to count for little at all. They labour on
steadily amid a huge indifference. The very material
of their appeal is vanishing. Fear which is the beginning of wisdom no longer terrifies a society which
sees orderly arrangements everywhere accepting the
secure as the normal. It cannot believe that, even
if any future world exists at all—of which existence
it is becoming increasingly doubtful—that future
world will not in essence re-establish the decencies and
commonplaces of the modern city state. There is
less material therefore to-day for the appeal—to the
general—of the revivalist preacher, with which Wesley
and Whitefield changed the face of eighteenth-century
England. The fleeing from the city of Destruction,
the crying out against the "burden" of sin, the
vision of the flames of hell flaring close to the
Celestial City, represent an apparatus of experience
that is alien to the present. " Religion," was Dolling's
testimony from Poplar, " has, so to speak, gone to
pieces. There is no opposition. We do not care

enough to oppose.   God is not in any of our thoughts :
we do not even fear Him.   We face death with perfect
composure, for we have nothing to give up and nothing to look forward to.   Heaven has no attraction,
because we should be out of place there.   And Hell
has no terrors."

And although this fading of the background is
perhaps less manifest in country than in town, and
less in the industrial provinces than in the capital, its
effect can be apprehended amongst all classes of the
community and throughout the whole of the modern
world.   The meaning is gone from phrases which
are still repeated, whose significance is becoming
historical merely.   The tide is ebbing within and
without the Churches.   The drift is towards a
non-dogmatic affirmation of general kindliness and
good fellowship, with an emphasis rather on the
service of men than the fulfilment of the will of
God.   Most modern activities of the great religious
bodies are coming more and more to enlarge themselves into efforts towards social or humanitarian
reforms.   Even the noisy warfare between the
various denominations may be interpreted less as a
sign of secure vitality than as evidence of uncertain
position ; a struggle excited less by confidence than
by foreboding.   Whirlpools of brave and often
feverish energy are maintained amid the prevailing indifference.   The children are everywhere persuaded
to attend the centres of religious teaching ; everywhere, as they struggle to manhood and womanhood
in a world of such doubtful certainties, they exhibit a
large falling away.   The sternness and severity and

compelling claims of the ancient injunctions to repentance and an ordered life become replaced by a general sense of vague and misty optimism, in which the former beliefs are less definitely denied than put aside as negligible and irrelevant to the business of the day. "The great bulk," is one general verdict of Mr. Booth's investigation, "seem to be incapable of attaining to that pressing sense of sin which is the common basis not only of these but of most other forms of Christian teaching." "Those who have any definite convictions," testifies a hospital chaplain, "are few and far between : they have for the most part put religion deliberately out of their lives, and dislike to be reminded of it." Another observer finds "a very great variety of aim, but an almost universal sense of disappointment." "All have empty churches," is the sweeping verdict over one large industrial borough, "and the general attitude of the people is that of complete indifference." "Those of the poor who attend religious services," is another general verdict, "are mostly bought." "They take their religion lightly," is perhaps the final word upon twentieth-century England, "and are much inclined to believe that it will all come right in the end." [1]

These changes amongst the wealthy and prosperous are perhaps negligible ; because—with of course many exceptions—in no society have "they that have riches" ever entered but hardly into the kingdom of any God. But among the Middle Classes—the centre and historical support of England's Protestant creed—

[1] *Life and Labour of the People. Religious Influences.*

the drift away is acknowledged by all to be conspicuous—by friend as well as by enemy. The
country is here following the town; and amongst
the industrial people the prophecy of Taine thirty
years ago would appear to be fulfilling itself
to-day: "By an insensible and slow backward
movement, the great rural mass, like the great urban
mass, is gradually going back to Paganism."

It is a European movement, conspicuous even to
the superficial observer. At intervals there are
efforts at diagnosis, even random efforts at cure.
Missions and revivals produce transitory tides invigorating the older faiths—like the Catholic reaction
in France after the disasters of 1870, or the rise of
the Salvation Army a little later in the great towns
of England. Despite such rallies, however, the
process continues. It continues without violence,
continuously, steadily, as a kind of impersonal
motion of secular change. It is the passing of a
whole civilisation away from the faith in which it
was founded and out of which it has been fashioned.
Mr. Hueffer, in his *Spirit of the People*, tells the story
of a neighbour who after a late evening service in the
village church suddenly discovered that he no longer
believed in the immortality of the soul. And that is
typical of the change in the world of to-day. It is not
becoming atheist. It is ceasing to believe, without
being conscious of the process, until it suddenly
wakes up to the fact that the process is complete.

Most attempted explanations fall into the quite
natural error of ascribing the indifference towards
the enterprise of the Churches of the English city

populations to those particular elements of their teaching or action which they regard as pernicious. In examination of these mysterious multitudes which have collected in the new towns it is always possible to find anything that one desires—drunkenness and temperance, happiness and misery, aspiration and indifference, cowardice and courage. This is specially true when the observer seeks to penetrate beneath the surface and to examine the actual spiritual beliefs and apprehensions accepted by large masses of men whose thoughts on such subjects are never clearly expressed. A few years ago a number of the religious leaders of this country collected in a symposium their explanation of this change.[1] And the replies are very characteristic in their reference of causes to things which are disliked or denied. Dr. Horton, from his study at Hampstead, opines that drink is the chief cause of the indifference to Christianity of the working classes. He would add also absence of good preaching. He judges from the crowds which come to hear the good preacher, that preachers of similar power would draw similar crowds beneath every pulpit. But it is just as possible, and perhaps more demonstrable by experience, that the good preacher only attracts the preacher-loving class from the bad preachers, without substantially recruiting the class from the indifferent outside. The water is decanted from bottle to bottle without increasing its bulk. And drink certainly does not separate from religion the Scotch or Irish in their own land, or the Irish in

[1] *Christianity and the Working Classes*, edited by George Haw.

the great cities of England and America. Nor is there any particular reason why drunkenness should exercise a more general estrangement than the other, more respectable of the deadly sins. Mr. Silas Hocking, again, dislikes war and sacerdotalism. He therefore announces that the Church's alliance with war and sacerdotalism are the cause of the modern falling away from religion. But the Church and war have lived in some condition of mutual tolerance for nineteen centuries. And as in his vision Christianity practically ceased to exist, "since in the early centuries it became corrupted by paganism," we may assume that here also some friendly agreement had been possible beforetime, which might not be impossible to-day.

Many social reformers very frequently ascribe the abandonment of the churches by the working classes to the fact that the Church has been the Church of a class, filled with respectabilities and caste distinctions, and hostile to the newer movements for the collective welfare of labour. Such reformers, that is to say, eagerly desire that the Church should abandon the stiff and formal ways of its class traditions, should become more friendly and universal in its appeal, and should concern itself actively and intelligently with the problems of poverty and social discontent. But it would seem impossible to assume that such a transformation of organised Christianity would bring back the people to the spiritual affirmation of their fathers. Letters frequently appear in the newspapers, alike pathetic and passionate, from those who have been sweated by "Christian ' employers, or have been offended by hearing clergymen openly supporting " wars of aggression " or opposing the franchise and free libraries.   But there is no evidence—because in the nature of things such evidence cannot be forthcoming—to prove that the correspondents or the crowd represented by them would be accepting the enormous affirmations of Theism or of Christianity if all these things were suddenly changed.

Again, many good men have perhaps too fatuously discovered and proclaimed that there is " no hostility to Christ" amongst the working men.   One observer in the symposium above quoted can find satisfaction in the fact that a crowd of men flung up their caps and cheered His name on Tower Hill.   " Such straws show which way the wind blows."   Such "straws" show nothing more than any noise and excitement have shown since the day of the riding into Jerusalem, or the scene in the Judgment Hall of Pilate.   Why should any one to-day be " hostile to Christ"?   And what relationship has such vague toleration or applause to anything in the nature of a vital and compelling faith?   All such sentiment belongs to the same class as that of the comfortable householder, leading a life of respectable and benignant self-indulgence, who will inform you in a burst of confidence that his religion is that of the " Sermon on the Mount," or one " of willingness to do good."   There is no more common illusion than the interpretation of ethical judgment as spiritual affirmation.   To all such advocates of an inexacting standard Christianity appears as a rule of common life, which has been somehow evaded or destroyed.   But

18

Christianity is something widely different from a rule of common life. It is a creed, not a system of morals. Religion is an attempt at some ultimate assertion concerning the being and purpose of the world. No tolerance of the virtues specifically Christian or admiration of a life lost in the distant centuries can guarantee that creed's validity, or restore a faith which appears to be slipping over the visible horizon of mankind.

There is morality without faith ; kindliness and devotion with no "consciousness of a divine inheritance or of the sin by which it is lost." Such is the testimony of Canon Barrett, from thirty years' experience of every class in English society. The people of East London especially are better mannered, better dressed, more respectable, more sober than the people of a previous generation. But they have " less idealism," " less superstition." " Joy " is in consequence lacking. Life is more respectable, less vivid. The salt of life is somehow losing its savour. Whatever scale of value is represented by the outlook upon larger spiritual kingdoms is vanishing. And the scale is in consequence contracting, truncated. " The desertion of the churches and the somewhat undignified efforts of the churches to attract congregations are equally the outward signs of spiritual failing."

Here is the kernel of the whole matter. Ethical advance is accompanied (as it seems) by spiritual decline. It was the process which so perplexed Mr. Gladstone more than half a century ago. Growth of morality is coincident with decline in religion.   Violent controversialists still endeavour to demonstrate the opposite, exhibiting murders, thefts, and adulteries accompanying the introduction of secular education or the disestablishment of a Church.   On a large survey the facts do not bear such an interpretation.   The work of civilisation steadily advances.   The vision of a universe beyond or behind the material steadily fades.

My effort here is confined to diagnosis, not prophecy. And prophecy concerning religion is of all forecasts the most impossible.   For never is it safe to assume that any piece of solid ground may not suddenly flare and tremble, or any common bush commence to burn with fire.   Remembering the historic failures in similar ages of rationalism, the contemptuous dismissal by Tacitus, in a kind of footnote, of the faith which was to transform the world, he would be rash who asserted that even to-day and in this secure civilisation there may not be the seed growing which will survive when this very society shall have vanished from the earth.   My own belief is that the so-called intellectual difficulties of belief are to-day less operative amongst the masses of mankind than certain other changes which are powerful in modern life.   I should put in the forefront of these the creation of the towns, with their machinery and their confusion; the condition of labour within their boundaries; and the establishment of security and order in the present "Roman Peace" which has come upon the western races of Europe.   The result, as Dolling saw it amongst his people in East London, is a life universally dull, decorous, decent. Nor can we estimate what developments may originate from such a condition of uniform comfort and acquiescence. General Booth in his Salvation Army, the most remarkable spiritual product of the present age, has shown how the inspiration may come in a sudden flaming up of the incalculable elements of the soul of man, amongst seemingly drab and unimportant people; with a craving for self-immolation, and the intrusion into commonplace accepted ways of the vision of blood and fire. The fruit and duration of such a state are equally difficult to foresee. Sidgwick concluded at the end of his days that "humanity would never acquiesce in a godless world." "If they do abolish God from their poor bewildered hearts," was Carlyle's fierce comment, "all or most of them, there will be seen for some length of time, perhaps for several centuries, such a world as few are dreaming of." The first experiment on a large scale of society organised on a positive basis came to a premature end: through the intrusion of Christianity and the advent of the barbarian. The second seems about to be established. It should prove an interesting study to any observer possessing the felicity of seeing alike its commencement and its close. But it is not impossible that the same two disturbing elements — the advent of the barbarian, intrusion of Christianity — may once again prevent the realisation, upon adequate scale and through any substantial period, of life seeking comfort in a rational society.

CHAPTER X

THE ILLUSION OF SECURITY

SUCH—in briefest outline—is the England which confronts the challenge of a new century. It represents a civilisation containing many of the elements of human welfare, and enjoying a widespread happiness and personal comfort. Such comfort appears as somewhat unjustly divided between class and class. A main body of adequately rewarded and generally satisfied workers are set between the unnaturally wealthy on the one side, on the other the unnaturally poor. The superficial appearance is of a "plutocracy" with riches extravagantly accumulated and extravagantly expended; a middle class industrious and a little bewildered; a labouring population industrious, and in times of prosperity contented; below, a life which cries almost unheeded from a condition of perpetual privation. In all cases prosperity has brought some especial dangers: a weakening of the willingness to work, a rejection of earlier simplicities, a too eager absorption in pleasure. Representatives of the rich, from the security and ignorance of the country house and the country-house outlook upon society, bring charges against the working man: of loafing and neglecting his labour; of betting, drinking, and idling; of organising trades unions as a tyranny on the "ca' canny" principle, designed to restrain the honest toiler from giving a fair day's labour for a fair wage. Representatives of the working people, on the other hand, inflamed to bitterness by the wretchedness and degradation of those who endure an animal life in the abyss, bring a fierce indictment against the wealthy: of luxurious living, of callous indifference to the wrongs they see around them, of the contented plundering of the poor. The fact is that each class, in its several station, has pretty much the same characteristics, impulses, desires. If the poor were suddenly made rich, in a short space of time the majority would find themselves able to enjoy super-fluous dinners, artificially created pleasures, and the satisfaction of an abundant life, without any sharp sense of judgment and condemnation in the know-ledge of the huge misery that accompanies all this waste. If the rich were suddenly made poor they would soon be forcing their children to leave school prematurely in order to earn wages at mean occupations, would be organising themselves into "tyrannous" trades unions, would be mitigating the monotony of their lives by the excitement of a shilling on a horse or the encouragement of alcoholic stimulation. Dives and Lazarus may some day experience that kaleidoscopic change which has been dear to the heart of the discontented in all ages: a reversal of the accepted social order in a poor man's Paradise. A very short time afterwards the child of Lazarus would be found faring sumptuously every day; indifferent to the descendant of Dives, lying at his gate, impotent, full of sores.

The observer will therefore not be greatly affected, in his choice of advocacy and action, by the particular arguments and appeals which may be advanced for the one side or the other. He sees a literature which vindicates an unequal distribution of wealth, in the necessity for leisure and a secured comfort for a certain proportion of the people, if there is to survive an amenity of manners, a cultivation of the arts, the traditions of a governing class. He sees a literature which stretches gaunt fingers over the costly clothes and furniture, and exhibits upon them the stains of blood. No reasoned or intellectual appeal will compel him to accept the one side or the other, to appear as the advocate of order or the advocate of change. Instinct, sentiment, temperament, upbringing in the case of the many; in the case of the few, a deliberate effort of the will, without much intellectual justification, and certainly as no nicely balanced adjustment of alternative, will direct statesmen or publicist to-day to choose the side of the rich or the side of the poor.

Among the many it is of little importance to any one but the individual which side is chosen. What is of importance is that, the choice being made, each man should see things clearly; should " clear himself of cant "; should realise that he is a soldier fighting for a cause, to be deflected from his purpose by no weakness and no vacillation. Whatever the future may bring, to him the matter of vital moment is that he should refuse to betray under any temptation those who have trusted him with their allegiance.

The reformers who have enrolled themselves with the advocates of change must not expect too speedily to realise even an appreciable percentage of their aims. Most men, setting out to move the mountain, will be content at the end if they have made some impression on the molehill. The divergence between the roseate vision of the ideal and the hard effort of practical affairs is a divergence which sometimes excites impatience and sometimes awakens suspicion of lethargy and compromise. Yet in a settled society, such as that of England to-day, where the overwhelming forces of the community are against any too sudden dislocation, we may be very content if some visible improvement can be estimated in a year or a decade. The forlorn and tattered flag "Work or Revolt," flapping dejectedly over a procession of the ineffectual unemployed, is more scornful and cruel in dissociation of promise and performance than any attack from outside. It exhibits a challenge to the forces of this country by those who would be mown down like sheep or massacred like flies if they gave any real trouble or excited any real anxiety amongst the governing classes of England.

And this "security" is exceedingly strengthened by the inability of the majority of mankind to picture any life but the life that they have always known. The defiance of the future by the present—the insistence of hard, tangible things against a kingdom of dreams and speculations—is a defiance too often forgotten by those who are impatient of the slow processes of change. They see evil to be overcome, visions of clearer horizons and a fairer dawn. They cannot understand why mankind round them—equally intelligent, equally pitiful—do not find their feet marching to the same militant melody. They fail to apprehend rightly the crushing effect of the present, especially as embodied in solid, material realities, upon the minds of the majority. To these, history is but a misty panorama of uncertain meaning, geography a story of things wonderful and strange, but remote and negligible. Here is the real world : the houses of commerce, four-square, of stone, ample Government offices, law courts, police stations, secure private dwellings. " Let him change it who can," their innermost souls declare, in a declaration which actually signifies, " It never will be changed at all." By the many, of all classes, the affirmation of the Psalmist would be readily re-echoed,—" He has held the round world so fast, that it cannot be moved at any time." Inhabitants of the earthquake zones are always convinced that each successive tremor will be the last tremor, that now, at length, the old earth, after a final shaking, has settled down to sleep. And the same is true of the shaking of the children of earth—the call, sounding to the nations in succeeding centuries, which has shattered custom, convention, security, and all the accepted ways. Each revolution is always the last revolution, the final effort of a violence which has expired in this ultimate convulsion. Now, at last, and after all the centuries, mankind is to be allowed to " settle down " in reasonable comfort to accept and to enjoy.

This tyranny of the present upon the imagination,

is perhaps the greatest of all obstacles to reform. It is not only that the inhabitants of London cannot picture what London was when the Abbey of Westminster stood up white from green gardens, and over the river where now dwell two millions of persons the roads ran on causeways through sullen marshes lit by will-o'-the-wisps and fever fires. It is that they are unable even to imagine a time when Cadogan Square was a huddle of slum tenements, and Islington an expanse of meadow land, and the places they now occupy, quiet fields. Lacking such imagination, they find it impossible to stand up and face the domination of the present with the naked vision of the future. Mr. Wells, at the end of his voyage into Utopia, has described the traveller returning, standing, after so adventurous a journey, at the familiar spot where the Strand debouches into Trafalgar Square. Everything is the same — the railway stations, the tall buildings with winking sky signs, the column and the lions of the Square, the long, low, brooding ugliness of the National Gallery. Amongst them move the busy people, hurrying, to-day as yesterday, to and from their sedentary occupations and their comfortable suburban homes. It all appears "so fast" that "it cannot be moved at any time." Utopia, before this intrusive reality—to be seen, touched, handled—rises from the earth and joins all other cloud cities "built in heaven." An ironical touch may be given by the sight of a squalid, tiny crowd gathered round one of these pillars, with banners demanding the speedy coming of "the Social Revolution"; mocked at alike by the solid architecture, the indulgent policemen, the indifferent multitude that passes by. Mr. Lowes Dickinson, in a dialogue recently published, confronted a banker, of enlightened views, with the protest of an idealist and reformer against present social injustices. The reformer — from a University common room — has much the best of the argument. Looking out from those pleasant paths and gardens, not only over the injustices of the present, but also over all time and all existence, he can reveal to the man of business the impossibility of these injustices continuing, the urgent necessity for change. The banker has but one argument, but with that he can overwhelm his antagonist. That argument is the actual existence of the present, in solid, appreciable reality. He can counter the reformer's acute and ready phrases with steamships and factories, Lombard Street, Pimlico, Manchester; against which the random Socialist, academic or anarchical, can make no more impression than a rat attempting to gnaw through the granite stones of the Bank of England. Here in part is the insistence of things against ideas, the dominance of the material; "the things" which, according to Emerson, are "in the saddle and ride mankind." Samuel Butler once pictured the revolt of the machine against its master, a kind of universal Frankenstein monster come to life and striking blindly in the dark, like the furious rebellion of some slave race which in the past has occasionally wiped out a civilisation in hideous ruin. But apart from the possibility of such revolt, no first visitor to the newer industrial centres but is aware of a certain shrivelling

up of man's importance before the aggregate of
material construction. The sense of proportion is
dwarfed by the mere divergence in size and stability,
as the weak, unprotected human body is contrasted with vast levers and furnaces which at any
moment could crack him like an eggshell, or shrivel
him up like sawdust. Human life and mechanical
life come to be pictured in permanence like those
gaunt and sullen streets of East London, where tiny
cottages crouch beneath tall encompassing walls so
high that between them men scarce can see the sun.
And behind the weight laid upon the imagination
by mass and matter is the perhaps more oppressive
weight of custom and convention. "Every body"
—so commences Newton's famous law—"continues
in its state of rest or motion in a straight line."
More than of any projectiles careering through space
is this true of the mind of man—continuing always,
unless forcibly and sometimes brutally wrested away
by impacting forces, in its motion in a straight line.
Bagehot tells a story of the "very conservative"
people of Fiji. "A chief was one day going over
a mountain path, followed by a long string of his
people, when he happened to stumble and fall; all the
rest of the people immediately did the same except one
man, who was set upon by the rest to know whether
he considered himself better than the chief." Fiji is
too remote a dwelling-place for such a leader. He
resides to-day in Dulwich, in Poplar, in Eaton Square.

Not only is the present in its resistance to the
future secure in its own armies and entrenchments.
It is continually trafficking—and successfully—with

the forces of the invader, purchasing them in single spies and in battalions. Every reform, successfully effected, transfers whole divisions and army corps from the attacking to the defending army. The giving of old age pensions, for example, at one stroke swings half a million aged persons passionately on the side of the *status quo*, passionately against any upheaval which would jeopardise, or might be thought to jeopardise, the regular reckonable dole of two half-crowns per week. And amongst individuals, nine out of ten at least of the men who would be competent to lead a movement towards change are to-day immediately caught up in the huge machine and provided outlet for their ambitions within a tangible and realisable present. How many potential Labour leaders and Socialists, through the operation of the huge sieve-net of the new scholarship system, are being swept into secondary schools from working-class homes? and thence, as clerks in great businesses, through university training, in subsequent Government or private employment, destined to be firmly cemented into the fabric of the present social order? Even the Labour leader, if successful, tends to become conservative, to despise the material he once organised, the masses of unskilled labour, as scattered dust or crumbling snow.

But the great majority of the children of ability in the industrial classes are being intercepted before the opportunity of becoming "Labour leaders" will arise. Their energies are being deflected from politics into commercial or industrial enterprise. Socialism seems

destined to be left to the idealist and the economic
failure, to the man with ready tongue and little stable
capacity for work, like the "Masterman" so cruelly
portrayed in Mr. Wells's "Kipps," to the reformer
who revolts from the harsh operation of present law,
but finds no allies except a proletariat from which the
intelligence has been steadily drained in early boyhood. We seem destined to pass from the antithesis
of the class war—the rich against the poor—to the
antithesis which Nietszche foresaw many years ago—
the Many against the Few; the demands of incapacity
to share in the benefits created by the competent. It
is under such circumstances that the very sombre
architecture of the present seem to smile down
derisive indulgence at the vapourings and pleadings
of those who still hope to change the world a
little. The infant, says Mr. Whiteing in *The Yellow
Van*, was blowing lustily upon a tin whistle as the
van of the land reformers passed under the walls
of Allonby Castle. "Nothing happened to the
walls."

Yet against this tyranny of the present the reformer, after all, has some sources of protection.
"He laughs best who laughs the last": and the
longest laugh is always on the side of the forces of
change. The hills are nothing, and flow from form
to form ; the mountains smoke at the touch of His
hand : "He washeth away the things which grow
out of the dust of the earth and destroyest the hope
of man." Researches in the great canyon of Arizona
have revealed not only an eating through miles of
solid rock by the flow of a quiet stream of water

in a gulf created through almost limitless time, but behind this, in incalculable space of years, a succession of previous operations, formation and upheaval of continents and their overthrow, swinging the plummet of the mind into abysses beyond the powers of that mind ever to comprehend. The sun and rain and delicate air are wasting away, not only the backbone of the mountains, but also the granite stones of the Bank of England. The Future has great allies. Despite the momentary insistence of the material in factory and furnace, the mind can find tranquillity in realisation that this is merely the Idea, clothing itself for a season and in a temporary habitation ; the Idea which can make the rocks dance to its music, and the solid ground tremble at its advent. Such has always been the vision of the poet ; of all who can see not beyond the present, but through the present, to the future. To all such insight

> " Cities and thrones and powers
>   Stand in Time's eye
> Almost as long as flowers
>   Which daily die."

And as of Nineveh there remains but a heap, and of Tyrus a spit of sandy shore, and of Sagesta but one solemn temple looking down the valley to the sea, so a triumphant imagination can fling off the yoke of the present, to see in solid England dynamic instead of static forces, and all the cities in motion and flow towards some unknown ends. This may not provide any peculiar satisfaction for present endeavour. There is no guarantee, because change is inevitable, that change will come along desirable ways. Nor does any consolation reside in the knowledge that one day, without a shadow of uncertainty, great London itself will become but a vast tomb for all its busy people, and of its splendour and pride not one stone be left upon another. But it does release from the tyranny of a present which sees no change possible. If change must come, then it may be deflected along desirable ways. The direction of forces is so much easier than the initiation of them. *E pur si muove* is the eternal affirmation, as much over societies which appear stationary as over societies which appear reckless in progress. For over each successive present, with its ample Government offices, its law courts, its police stations, its secure private dwellings, there will be written as epitaph the inexorable law of a universe, not of Being, but of Becoming: "A wind passeth over it. It is gone. The place thereof shall know it no more."

And of all illusions of the opening twentieth century perhaps the most remarkable is that of security. Already gigantic and novel forces of mechanical invention, upheavals of people, social discontents, are exhibiting a society in the beginnings of change. It would seem likely that the very rapid disintegration, which has taken place in a period of external tranquillity, in beliefs and ideas, may be giving place to a reverse condition: of a time of internal quietude accompanied by large external transformations. With Europe facing an international discontent amongst its industrial peoples, the nations, as an armed camp, heaping up instruments of destruction, the East suddenly awake, the people in England and America writhing in the grasp of a money power more and more concentrated in the hands of enormous Corporations, he would be but a blind prophet who, looking to the future, would assert that all things will continue as until now.

A few years back men loved to anticipate an age of innocence and gold ; with humanity at last tranquil and satisfied, in the socialistic millennium or the anarchic heaven of childhood. To-day the critic of a less sanguine outlook openly proclaims that modern civilisation carries within itself the seeds of its own destruction. Two great imaginative writers, M. Anatole France in Paris, Mr. H. G. Wells in London, have presented their visions of the coming end of an age. The picture of the former is more ironical, more completely the cry of Vanity in a world of disillusionment. The picture of the latter is more scientific. Here is one way at least in which the thing may happen, in which the end may come. And if not in this way, yet in any similar and entirely unexpected fashion, arising out of that present danger : the instability which of necessity must prevail when vast implements of destruction are placed in the hands of a civilisation imperfectly self-controlled, and subject to panic fears and hatreds. It is in the realisation of so remarkable a danger that the story of the outbreak of aeriel warfare becomes not so much a nightmare vision of the future as a vigorous criticism of the present. Mr. Wells had formerly

19

demanded supernatural machinery to effect his outpouring of calamity and terror. A comet, bearing a strange gas, will make every one sane. With a sudden gasp of amazement, they will realise the essential insanity of the life which they had hitherto regarded as natural to mankind. Martians, descending from the darkened sky, with irresistible powers of heat ray and poisonous dust, will wipe out humanity as a man will wipe out a wasp's nest. But here[1] he has returned to the solid ground, and without any assumptions but those of but a slight advance in mechanical invention, exhibits the forces which make towards a cosmic overthrow. The apparatus required is not much more than will undoubtedly be furnished within the next half-century. "Flying" is now assured; has come to stay. It is merely a matter of years or perhaps months before every external apparatus that the author requires for his apocalypse will be at the disposal of mankind. And with that invention there comes a new epoch in the history of humanity. Given effective flying—to be utilised in war not for the transference of men, but for coercing a nation into submission—the march of events appears to follow a possible chain of sequence. Each nation, armed to the teeth in a world which has scarcely apprehended war—a city-bred people—is to-day restrained from fighting by fear of consequences. Each nation—in this grim forecast—thinking itself secure in the possession of a new invincible weapon, plunges into effort for the overlordship of the world. The German air fleet

---

[1] *The War in the Air. By H. G. Wells.*

invades New York. The city, "drinking up the
wealth of a continent as Rome once drank up the
wealth of the Mediterranean, and Babylon the wealth
of the East," after a hopeless resistance, capitulates.
The poor, neglected in their quarters of squalor, like
the poor in Paris in 1870, raise the cry that they are
betrayed. Sporadic violence against the invader
breaks the truce. The Germans, enraged, determine
to make an example which will crush out the need
for further effort in a cruelty which is ultimately to
prove a kindness. Fire and brimstone rain down
from the airships, like the fire and brimstone which
rained down upon the cities of the plain. At the end
New York is a smoking mass of ruins: a cemetery of
a million dead. The assumption of terrorism would
have been justified had war been operating under the
old conditions. Rage and a fury of revenge on such
occasion will always overcome cowardice; man, in
a kind of madness, will be content to be destroyed,
if only he can destroy. It is only when the resistance
becomes obviously senseless—when he has no means
of hurting his enemy—that he finally accepts the
inevitable. But in the new conditions of air-fighting
such an equilibrium would never be attained. There
are no frontiers that can be guarded. Desperate
men, equipping these new craft, can always exact
terrible reprisals. In return for New York's destruction, Berlin is smashed to powder by American
airships; in return for Berlin, other American cities.
Madness and delirium seize the people: the whole
world is at war; modern civilisation blows up and
vanishes from the world.

With the destructive fury of the war comes the collapse in the whole edifice of credit which maintains the economic efficiency of the industrial system. Men demand gold as in America in the last crisis, hoarding it in their stockings or burying it in their gardens. The stock of gold becomes exhausted, bonds and shares waste paper. Factories close. The city populations find neither work nor bread. In peril of imminent destruction from the enemy above, men claw and mow at one another in blind struggle in the starving cities, reeling back visibly into the beast ; as they will do in extremity even when an earthquake has shattered their city and death sits waiting at the door of their houses. After the fighting comes the famine, after the famine the great pestilence. The organisation of society is broken and fissured. The vast multitude perish. The few that remain, like the few that remained of the Roman civilisation after the impact of the barbarian, are found at the end, in village communities or isolated huts, or encamped in the ruins of once populous towns. Amid the nettle and the ivy the survivors of London wander forlorn through the empty labyrinths : as the survivors encamped in the ruins of Rome in the long twilight which preceded the Middle Age. After the three hundred years of diastole there came " the swift and unexpected systole, like the closing of a fist." " They could not understand it was a systole," writes Mr. Wells. " They could not think of it as anything but a jolt, a hitch, a mere oscillatory indication of the swiftness of their progress. Collapse, though it happened all about them, remained incredible.

Presently some falling mass smote them down, or the ground opened beneath their feet. They died incredulous." So incredulous indeed died Babylon, Tyre, Rome; each refusing to believe that it was witnessing the end of a world.

How far is this sombre vision a nightmare merely? How far a warning of the things which may come to pass? Mr. Wells requires for his *Götterdämmerung* no fresh influx of barbarian hordes to smash civilisation brutally to pieces, such as is feared by some: not even the upheaval from below, in the consolidated masses of the poor, which has seemed to M. Anatole France and others a force destined to consume civilisation in fire and blood. He had accepted the undeniable note of the age, that material advance has far transcended moral progress, and that this inequality is full of the elements of danger. Man has wrested secrets from sun and star, equipped himself with apparatus which should make him rival the older gods, stolen, like Prometheus, the fire of heaven to be his servant, and made the earth and the air to obey him. Yet this unparalleled control of dead things has failed to eliminate his silly national jealousies, his little prejudices and selfishnesses, his clumsy determination to make his life a brutal, irrational thing. Mr. Wells outpours his vials of wrath upon the Crowd: the vacant street-bred people, the "common abundant life," "flowing, in its cheerful, aimless way," towards the Abyss. His hero, one of this Crowd, Mr. Bert Smallways, is one of "the sort of men who had made England and America what they are." "He had lived all his life in narrow streets, and between mean houses he could not look over, and in a narrow circle of ideas from which there was no escape. He thought the whole duty of man was to be smarter than his fellows, get his hands, as he put it, 'on the dibs,' and have a good time." But the author need not have gone to the Crowd for his illustration. No lunacy that flourishes amongst the little but is intensified amongst the great. The German Professors, the conversation of an Oxford College Common Room will exhibit as dangerous a combination of truculence and terror as any gathering of patriots at a public-house bar. The war scare of a halfpenny paper, with its frantic appeals to race prejudice and passion, is revealed in deepening imbecilities in sixpenny magazines which circulate amongst the country clergy, or half-crown reviews which lie upon the table of country houses. Countless millions in Europe and Asia and America, "instead of being born rooted in the soil, were born struggling in a torrent they never clearly understood. All the faiths of their fathers had been taken by surprise, and startled into the strangest forms and reactions." Everywhere in the early twentieth century this observer finds " a sort of heated, irascible stupidity "; everywhere " congested nations in inconvenient areas, stopping the exchange of population and produce with each other, annoying each other with tariffs and every possible commercial vexation, and threatening each other with navies and armies that grow every year more portentious."

" The houses were never high enough to satisfy the people," says M. Anatole France of his " Penguins."

" They kept on making them still higher. They built them of thirty or forty storeys, with offices, shops, banks, societies, one above another. They dug cellars and tunnels ever deeper downwards. Fifteen millions of men laboured in a giant town." Everything here was constructed efficiently for the production of wealth. The organisation was perfect. The ancient aristocracies and democracies had alike departed. The Trusts, with their Directors, were omnipotent. "Like all true aristocrats, like the patricians of Republican Rome or the squires of old England, these powerful men affected a great severity in their habits and customs. They were the ascetics of wealth. At the meetings of the Trusts an observer would have noticed their smooth and puffy faces, their lantern cheeks, their sunken eyes and wrinkled brows. . . . Denying themselves all happiness, all pleasure, and all rest, they spent their miserable lives in rooms without light or air, furnished only with electrical apparatus, living on eggs and milk, and sleeping on camp beds. By doing nothing except pressing nickel buttons with their fingers, these mystics heaped up riches of which they never saw the signs, and acquired the vain possibility of gratifying desires that they never experienced." Society, as a whole, became organised on a plutocratic, as once on a military, basis ; and all classes endeavoured to approximate themselves to the ideal standard set from above. Like insects, the huge hive laboured night and day, driven forward by the blind, furious instinct for accumulation. "All passions which injured the increase or the preservation of wealth were regarded as dishonourable. Neither indolence, nor idleness, nor the taste for disinterested study, nor love of the arts, nor, above all, extravagance, was ever forgiven. Pity was condemned as a dangerous weakness." "The State was firmly based on two great public virtues: respect for the rich, contempt for the poor." As they devoted their whole intelligence to business, they sought no intellectual pleasures. The theatre was reduced to pantomime and comic dances. The very rich formed only a minority, but their collaborators were the entire people. The agents of commerce or banking, the engineers and managers of factories, received immense salaries, and were recruited from the talent to whom this supreme career was always open. The system sucked the efficient and enterprising from the populace below. What remained, a spongy morass of low-grade life, shepherded, controlled, fed, and housed by their masters, presented every sign of physical and moral degeneration. "Of low stature, with small heads and narrow chests, they were further distinguished from the comfortable classes by a multitude of physiological anomalies, and, in particular, by a common want of symmetry between the head and the limbs." The more robust of them became soldiers. From the remainder the employers continually and methodically selected out the enterprising and talented, leaving alone "labourers who were incapable of defending their rights, but were yet intelligent enough to perform their toil, which highly perfected machines rendered extremely simple." "In a word, these miserable employees were plunged in a gloomy apathy that nothing enlightened and nothing exasperated. They were necessary instruments for the social order, and well adapted to their purpose."

Civilisation seemed to have at length attained its ideal, and to have finally established a coherent, organic society. A system founded on "what is strongest in human nature, pride and cupidity," would seem to have been guaranteed an earthly immortality. Yet there were grounds for uneasiness, especially on the score of physical health. "The health of the poor is what it must be," said the experts in hygiene, "but that of the rich leaves much to be desired." The multi-millionaires were bald at the age of eighteen. Some showed from time to time a dangerous weakness of mind. Overstrung and enfeebled, they gave enormous sums to ignorant charlatans, and there suddenly sprang up in the town the medical or theological fortune of some trumpery bath-attendant who had become a teacher or a prophet. The number of lunatics increased continually. Suicides multiplied in the world of wealth.

M. Anatole France requires no visitants from another world to ensure the destruction of his nightmare. He does not even need the national jealousies and insanities of Mr. Wells equipped with new weapons of destruction. His vision of a Penguin Chicago at Paris finally falls to pieces from its own internal rottenness. Anarchists, wielding tremendous explosives, accepted as deliverers by the enslaved and degenerate proletariat, smash Society into pieces. One of them, a clerk in the Electricity Trust, an afternoon in June, from the heights of Fort Saint-

Michel, witnesses the beginning of the end. To a little child, playing there all unconscious of the coming cataclysm, he tells the story of human progress. "A fisherman once threw his net into the sea, and drew out a little sealed copper pot, which he opened with his knife. Smoke came out of it, and as it mounted up to the clouds the smoke grew thicker and thicker, and became a giant, who gave such a terrible yawn that the whole world was blown to dust." The "yawn" is the weariness of a vast disillusionment: the awakening of a slave population to the futility of its further continuance. At first the Anarchists waged war on the Trusts, while the people stood aloof, resentful, indifferent. Later, in the panic that accompanied the immense ruin of property, the mob ceased work and indulged in a pandemonium of destruction. Men fought for food and for plunder in the darkened ways of the city. Society lost its structure and deliquesced into a kind of sloppy morass. Epidemics followed the fighting, bred from unburied corpses. Famine carried off those whom pestilence had spared. "Reforms were introduced into institutions, and great changes took place in habits and customs; but the country never recovered the loss of its capital, and never regained its former prosperity. Commerce and industry dwindled away. Civilisation abandoned those countries which for so long it had preferred to all others. They became insalubrious and sterile. The territories that had supported so many millions of men became nothing more than a desert. On the hill of Fort Saint-Michel wild horses cropped the coarse grass."

The diastole had been followed by a systole. Mankind after the European, as after the Roman, civilisation fell back into darkness. A catastrophe of centuries was occupied by the evening, the midnight, and the dawn. As once the barbarians walked with wonder along the deserted Roman roads or suddenly emerged from forest and plain to gaze astonished on the vast ruins of aqueducts and coliseums and once populous cities, so the new child peoples which survived the cosmic catastrophe contemplated the embankments, the crumbling bridges, the tattered, torn fragments of deserted towns which marked the memories of our dead race. The wheel of history slowly revolved through the centuries, and after a time once again the unending cyclic process was renewed and another " civilisation " erected which thought itself the last word of human progress.

" Days flowed like water from the fountains, and the centuries passed like drops falling from the ends of stalactites. Hunters came to chase the bears upon the hills that covered the forgotten city. Shepherds fed their flocks upon them. Labourers turned up the soil with their ploughs. Gardeners cultivated their lettuces and grafted their pear trees. They were not rich, and they had no arts. The walls of their cabins were covered with old vines and roses. A goat-skin clothed their tanned limbs, while their wives dressed themselves with the wool that they themselves had spun. The goat-herds moulded little figures of men and animals out of clay, or sang songs about the young girl who follows her lover through woods or among the browsing goats ; while the pine trees whisper together, and the water utters its murmuring sound. The master of the house grew angry with the beetles who devoured his figs. He planned snares to protect his fowls from the velvet-tailed fox, and he poured out wine for his neighbours, saying, ' Drink ! the flies have not spoilt my vintage ; the vines were dry before they came.'

" In the course of ages the wealth of the villages and the corn that filled the fields were pillaged by barbarian invaders. The country changed its masters many times. The conquerors built castles on the hills. Cultivation increased : mills, forges, tanneries, and looms were established. Roads were opened through the woods and over the marshes. The river was covered with boats. The hamlets became large villages, and, joining together, formed a town which protected itself by deep trenches and lofty walls. Later, becoming the capital of a great State, it found itself straitened within its now useless ramparts, and it converted them into grass-grown villas. It grew very rich and large beyond measure.

" The houses were never high enough to satisfy the people. They kept on making them still higher. They built them of thirty or forty storeys, with offices, shops, banks, societies, one above another. They dug cellars and tunnels ever deeper downwards. Fifteen millions of men laboured in a giant town." [1]

After a time, says a great writer, the earth grows sick of her children, like exhausted ground that will

---

[1] In these summaries and quotations I have used the excellent translation of Mr. A. W. Evans's *Penguin Island* (John Lane).

bear fruit no more. It is impossible that society could "blow up" with such rapidity as is here pictured; the process is, in any case, foreshortened. But any student who has followed the history of Rome's destruction—the gradual disintegration of a society exceedingly complex and rational—will never conceal from himself the possibility of similar vast changes in the world of to-morrow. The process is always incredible to those who think that mankind henceforth has but to settle down and be comfortable in a world where tranquillity is secure. Dr. Dill has described such a life under the Roman peace, with the municipalities competing in magnificence of building, the arts of life secure, the farmhouse (in one picture) with the peacocks in the garden under the sunlight, and every accompanying element of enjoyment and repose. The only sorrow which disturbed such an age was the sometimes transient regret that all the great things had been accomplished; that humanity, in a completely rational society, had nothing to contemplate in the future but a continuous repetition of the present—an endless end of the world. A few generations later that farmhouse lies deserted, the cities are crumbling into ruin, society itself has fallen to pieces, terror, and with terror childlike superstition and ferocity, have achieved dominance. Night has resumed her ancient Empire. What guarantee does the present offer against the repetition of a similar catastrophe? Civilisation possesses weapons adequate to protection against forces without. It has no protection against forces within. One of the passing figures in Mr. Wells's

vision of desolation mourns over the vanishing of all
the bright hopes of a transfigured world. " The
sense of fine beginnings! It was all a sham. There
were no beginnings. We're just ants in ant-hill
circles, in a world that doesn't matter: that goes on
and rambles into nothingness. New York—New
York doesn't even strike me as horrible. New York
was nothing but an ant-hill kicked to pieces by a
fool."

These observers are justified at least in one con-
tention: that the future, whether in orderly progress
or with sudden or gradual retrogression, will be
astonished at the "illusion of security" in which
to-day society reposes; forgetting that but a thin
crust separates it from the central elemental fires,
that the heart of the earth is a flame. There are
forces of resistance to disintegration and decay, even
amongst this shabby crowd which appears to the
indignant observer but an aggregation of aimless,
impossible lives. Mr. Wells himself in earlier work
has shown us the humanity and romantic ardour of
Mr. Hoopdriver and the resolute hope of Mr. Lewisham, even if in later effort he can see little but the
fatuous ineptitude of Mr. "Art" Kipps or the ineffective blunderings of Mr. Bert Smallways. Mr.
Anatole France has revealed in his studies of contemporary life kindly intelligent citizens, doing bravely
the work of the day. In no panic fear, certainly
with no acquiescence and despair, the reformer to-day
will contemplate the possible future of a society
beyond measure complex, baffling and uncertain in
its energies and aims. But the warning, always useful,

but now more than ever necessary, cannot be too strongly emphasised: that with the vertical division between nation and nation armed to the teeth, and the horizontal division between rich and poor which has become a cosmopolitan fissure, the future of progress is still doubtful and precarious.   Humanity —at best—appears but as a shipwrecked crew which has taken refuge on a narrow ledge of rock, beaten by wind and wave; which cannot tell how many, if any at all, will survive when the long night gives place to morning.   The wise man will still go softly all his days; working always for greater economic equality on the one hand, for understanding between estranged peoples on the other; apprehending always how slight an effort of stupidity or violence could strike a death-blow to twentieth-century civilisation, and elevate the forces of destruction triumphant over the ruins of a world.

CHAPTER XI

POSTSCRIPT

SO at the end we are compelled to confess an essential ignorance. To-day's "human comedy" still remains unwritten. Those who have essayed it are always unconsciously or deliberately foreshortening or distorting: exhibiting excess of darkness or sunshine. We know little of the forces fermenting in that strange laboratory which is the birthplace of the coming time. We are uncertain whether civilisation is about to blossom into flower, or wither in tangle of dead leaves and faded gold. We can find no answer to the inquiry, whether we are about to plunge into a new period of tumult and upheaval, whether we are destined to an indefinite prolongation of the present half-lights and shadows, whether, as we sometimes try to anticipate, a door is to be suddenly opened, revealing unimaginable glories.

In face of such uncertainty, the verdict is often one of criticism and despair. "The wisest man has warned us"—so runs a mournful verdict—"not to expect the world ever to improve so much that the better part of mankind will be in the majority. No wise man ever undertakes to correct the disorders of the public estate." "He who cannot endure the madness of the public, but goeth about to think he can cure it, is himself no less mad than the rest."

Such a verdict, however, pays little heed to the effort of those whose unregarded labour, now in patient adherence to duty, now in "something more heroical than this age affecteth," has bought the good things which are the common heritage of to-day: a wide-spread comfort, opportunities for happiness and content, freedom which is always but hardly won and but hardly maintained.

Optimism and pessimism, in face of any civilisation in a changing world, are equally untrue, equally futile. All human societies mingle selfishness and sacrifice, exultation and weariness, laughter and tears. No one age is especially wicked, especially tired, especially noble. All ages are wicked, tired, noble. Progress is always impossible and always proceeding. Preservation is always hazardous and always attained. Every class is unfit to govern; and the government of the world continues. Austerities, simplicities, and a common danger breed virtues and devotions which are the parents of prosperity. Prosperity breeds arrogance, extravagance, and class hatreds. Opulence and pride in their turn breed national disasters. And these disasters engender the austerities and simplicities which start the cycle again anew.

To accept all and to reject all are in this case equally desperate courses. To turn aside in despair, to hold aloof in disdain, to proclaim from the heart of comfort an easy approval, are policies traitorous to the public good.

20

A king of France—so runs the medieval legend —when travelling in Catalonia, discovered an ancient man engaged unremittingly in the planting of date-kernels. "Why?" he asked, "do you sow the seeds of a tree of such tardy growth, seeing that the dates will not ripen till a hundred years be passed?" "Am I not then eating," was the answer, "the fruit of trees planted by my forefathers, who took thought for those who were to come? And shall not I do like unto them?" [1]

It may be that the men "who took thought for those who were to come" will be found upon the winning side.

[1] *Gentlemen Errant. Mrs. Cust.*

INDEX

out there, with the use of that instrument — the Democratic instrument of Government—which gives to the people full control over its own fortunes. To-day each citizen of the crowd " compares with sadness his political power with his economic dependence : humiliated every day with the contrast between his divided personality—on one side a *misérable*, on the other a sovereign : on one an animal, on the other a god."

The increasing apprehension of this contrast, and the increasing consequential effort at readjustment, will furnish the guiding thread to the various political and social changes of the twentieth century. It will influence and control the rise and fall of political parties, each doing the work all unconsciously of forces which it does not understand. It will lead in various ways, and through all oppositions and reactions, towards an organised society profoundly differing from our own.